CONFLUENCE

CONFLUENCE

John Gottschalk's Life
of Duty, Service, and
the Business of News

George Ayoub

Confluence: John Gottschalk's Life of Duty, Service, and the Business of News

Copyright © 2020 Carmen and John Gottschalk Foundation

Published by Teewinot Publishing, www.TeewinotPublishing.com

Hardcover: 978-1-7341709-1-7
Paperback: 978-1-7341709-2-4
Mobi: 978-1-7341709-3-1
EPUB: 978-1-7341709-4-8

LCCN: 2019916500
Library of Congress Cataloging-in-Publication data on file with the publisher.

Author photo: iNk Photography, Grand Island, Neb.
www.pathogenink.com

Design and production: Concierge Publishing Services

Printed in the United States of America
10 9 8 7 6 5 4 3 2 1

Contents

For Jacalyn,
who is especially beautiful
with a book in her hands

Preface

As recently as 2016, ink-smudged printer's blocks filled a wall of shelves in the basement of Hinn's Ace Hardware and Furniture Store on Main Street in Rushville, Nebraska, population 856. Nearby, two buckets of leaden type sat on the concrete floor, each holding a mishmash of letters and symbols, the basic imprint for hundreds of thousands of stories, ideas, and commercial appeals, the lifeblood of a newspaper.

These printer's tools, these implements of democracy, were neither out of place nor ill-suited to a hardware store. Hinn's back room was for years home to the printing press of the *Sheridan County Star*. The *Star* was the newspaper of record for Rushville and nearby residents of the rolling farm ground tucked away in Nebraska's Sandhills just west of the 100th meridian. The printer's blocks and type remained long after the newspaper was gone, a fading reminder of what once was.

On the wall outside the door to Hinn's back room, among a hodgepodge of old notes, invoices, and business cards, was a photograph of six-year-old John Gottschalk. He sits atop a snow drift, sporting woolens and a smile wider than a center pivot sprinkler, just days after the Blizzard of 1949 had devastated a broad stretch of Middle America, including Rushville and Sheridan County.

John was on familiar ground. His family published the *Star*. He would cut his teeth in the newspaper business first at the end of a broom, then on a Linotype machine setting hot type, the same leaden slugs still found in buckets in Hinn's basement many years later. Before he was old enough to vote, John Gottschalk knew how to run a small-town newspaper.

Four hundred miles east of Rushville, the printing hub for the *Omaha World-Herald* graces four city blocks in downtown Omaha. It has three, five-story, state-of-the-art presses, which can print seventy-five thousand newspapers an hour. The facility can house three thousand rolls of newsprint, each ten miles in length.

The magnificent glass and steel facility, the John Gottschalk Freedom Center, was named for the former publisher and CEO of the Omaha World-Herald Co. A newspaper guy through and through, he started his journalism career sweeping floors at the *Sheridan County Star* and finished it as one of the nation's most successful and respected newspaper publishers. John built the Freedom Center. His successor in the publisher's office, Terry Kroeger, named it after him.

The distance from Rushville to Sidney to Omaha is 536 miles. Neither those dots on a map nor the sheer drama of advancing technology expresses the distance his life traveled. As a newspaper publisher, philanthropist, and powerful force on national boards, John built a record of depth and excellence at each stop along his professional and personal journey.

This biography's genesis came about when John and his longtime colleague and former *Omaha World-Herald* editorial page editor, Frank Partsch, began thinking about how best to tell the modern history of the *World-Herald*. Frank, who edited this book with massive doses of patience, skill, and humor, and for whom I'll be forever grateful, sought me out after the pair realized that a considerable stretch of the newspaper's growth and maturation took place during John's thirty-two-year tenure. Still, the newspaper's story and the John Gottschalk story would best be told separately.

So began the sizable task of putting together the book now in your hands, a project shaped by winnowing the massive amount of material from a life well-lived and considerably larger than most. John proved to be a willing and committed subject and a first-rate, detailed database of information. He and Frank presented me a compilation of cross-referenced subject matter as disparate as Omaha city government and the state's "water wars." I also plowed through six years of *Square Talk*, John's in-house communiqués to *World-Herald* employees. These monthly newsletters gave me insight into his management skills on several fronts, including a powerful ethical streak he applied to the business of newspapers and the newspaper business. His inner drive to solve problems also showed up in boardrooms and philanthropy circles, where he not only led successful teams but showed a deft hand at putting them together.

Former *Omaha World-Herald* reporter Leslie Reed and I interviewed dozens of colleagues, friends, family, and foes of Gottschalk. Leslie's steady and professional touch and considerable interview talents were immeasurably important in completing the story. I would be remiss without acknowledging the work of Donna Grimm, John's exceptional assistant, who added to the project both as a contributor to the story and as the gracious and irreplaceable captain of the ship at Three Cedars office building in Omaha, where I had a temporary space to work.

Rushville framed John's remarkable birth and rebirth, the small Sandhills crossroads imprinting his values via family, coaches, scout leaders, the land, and the beckoning horizon.

Together, they prepared him for a life of leadership, of standing at the helm and making those around him better. He showed his leadership chops early, whether working at the paper, calling signals as quarterback for Rushville High, or participating as an enthusiastic Boy Scout in an organization whose national board he would one day lead.

When John arrived at the University of Nebraska in Lincoln in 1961, he became a Phi Gamma Delta fraternity brother of Bob Kerrey, the start of a lifelong friendship with the former Nebraska governor and United States senator. Coincidentally, Kerrey's fellow Nebraska senator from 1997 to 2001, Chuck Hagel, was a schoolmate of John in Rushville. As with the Boy Scouts, John's connection to the "Fijis" was to be lifelong. As an undergraduate, he was the house president; three decades later he served on the fraternity's national board for six years including two as president.

In 1964, the summer before his senior year at NU, his family purchased the *Sidney Telegraph*. John took a break from school and returned west to help his mother, Mary Jane, run the *Star* in Rushville. His father, Phil, spent his time in Sidney with the *Telegraph*, which published three times a week.

Mary Jane and Phil then divorced, and Phil headed to Columbia, Missouri. John moved to Sidney in 1965 and found himself dividing his time between the family's Rushville and Sidney newspapers, logging long days and many miles on Nebraska Highway 385. He became co-owner of the *Telegraph* with Jack Lowe in 1968 and sole owner in 1971 when Lowe retired. Before he left Sidney in 1975, John had put in time on the city council, served two years as mayor, and undertook a run for the University of Nebraska Board of Regents.

John married his high school sweetheart, Carmen Beck, in 1964. After selling the *Telegraph* in 1974, the Gottschalks with daughters, Jodi and Christina, arrived in Omaha in 1975 when John started his *World-Herald* career.

He joined the newspaper after a chance meeting with Publisher Harold Andersen at a Fiji function in Lincoln. John was considering other post-*Telegraph* careers, including banking, but Andersen encouraged him to stay in newspapers. Shortly afterward, he offered John a job at the *World-Herald* as part of the senior management team.

Fourteen years later John Gottschalk would succeed Andersen as the newspaper's fifth chief executive. In that time John immersed himself in the *World-Herald's* operations and culture, rising steadily through the ranks of responsibility and influence. He took the reins in November of 1989, applying years of leadership experiences to running the nation's largest employee-owned newspaper.

During his tenure in the publisher's chair, John presided over unprecedented growth in the company. Employee ownership was a legacy at the *World-Herald* left by the previous owner, Peter Kiewit. Annual growth of nearly 20 percent created stability at the paper and wealth for its employee owners. The employee-ownership era ended in 2011, when Warren Buffett and Berkshire Hathaway Inc. purchased the *World-Herald*.

There were challenges, not the least of which was the transformation of the industry as technology played an ever-larger role. New ownership nationwide began looking at newspapers as mere "properties," prized more for their earnings potential than for their role in the advancement of a self-governing society. During his tenure, John steadfastly challenged the state's gambling interests on the newspaper's editorial page. In Omaha, the collapse of the Franklin Community Federal Credit Union opened an unseemly and rumor-fueled saga that greeted John in his first days on the job. While the Franklin scandal amused some in the city with tawdry tales, John kept the *World-Herald's* tiller steady, balancing his leadership and ethical responsibilities while friends and colleagues faced an onslaught of innuendos and outright lies.

Not everything worked. Much of how John dealt with setbacks was embodied in the *World-Herald*'s attempt to buy Stauffer Communications in 1995. Even though the details of the *World-Herald*'s bid were stunningly precise and exhaustive, a Georgia company carried the day. The planning, execution, and aftermath revealed both the style and substance of a John Gottschalk initiative and his approach to managing complex projects.

While his work at the paper moved the *World-Herald* forward within the confines of its culture, John's local philanthropic and civic footprint outside the office was considerable. Institutions such as the Holland Performing Arts Center, Joslyn Art Museum, Peter Kiewit Conference Center, and Baxter Arena benefitted from his leadership, as well as citywide K-12 initiatives and the advancement of learning centers and causes from the arts to the humanities to those in need.

With Carmen, Jodi, and Christina as constants in his corner, John and Carmen offered direct love and support to Omaha's most vulnerable children. The Gottschalks provided emergency foster care in their home to nearly one hundred at-risk newborns over a thirty-year period, caring for a baby sometimes as long as six months.

John was a mainstay on national boards, rising often to the leadership roles where his firm hand at management and problem-solving helped chart new courses for national companies and concerns as disparate as the USO, the National Benevolent Association, Pacific Life Insurance Co., the Boy Scouts of America, Phi Gamma Delta, Cabela's, Pheasants Forever, and the University of Nebraska Foundation.

After his retirement in 2007, John Gottschalk spent many hours fly fishing near Jackson Hole, Wyoming. But he didn't leave the leadership game. People still wanted his name, his advice, and his wisdom to be a part of their projects, whether constructing the beautiful new Modisett Baseball Park in Rushville, establishing Yanney Park in Kearney, helping to preserve local ownership of the newspaper in Jackson Hole, building storm shelters at a Boy Scout camp in western Iowa after tragedy struck there—or any number of initiatives advancing the well-being of Omaha and the rest of Nebraska.

At its very core, the John Gottschalk story is a Nebraska story. It embodies values true Nebraskans cherish: character, compassion, duty, ethics, and leadership. These form the professional, personal, and public tributaries of this newspaperman from Rushville. Professional, personal, and public may appear to be separate currents flowing downstream from the Sandhills to Sidney to Omaha. But they're not. The indefatigable pull of his life merged them into a single remarkable river.

George Ayoub
Grand Island, Nebraska
July 2019

ONE

Beginning, Beginning Again, and Rushville

Here is a person who was, in effect, orphaned and then reclaimed—creating in him both wariness and an ability to accept unconditional acceptance.

-MIKE MCCARTHY

On New Year's Eve 1988, forty-five-year-old John Gottschalk was winging his way from Omaha toward Rushville, his hometown in the northwest corner of Nebraska. He was only a few months from becoming the publisher and CEO of the *Omaha World-Herald*, a top-fifty metropolitan newspaper and the largest employee-owned paper in the country—a reality he had nurtured and shepherded into a stunning success. Flying in his own twin-engine plane spoke volumes about the position his hard work and leadership had afforded him.

Aside from the pilot, the only other person on board was Marjorie Wasserburger, John's high-school English teacher. She had been in Omaha visiting her daughter. John found out she was there and offered her a ride home. Wasserburger had left teaching and earned her PhD to become a clinical psychologist. She had been a taskmaster in the classroom, even for John, who had done well at Rushville High, writing with relative aplomb and accuracy. He was to recall that, in Wasserburger's class, a half-inch margin was a half inch—not three-eighths, not seven-sixteenths, but a half inch. English essays in the late 1950s were typed without the benefit of correcting tape or erasers. John admitted to typing far more papers than he actually turned in, always growing uneasy as he worked his way toward the end of the paper and then made a typing error. Retype the page—it must be perfect.

One assignment in particular stuck in John's mind. "It was a book report on some really droll piece of literature that everybody was supposed to know about. The paper came back with a big red A+ up in the corner, and then a note in her perfect script: 'John, you can do better than this.' That made no sense to a high-school kid. I consulted my father. He said, 'John, what she's telling you is that you are smart enough to write a good paper, but she knows it wasn't your best work and she wants everything you've got. So start giving it to her.'"

Her note resonated long afterwards. "It is an A+ but you can do better. If we held those standards today, let alone achieved them, where would our children be?" John said. "The great thing about growing up in a small town is that they exaggerate your victories and they assuage your defeats."

And they know when good was not your best.

The plane ride was a symbolic connection of John Gottschalk's past, present, and future: The small-town boy from northwest Nebraska, poised within grasp of a career pinnacle, flying through the Nebraska sky with his high-school English teacher, who, among others, had prodded him into excellence on his journey. This juxtaposition of events spurred a sense of introspection in John, so much so that he took to a journal the next day, January 1, 1989, to chronicle the moment.

It just seemed to pour out—at ten thousand feet on the way to Rushville. Dr. Marjorie Wasserburger—my high-school English teacher who later completed her doctorate, did family counseling in Minneapolis, then returned six or seven years ago to retire—was listening.

She was a great teacher—and today I shared with her my joy that this first entry into what I hope will be a lifetime journal will include her, a great inspiration in high school. Probably the best teacher I ever had. I told her I was compelled to begin this project as I reflected on Andy's (Omaha World-Herald Publisher Harold Andersen) retirement. There have only been four CEOs of the Omaha World-Herald. And soon I'll be its fifth...

I told Dr. Wasserburger I felt somehow my life will result in something permanently good on this planet— and if it does, someone will someday have an opportunity to want some insight into how and why it happened. Maybe these scribblings will help. I don't view myself as important. True, I've had considerable responsibility for leadership. And I've enjoyed much success in my life. I have tried to be humble about my role. It is, and will always be, the result of associates. Nothing that has happened around me has been exclusively my doing...In fact, my greatest failings have been in endeavors where I have been alone—without a team. Perhaps playing the clarinet in high school was the only thing I ever did well by myself—but even then I had an accompanist....

Thank you for hearing me out, Marj Wasserburger— and thanks to so many who have influenced my life to date, bringing me this opportunity....

The prologue is done. It is now time to chart the final and exciting chapters of a life which lies ahead.

∾

Rushville lay two degrees west of the 100th meridian, the line of longitude roughly marking the eastern edge of the Great Plains on maps and in legend. As Wallace Stegner chronicled in *Beyond the Hundredth Meridian: John Wesley Powell and the Second Opening of the West*, the land Powell and others saw was the result of the inevitable, incessant, and normal movement of wind and water from the Gulf of Mexico. Andrew Moore's spectacular 2015 book, *Dirt Meridian*, captured the consequences of nature and the spirit of humans as they first claimed and then called this land their own.

To the east of the dirt meridian lay rolling grassy prairies where straight lines and mile roads divide a sea of cropland. To the west sat semi-arid rangeland, less genial to the farmer than the stockman, a place where vast sky and endless horizon stirred a different kind of soul making its way across America.

Nearly twelve hundred people called Rushville home in 1945, about the time John Gottschalk arrived in the place he contended shaped him like no other. His was a singular journey, from the unusual circumstances of his beginnings to the formative events of his childhood and young adulthood. His origins were a process that infused his veins—and, most important, his heart and mind—with character from the soaring vistas of the 100th meridian and the ink from a lifetime of newspapering.

Living west of the 100th meridian took a particular constitution and outlook on life. For Bill Barnes, John's maternal grandfather, it also took a piano. A budding opera star from Kansas City had stolen the big, rough Irishman's heart in Belle Forche, South Dakota, where he worked as an engineer building a railroad. He married the opera singer and persuaded her to stay in the Great Plains. She agreed to stay, but only on one condition.

John heard the story from Bill at a special moment. "The night before my wedding I asked him, 'How did you ever get Grandma Ruth out here?' He said, 'I promised her a piano.' And fifty years later, the piano was still sitting in that house."

Bill and his sister, Mabel Grimes, ran a little livestock weekly newspaper in South Dakota before eventually moving it to Hay Springs, Nebraska, thirteen miles west of Rushville on Highway 20. There they bought the *Hay Springs News*. In time, Bill saw more opportunities up the road in two newspapers, the *Rushville Standard* and the *Rushville Recorder*. Bill and Mabel were able to acquire these and merge them to form the *Sheridan County Star*. Mabel, Bill, Ruth, and their daughter Mary Jane—John's mother—moved to Rushville after Mary Jane's graduation from Hay Springs High School in 1935.

According to Margie Hinn, John's third-grade teacher, matriarch of a long-time Rushville family, and, at eighty-four, still running Hinn's Hardware Store on Main Street, John's Great Aunt Mabel was a news hound. "She was the roving reporter. She came in here every Monday morning to get the news, and she would go to all the businesses. They don't do things like that nowadays."

Mabel Grimes at her *Sheridan County Star* desk.

Bill Barnes embraced Rushville and became a mainstay moving the town forward. He led the town's seventy-fifth anniversary celebration in 1950, a huge event inspired by the Black Hills Passion Play, which Bill had witnessed in his South Dakota days. The Rushville gala was so big the organizers had to move what was essentially an outdoor theater to the town's ballpark to accommodate the throng of participants and spectators.

Bill's generosity around town was obvious, from purchasing uniforms for the high-school band to making sure that Rushville graduates had tuition money for Chadron State College, just a half-hour west.

John was a junior in high school when he realized that a fellow football player, "a pretty good kid," had no way of going to college "without Grandad's tuition gift." His grandfather's generosity had a "profound impact" on John. He wondered, "Why would he do that for someone else's child? I never talked to him about it, but I was learning that he was a guy who would get things done—the right things."

The Presbyterian Church was clearly on Bill's radar, as he was a regional officer of the Presbytery. New choir robes and a new church organ were evidence of his philanthropy.

Lynn Roper, John's sister, said the family learned about philanthropy from their grandfather. "I know he paid the college tuition for one of my classmates. Mom was on the library board. It was a Carnegie Library and the roof was flat and leaked. She helped raise the money to fix the roof. We grew up knowing we had a little more than others, so we were expected to give it away."

John remembered his opera-singing grandmother, Ruth, as "spectacular," and as good in the kitchen as she was with an aria. John could count on her banana cream pie every birthday. Her culinary prowess came with a "signature" of sorts.

"Even though she had a hand roller for her dough, she insisted on using a large glass 7-Up bottle filled with water to roll her crusts," John said. "What I remember is the label was slightly raised because it was somehow etched in the glass; it wasn't a stick-on label. When finished, there was always a large '7' baked into the crust."

Ruth and Bill's only daughter, Mary Jane, was known in Rushville as Pug. She left in 1935 for Columbia, Missouri, to study journalism at the University of Missouri. She spent a summer as a hostess for the Disney bus tours in California. After graduating in 1939, she landed a job at a newspaper in Sheboygan, Wisconsin, and later moved to a newspaper at Alpena, Michigan, in that state's north woods. Along the way she took flying lessons and acquired a pilot's license.

When she wasn't reporting the news, Mary Jane was flying around the Great Lakes on Civil Air Patrol search and rescue missions. With war clouds gathering, CAP pilots were instructed to be on the lookout on the chance a German U-boat might make its way through the Saint Lawrence Seaway into the Great Lakes.

While at MU, Mary Jane met and fell in love with the irrepressible Phil Gottschalk, an eventual *summa cum laude* graduate with majors in history and economics. Phil's journey to Columbia proved to be just slightly less astonishing than John's own path to Rushville.

Philip Anderson was born in Detroit in 1917 to Paul and Blanche Anderson from Lansing, Michigan. Blanche did not survive the birth. A month later Paul succumbed to the shock and distress of her death and took his own life, leaving little Philip an orphan. He was sent to live with Blanche's sister, Helen Gottschalk, in Jefferson City, Missouri. Helen's husband Ed was the chief purchasing agent for the city's power plant. Helen and Ed raised Phil as their own, alongside their son Roger, who became a heart surgeon. Phil did well in school and parlayed his mellifluous voice into his own radio program in high school, a considerable undertaking for a teenager. While a University of Missouri undergraduate, he decided to change his name legally from Anderson to Gottschalk. "I remember seeing a couple of letters that my father had written," John said. "When he was a sophomore or thereabouts, he wrote Helen and Ed and told them that they had done so much for him and they were clearly his parents and he wanted to change his name from Anderson to Gottschalk."

Phil Gottschalk and Mary Jane Barnes, by then a couple, both graduated in 1939. While Mary Jane began her career in journalism and stepped into a historic role in the early war effort, Phil began working for an economic survey company. As war grew ever more imminent for the United States, he volunteered for the draft. He went through Officer Candidate School and was commissioned as a second lieutenant, becoming an artillery officer.

As Germany ramped up its war effort, England was ill-prepared. To mitigate its shortcomings, England entered into the Lend-Lease program with the United States to build up its materiel readiness. The U.S. would ferry war planes to England filled with gasoline in huge bladders for the arduous journey across the Atlantic. With America still maintaining neutrality, the U.S. could ill-afford to have military pilots flying these bombers to England. Instead the government hired women with pilot's licenses to fly the planes. These women would pick up planes in Omaha and fly to Gander, Newfoundland. From there they would fly on to England, leave the planes, and return home by ship. Mary Jane Barnes was one of these pilots.

John knew little of the extent and drama of Mary Jane's flying exploits until much later. When he started to help her through the maze of applying for Social Security benefits, more was revealed. "I did know she had a pilot's license. I suppose I was probably twenty-five before I found out about this other stuff. She died at sixty-two. I remember when she turned sixty-two she was incapacitated with emphysema. We moved her here to Omaha and I went down to Social Security to start her benefits. The clerk asked me if she had been in the service. I said, 'I don't think so, but she flew bombers to England during the Lend-Lease program.' The clerk tapped her keyboard and said, 'Yeah, they're giving her credit even though these women weren't inducted into the military.' It raised her Social Security about four dollars a month."

The U.S. entry into the war grounded Mary Jane from flying military planes across the Atlantic. She continued to work at the newspaper while Phil was an artillery officer stationed in Fort Sill, Oklahoma. After one of his leaves, Mary Jane found out she was pregnant.

Time and place made life exceptionally difficult for unwed mothers in 1942. The wide midsection of America was particularly unforgiving of a pregnant single woman. The Center for Disease Control put the number of births to unmarried women ages twenty to twenty-four in 1940 at 9.5 per 1,000 compared to nearly 40 births per 1,000 twenty-five years later.

"In those days it was clearly a scarlet letter," John said. "I think that the culture and the acceptance out in the Plains for that kind of thing was probably less than it was anywhere else, and it wasn't very acceptable anywhere else. The horror of birthing a child weighed heavily on her. I learned later from my father that this had a significant impact on her mentally, to the point that whether to proceed with this pregnancy or not was a big issue. In looking back, from what little I know, the fact that I'm even here—clearly, she decided to go through with it, but I do know that there was significant angst."

Her decision would set in motion a series of momentous events, the first of which was John's birth.

$\sim$

John Gottschalk was born June 12, 1943, in Dayton, Ohio, where his mother had taken a job with the Army Air Corps Public Information Office. His birth certificate identified him as the son of Mary Jane Barnes and Phil Gottschalk. Mary Jane placed him in foster care in Dayton. Nearly two years later, after Phil and Mary Jane married and settled in Rushville, Phil would return to Dayton to claim their son, essentially giving him birth a second time.

John had no idea and obviously no recollection of his two years in Dayton. Nor had any paper trail come to light to suggest who took care of him during that time. Mary Jane had determined she could not raise a child in wartime circumstances, so she went back to her job and Phil went back to the war. John stayed in Dayton in what he came to believe was "some sort of foster home."

Before the war ended, Phil and Mary Jane married. But there was still the matter of their son in Ohio. In stories Phil told John when he was in high school and becoming aware of his remarkable beginnings, the choice between leaving him in Dayton as an orphan to be adopted, or starting a new life in Rushville with his biological parents, was a "big to-do."

The decision changed the course of John's life and the lives of many other people and institutions. Phil and Mary Jane decided to start a new life with John in Rushville.

Phil took the train to Dayton. Mary Jane stayed behind to confront what she had not wanted to face two years earlier. She was spared some of the awkwardness when Phil arrived in Rushville with the story that he was bringing home their "adopted" son. The hope was that this story would overcome the curiosity of friends and neighbors in Rushville, but most especially of Bill and Ruth Barnes. John never found out what transpired in the days following Phil's return.

"I don't know how that introduction went with my grandparents," John said. "I don't know if while I was in Dayton they knew I existed or if (Mary Jane) was going to 'adopt' me. I have no idea how they handled all of that. She can't just show up with a kid and say, 'Here we just adopted this kid.' But anyhow, that was the story and I didn't know the difference."

Contributing to any awkwardness surely was the fact that Mary Jane was pregnant with John's brother Mike at the time of John's arrival. A telltale item appeared in none other than the *Sheridan County Star* when Mike Gottschalk arrived. Proud grandpa Bill Barnes, in a column he periodically wrote for the *Star,* welcomed his "first" grandson, a nod to the mores and attitudes about adoption in the 1940s. John recalled his own incredulity when confronted with the notion that he was something other than a full member of the Gottschalk clan.

Bill Barnes at the *Sheridan County Star.*

"Somewhere along in grade school, maybe fifth or sixth grade, my best friend, Charlie Bare, told me I was adopted. I said, 'You're crazy. Where did you get that?' He said, 'My mom told me you're adopted.' I said, 'Well, tough luck.'" But John recalled a relationship with his grandfather that in hindsight spoke volumes about whether Bill Barnes was absolutely clear about John's extraordinary journey to Rushville.

Though Bill treated John warmly, John recalled, "Mike was really the apple of his eye because Mike was, presumably, his first grandson. I had a good relationship with Bill Barnes, but he had an understandable special relationship with Mike. I think part of the reason was they were laboring under this adoption business for a long time. My grandpa would go to Omaha to sell his cattle. By that time, he had sold the *Sheridan County Star* to my mom and dad and acquired a ranch south of Nenzel. He had an Angus operation and would often take Mike to the ranch. When he would sell his cattle, they'd ship them by rail and he'd drive to Omaha. Mike would frequently go down with him. Sometimes I could go, too. I guess what little recollection I have, I always felt it was unusual that he had such a close relationship with Mike and not me. It wasn't a distant relationship (with me). It was a very affectionate relationship, which I guess tells me now in retrospect that he didn't know that I wasn't adopted. I'll tell you, I've got pictures of Mike and me, and it's got to be patently obvious (that we were biological brothers). But I don't know that the record was ever straightened out. It had to have been before Bill's death, because by then I was in my twenties and it got straightened out with me probably late in high school. That's when I learned this whole story."

By no means did the revelation of his unusual beginnings diminish his wonderful life growing up in the bucolic northwest corner of Nebraska. "I knew about my mother's flying, and I knew my dad was in the war, and fortunately in those days you actually read history books and knew what was going on, unlike today. So I knew when the war was and what they were doing, and I knew war was hell and I knew things stop and go and there are all kinds of things that happen. So it was entirely rational to me. I had no animus at all about being on the threshold of abandonment, a fact I had no recollection of at all."

If John's twice-born beginning was dramatic and unusual, it had no visible effect on his development, ability, or his relationships, especially with his father, with whom he was quite close. John remembered both his parents as being very nurturing and maintaining high expectations for him, Mike, and sister Lynn.

There was work to be done at the newspaper. Mary Jane shared the workload with Phil, setting type, keeping the books, and doing whatever else was necessary to meet deadlines. "At the end of the day, you're covered in printer's ink," John remembered. "It was an old, four-aught, Miehle press. That's a dirty thing. My mother also cooked our dinner, cheered us on, and the paper went out every Thursday."

Phil and Mary Jane "hang" lines of type on the Linotype machine in the back shop of the *Sheridan County Star*.

Soon the workload came to be shared with John and Mike. The brothers would spend their Saturday mornings sweeping the trimmings from the folder, tearing down the pages, melting the lead slugs, and pouring the elongated metal "pigs" to feed the Linotype for the coming week's paper. The chores became lessons for John. "We had to sweep, and then we had to throw in all the individual letters used for the headlines. They were handset so we had to throw in all the handset type so all the letters would be ready for assembly into next week's paper. We learned a California type case at probably ten or eleven."

By the time John was a freshman, activities at Rushville High were front and center, especially participation in a solid music program and an elite football team, which rarely found itself on the wrong end of a Friday night scoreboard. John starred as a linebacker and quarterback for the Longhorns. "I think we lost a couple of games in four years. It was extraordinary. Saturday was always a day off for the players. Not Mike and me, though. We had to go down and sweep. One day we figured out a way to sleep late on Saturday. We went down to the shop, got all our work done in the middle of the night, went back home, and went to bed. And of course, first thing in the morning, Dad opened the door and hollered that it's time to get going, and we chuckled to ourselves and went back to sleep. When he saw through our plan, he said, 'Boys, have you thought this through? You spent all night up so you could sleep in the morning? That isn't that big a deal. It didn't change the amount of work. It didn't change the amount of time you worked. What did you gain by this?'" John was later to realize that growing up in Rushville, and in the Gottschalk household, brought lessons about what's important and what's not.

While John learned the newspaper business starting from the ground up and found his extracurricular niche on the football field and in the music room, he proved to be an exceptional student and classroom leader, prodded both at home and by the likes of Marjorie Wasserburger. His excellence in school showed up early. According to Margie Hinn, John was not simply a bright young man but a considerate one, too. "He was a nice, jolly little kid and a very good student. He had a compassionate heart. I had thirty-three kids in the third grade then. Of course, that was not when you had any helpers or anything like that. There was everything from genius kids to slower children. John was very helpful to anyone that was having trouble. He was a very kind little kid."

Expectations in a place such as Rushville were built into the culture. It was a place where everyone knew your business whether that be your grades in school or your reputation around town. Some found small-town America suffocating and inhibiting, but for John Gottschalk, who embraced and thrived in such a milieu, Rushville, in aggregate, became a sort of nurturing relative.

"In little towns, everybody knows everybody and everything. If there ever was the concept of a village raising the child, it seems to me, at least in my reckoning, Rushville was like that. I saw my father do this and I'm sure my brother and I were, more than once, the victims of this same thing: if you were screwing around, doing something stupid, just about anybody would tell you to knock it off and you would."

His theory played out many times, but was brought into clear relief one afternoon outside the Modisett Men's Club, an alcohol-free social club in Rushville where ranchers could sit and relax in town while their wives shopped. The Modisett family was well-known in Sheridan County as signature philanthropists, making the Modisett name synonymous with the area. A handsome new baseball stadium and field on the west side of town—rebuilt in 2014 through John's leadership and financial support—was called the historic Modisett Ball Park.

That afternoon, John and Mike were behind the club with a bat, ball, and undoubtedly dreams of the Major Leagues.

Sure enough, the baseball found a window, shattering it. John and Mike went directly to the court house to find Joe Baldauf, the county veterans service officer, who also looked after the Modisett Men's Club.

"We told him that we had knocked a ball through the window and he said he'd get the thing fixed. He talked to dad about getting paid, and we told him we were sorry and that's the way it should be. Years and years later, I ran into his daughter somewhere, and the first thing she said to me was, 'My dad still remembers you guys coming to him because you did that, and you could have walked away.' True, but that's not the way we were raised. You didn't have to worry whether someone saw you or not. It's a lot easier to just live clean."

Carmen Beck, the love of John's life, his soulmate, and his wife for more than five decades, remembered Rushville with a fondness gleaned from the experience of an "outsider." She moved there in her early teens from Mission, South Dakota, to live with her sister, Verleen. The move took some of the pressure from Carmen's mother who was trying to raise five children. Other than room and board from her sister's family, she was responsible for herself. At age thirteen, she worked as a waitress during the morning rush at the C and L Café, and then filled in at Levi Jones clothing store after school.

From the very beginning Carmen found a home. "The people were so warm in welcoming me, I felt as though I had lived here forever," she said. "Rushville became my family and I am indebted to these people." Carmen remembered one-on-one attention from teachers in a school where excellence was expected in the classroom and in activities.

She and John began dating their junior year in high school, married in 1964, and made Omaha their home after 1975. Still, for Carmen, the Sandhills and Rushville always remained "like no other place."

Striking a classic teenage pose with Carmen Beck, the future Mrs. Gottschalk.

While Rushville was a nurturing place for children of the 1950s and 1960s, in the Gottschalk house, expectations were high, according to Lynn Roper. "Our father said a thousand times, 'A's in grade school are B's in high school are C's in college.' I mean the expectations were that you're going to put your nose to the grindstone. In other houses they didn't probably have those kinds of expectations. I knew that my parents had college degrees and most other people didn't."

West from Rushville and the dirt meridian, the broad and boundless high plains eventually gave way to Wyoming's spectacular skyline: the Bighorns, the Wind River Range, and the Tetons. Millions of tourists were drawn to the state each year to ski, hunt, fish, hike, camp, and enjoy the unspoiled beauty of the Northern Rockies and their eastern slope. Preserves such as the Gros Ventre Wilderness, Grand Teton National Park, and Yellowstone beckoned both those at home in the rugged and pristine outdoors and those for whom some of the planet's most unspoiled land touched a part of their souls nowhere else can.

So it was for John Gottschalk, who high in the Tetons had his life changed at a place called Jenny Lake in the mid-50s. The mountains spoke to him via his love of the Boy Scouts, an organization he would lead many years later when he became the national president of the Boy Scouts of America. After World War II, a Rushville insurance man and huge supporter of scouting, Gene Leahy, homesteaded 160 wooded acres near Sheridan, Wyoming. John's scoutmaster arranged with Leahy for his scout troop to camp there for a few days on the way to the Tetons.

After camping at Leahy's, they arrived in the magnificent range south of Yellowstone, making camp near Jenny Lake. "Two of the adult chaperones rented a canoe and had fishing rods. I showed an interest in what they were doing. They let me come along. I caught a trout, maybe my first ever." John was twelve years old. He never forgot the thrill. He was to return again and again to the trout waters of northwestern Wyoming. Eventually he and Carmen purchased a home there.

John cradles a beautiful cutty. Cutthroat trout are indigenous to the Tetons where John caught his first trout at age twelve.

Aside from hiking, camping, and developing his newfound love for fly fishing, John earned his lifesaving merit badge on that trip—but not without searing the incident into his memory. "We went up to a place called Lake Solitude, surface elevation is 9,032 feet. So that's where we were going to do our lifesaving merit badge. The water temperature was fifty-five degrees, maybe sixty-five. It was incredibly uncomfortable. Spending time in that icy water was perhaps one of the dumbest things I ever did. But we got the merit badge. We hiked into the Tetons a bit and learned a couple of things."

Later John would earn admittance to the scouts' prestigious Order of the Arrow, undergoing a twenty-four-hour vigil alone in the woods. This required him to find food and shelter and make his way back to camp using his wits, intuition, and skills learned both in scouting and at home. Who could have guessed that fifty years later he would lead the Boy Scouts of America national organization—four million boys and a million volunteers—using the same skills and practical knowledge that led him out of the woods many years before?

He returned to the Tetons a couple of years later on a rare Gottschalk family vacation on the Fourth of July holiday. He was fourteen by then, and the magnificence and pull of the range was exerting a lifetime allure. The holiday getaway was unusual because running a weekly newspaper afforded the family very few days off save a press convention here and there, which for Phil and Mary Jane Gottschalk were single-day sojourns to mix and mingle with the state's newspaper community.

During one of their trips, John found himself alone at the *Star* busy with the details of newspaper work. The *Star* published on Thursdays. In the previous edition, John had written a piece about a milk price dispute. Although he and Mike still had Saturday morning clean-up duties, by high school John could set type, edit copy, sell an ad, produce a story for the front page, and operate the Linotype, press, and folder. He essentially could run the newspaper. That Saturday morning, he also had to stand up to the kind of criticism that journalists traditionally learn to face.

South of Hay Springs in an area called Mirage Flats, dairy farmers had participated earlier in the 1950's version of the "milk wars," dumping milk to protest prices at market. These protests were part of a nationwide call to action against stagnating prices, caused, they claimed, by excessive regulation, and finding themselves too often at loggerheads with the trucking union. John's short story detailed these events and attempted to ascertain what effect the dumping produced. He concluded his piece, he said, with "something to the effect that in spite of the dumping, milk prices had not changed."

Two days after the article ran, two pickups from Mirage Flats pulled up to the front door of the *Star*. Four "unhappy looking men," as John recalled them, strode to the counter and demanded to know, "Who's the guy in charge?"

With his parents gone and no one else around, John had few alternatives.

"I'm the guy in charge."

"Well, who the hell wrote this story?" the quartet demanded, Thursday's paper in hand.

"I did. Is there a mistake in it?"

They had no quibble with the facts, only that they saw the story as invalidating their milk dumping, so the men spent the next ten minutes scolding the "guy in charge." The dustup proved instructive. Years later, as publisher of the *Omaha World-Herald*—the guy in charge—John would once again take on an angry group of agricultural producers who objected to a report of facts they could not refute but nonetheless were angered at seeing in print. It involved the powerful and well-heeled cattlemen's association over a story on the E. coli bacteria.

John often found himself at the head of the class in Rushville, whether by default or by design. The high school—home of the Longhorns—carried a reputation for excellence in academics, music, and athletics. A faculty, populated with the likes of Marjorie Wasserburger and John's football coach Bill Stephenson, honed his leadership skills, whether he was learning to write a clear declarative sentence or taking snaps as the Longhorns' quarterback. Also in his stable of mentors was the Rev. Herman Heuser at Rushville's Presbyterian Church, whose flock included the Gottschalks and Barneses and L.E. "Bud" Mitchell, his scoutmaster.

Younger Longhorns cheered him on football fields on Friday nights and then watched how he carried himself on Main Street the next day, more than likely coming to and from the *Sheridan County Star*. As it is with small-town heroes, John Gottschalk was someone they hoped to become someday.

Among his admirers was Chuck Hagel, who went on to have a spectacular career himself as U.S. senator from Nebraska and the secretary of defense in the Obama administration. His counsel and input was sought from universities to think tanks to the highest offices of government. But once, he was on the sidelines in Rushville, Nebraska, watching John lead and excel.

"I got to know John when we moved to Rushville in 1955 from Ainsworth," Hagel said. "He was three years older. His parents had the newspaper there. My dad ran the local lumber yard. I went to a different school, the Catholic grade school. There were only twelve hundred people, if that, in the town but there was a Catholic grade school. I was in junior high and he was in high school. But in a small town you know everybody. I got to know his sister, Lynn, very well. She was a little younger than I and I got to know his brother Mike a little better through scouts. He was a year older. John was always very involved in scouts. But when you're in that age group, if someone's two or three years older than you, that's a big leap. I got to know John a little bit and watched him. And I always admired him. On Friday nights, we'd go over and watch the games. The football field was like an open prairie in those little towns. It was only about a block from where we lived. He was a kind of hero of all the kids because he was a very good football player and a quarterback."

John was a quarterback and linebacker on the undefeated Rushville Longhorns, a Friday night football hero to the kids in town. One of his young fans was Chuck Hagel, who went on to become a U.S. senator and secretary of defense.

Hagel's family moved to Scottsbluff, 110 miles south and west of Rushville, but he reconnected with John in the 1970s when he was working for John McCollister, a GOP congressman from Omaha, and John was starting his career at the *Omaha World-Herald*. The friendship would endure and Hagel would call upon his childhood friend to help save the USO some years later.

When you're the quarterback, leadership is expected, just as it is when you're the "guy in charge," either by your place on a masthead or by default. But sometimes, leadership could come from the strangest quarters—and still produce a positive result.

Between John's sophomore and junior years in high school, he decided to pad his bank account by accepting a summer job on the Forney Ranch, several thousand acres of hay and grazing country south of Rushville. The ranch was founded in 1906 by Stanley Forney, who had migrated from Casper, Wyoming. He and his son Hubert both filed claims on land near that of Old Jules Sandoz and the massive Spade Ranch near the turn of the twentieth century.

In the summer of 1958 John signed on to be a scatter raker for $125 a month, cleaning up after the sweeps had made their way down the windrows carrying hay to the tall slide stackers. Don and Olive Forney were friends of Phil and Mary Jane Gottschalk. The couples always celebrated Phil and Olive's December twenty-third birthdays with a party. The Forneys lived deep in the Sandhills. John wanted to earn money but took along his football shoes to run in the sand and get ready for fall on the gridiron. The ranch hands were weathered guys, stretching in age from just older than John's tender teen years to nearly sixty.

"Most of these guys were in the bunkhouse with some younger guys from Scottsbluff," John remembered. "The ranch had another house, just a small little house, and I think three of us were in there. So we were separated from the rest of the hay crew. Don took us to this house, and we unpacked and went to bed at eight o'clock."

Shortly after they had hit the hay, Don Forney returned, banging on the door and barging in.

"Did you get those cows milked?"

What?" I asked.

"Did you get those cows milked?"

"No."

"Well, you'd better get a bucket and get them milked."

"I don't even know which end to start at, Mr. Forney."

"Well, I'll go out there with you and show you."

John and his bunkmates picked up the buckets, hobbled the cows, and went to school, learning in short order the finer points of cow milking. "Milking the cows was a good learning experience, not necessarily in my job description, but after all, this was not a union."

Nor was patience in the job description, but John needed a measure of it as heavy rains came within a few days of his arrival. The older guys dug out auto gates, fixed fences, and tended to other needs on the ranch while John and his bunkmates sat inside with nothing to do. Eventually, the rain stopped and everyone went to work haying, under the keen and watchful eye of Joe Bolek, the diminutive but tough foreman. "He was probably all of five foot seven but had a couple of sons who were probably six foot two, high-school seniors, big guys, football players," John said. "Dad was short, but he was stout. He was one tough scary boss. He growled a lot, didn't say a lot. So we were kind of behind because of the constant rain. We started working nearly from sunup to sundown, seven days a week. That went on for at least four weeks."

Even though the crew didn't bunk together, after dinner John and his two bunkmates always went to the bunkhouse to shoot the breeze with the guys. "Some of the younger ones were getting a little randy, which I didn't know too much about at the time. They were grousing and bitching. They said, 'We need to go to town. We're out here as slave labor.'"

Eventually one Friday night the complaining came to a head. The plan was to "shut this damn thing down and go to town Saturday." The argument was that for over a month they had been at it from sunup to sundown with no break. John was on board with the plan. It didn't go as planned.

"So it came around to five or six o'clock. I'd just pulled my tractor over by the gas tank wagon and shut it off. There wasn't exactly a big parade behind me. Not that they didn't want to go, but they didn't have the courage, I guess, and I was too dumb to know. It wasn't a joke; I was just the only guy to do what we had agreed to. I was sitting at the tank wagon and Don drove by in his truck. He waved and I waved back at him."

Twenty minutes later others showed up. The foreman wanted to know what was the matter? When John told him all was well, he demanded to know, "What the hell you doing over here? We've got work to do."

John told him the gist of the complaint session, explaining that they had been working four straight weeks and needed to go to town. "I was fifteen years old, the spokesman of the group. I was catapulted into the role and didn't have a clue why they were so all-fired up to go to town."

Joe grunted and they drove to the headquarters' dining hall where the twenty-man crew was eating its evening meal prepared by Olive Forney. While dinner was never a raucous affair, this night you could only hear forks clanking on plates. John took the silence as a bad sign. His perception was accurate. After dinner Joe told John that Mr. Forney wanted to see him at the house. "I thought, oh, shit." John walked over to the house where Don Forney answered the door.

"I did not step in, nor was I invited. His opening line was, 'John, I understand you don't want to work here anymore.'"

The thought "oh, shit" came to John for the second time in a few minutes. "Mr. Forney, it's not that. I think we're all just kind of pooped."

"Well, I'll take you to town tomorrow, John." John had yet to earn his driver's license.

"Mr. Forney, the second worst thing that could happen to me, besides getting fired, is for my dad to come home and see me sitting on the steps. That won't sit well with him, and it doesn't sit well with me either."

At which point Don gave John a short course on ranching. "Son, you've got to understand something. Have you ever heard the expression, 'Make hay while the sun shines?' We're way behind, we only have so much time to do this, and that's what we're here for, and that's what you're here for. So that comes first. We've got cattle to feed this winter. Now, if you want to reconsider."

"I have no desire to not work here, I want to work."

"Okay. By the way, I'm giving the guys a day off tomorrow. Do you want me to take you in?"

"No, no. I think I'll just stay here."

John, who would lead a newspaper company with thousands of employees and sit on boards whose policies affected hundreds of thousands of workers, had told the ranch story many times, always emphasizing that he learned labor relations from Don Forney.

Fifty years later, on the occasion of a big civic surprise dinner for John when he stepped down from the *Omaha World-Herald*, Don Forney was in attendance. At the conclusion of the event, Don handed John a wrapped shoe box and asked John to open it. Inside was a custom made pair of silver and copper spurs bearing his initials. "John," said Don with a firm handshake, "you've earned these." Don Forney passed away a week later.

～

Labor relations came in handy for John after he returned to Rushville the summer following his freshman year in Lincoln at the University of Nebraska. That's when he and Mike became businessmen, leasing and operating Dobry's Quick Serv Drive-In in Rushville for three successive summers.

During Christmas break John's freshman year, Phil Gottschalk told John and Mike, who was still in high school, that a lucrative opportunity might be available for them the following summer. According to John, Phil easily sold his sons on the idea: "Mr. Dobry talked to me and he owns the Quick Serv and has run it for a number of years. He said he's getting too old and he thought this would be a good venture for you and Mike. The terms of the deal are that you would lease the facility from Mr. Dobry for $1,000 from Memorial Day to Labor Day, about a hundred days roughly. Mr. Dobry tells me he makes good money and there's no reason you shouldn't be able to do this. You are smart guys, upstanding, and hard workers." That was enough for John and Mike, who loved the idea but wondered where they were going to get a thousand dollars. Phil suggested a trip to the bank.

"I swear to you, and it didn't occur to us then, but I'm positive he had this thing worked out." John and Mike made their way to see Mr. Johnson at the bank who sat the intrepid duo down and asked how he could be of help. John did the talking.

"We want to borrow some money to lease Mr. Dobry's drive-in."

"Oh, really? How much do you think you're going to need?"

"We're going to need a thousand dollars."

"I think that sounds reasonable. We've had the account for quite some time, and Mr. Dobry has a good business there. Now, what have you got for collateral?"

The boys exchanged glances and asked, "For what?"

"Collateral. When we loan you this money, you know you have to pay it back. But in the event that you don't pay it back, we'll have to recover the money because it's really not our money, it's our depositors' money. So you're going to either have to get some equity in there or you're going to have to have some collateral."

John confessed, "We don't know what collateral is."

Johnson continued the banking seminar, hitting on revelation after revelation for the Gottschalk brothers. "It's something that if we had to, we could sell and get our money back."

John and Mike offered up two 20 gauge, single-shot shotguns and a 1955 Ford.

"Well, I think you're a little light," Johnson said.

"We don't know much about this. Are there any other things that we could do that could help this?"

"You might look for a cosigner."

"What's a cosigner?"

"That's somebody who actually signs the loan with you and if you don't pay, they'll have to pay. So we're assured we'll get the money back."

John and Mike thought for a moment. "Man, who would we get for a cosigner? Could we use our dad if he'd do it?"

"I suppose. You'll have to talk to him about that."

The boys left the bank, walking the half block down to the newspaper office. "I'm sure he was sitting there grinning, but he had to see us coming, and he knew exactly what was going on, I just know he did."

John and Mike told Phil their tale, that they talked to Mr. Johnson and the shotguns and the '55 Ford weren't enough for collateral.

Phil played along. "Oh, really? What are you going to do?"

"He said we would need a cosigner. So would you cosign the note?"

"You know what that means, don't you? It means if you two don't pay the money, your dad's going to have to pay it."

"Would you do that for us, dad?"

"Yeah, I think so."

Whether Phil had set the bank loan wheels in motion—John was later to conclude that he certainly had—Dobry's Quick Serv Drive-In was under new management the summer of 1962.

That first summer John and Mike, still teenagers, spent most of their time there, making burgers and hot dogs and hawking ice cream through the Quick Serv's walkup window. "And we sold Aunt Mabel Grimes's potato salad there, too," Mike recalled. The drive-in was open from six in the morning until ten at night—seven days a week. There were no carhops at the Quick Serv. Sister Lynn was also a fixture at the Quick Serv, making the enterprise a complete Gottschalk sibling affair.

They made $7,000 in one hundred days. "I've still got the books," John said. "The books consisted of the checking account, which had both deposits and withdrawals. We had to pay off the loan. That's a thousand for the bank and three each for Mike and me. Room, board, books, and tuition at the university was two grand."

With a summer's experience and money in the bank, John and Mike, who was also now in college, looked forward to making more money the next year. It didn't quite work that way, though, as labor became part of the Quick Serv story.

"Our second year, we're ready to do this again, except we got to thinking, you know, that's pretty tough. Maybe what we need is have one of us there all the time, and we maybe ought to hire somebody."

They hired Tony Hixon, the postmaster's son. He proved to be an excellent part-time worker and a huge help to Lynn, who ran the place until the boys returned from college. It also introduced the boys to the concept of tax.

"We told Lynn that we would pay her all the silver dollars and all the two-dollar bills we received for the entire summer. She loves telling this story. She said fine and she was true to her word. I don't recall the exact amount, but I do know that we had maybe four or five silver dollars and maybe one two-dollar bill. She helped us throughout the summer for six bucks."

Lynn also remembered a financial idiosyncrasy that developed the first summer: the ironing of cash. "We'd bring the money home at night and iron it. Yeah. We'd iron the one dollar bills. (John, Mike, and their friends) would play poker with them because we had all these ones. We spent every day, all day at the drive-in."

The brothers actually had to pay Tony, so the second summer the account topped out at $5,000, another lesson the young entrepreneurs grasped immediately.

"That's a learning experience: labor can give you bad heartburn. Then we got to year three. This time we both were in the fraternity house, Phi Gamma Delta. I was then president of the house. We had four or five fraternity guys who came out to Rushville to spend the summer. They were mostly working construction."

Among the fraternity brothers in Rushville was Bob Kerrey, who remained one of John's oldest and most cherished friends. He did his pharmacy internship with Fritz Wefso at Wefso's Pharmacy. By now the brothers were paying two employees, but more problematic was that the crew from Lincoln and other friends would show up hungry—often about midnight.

"So we'd go back in and start eating the inventory," John said. "We got out of there that third summer with about a thousand bucks apiece. We got a lot of business experience backwards. Usually you start low and work your way up. But in a way it was really an education. Because when you're trying to climb up to the top you might not get to the top. But when you start at the top you know what it's like.

"It isn't necessarily because of the drive-in, but one of the visioning exercises I talk about in business is the concept of taking the hill. If you want to climb a mountain, you stand at the bottom and you can see the peak just clear as a bell. You can point at it and you can line it up with the road or the tree or whatever you want to do and you go right to it. The problem is you get in the trees first and it gets dense and you can wind up with a river crossing. You can wind up on a cliff. You can wind up with all kinds of bad stuff, so that doesn't always work just taking the hill. So what you've got to do is transport yourself mentally to the peak, your objective, and then look backwards. Because if you're at the top of a mountain and you look down, you can see every feature on the way up. And you know if you go straight, you're going to run into a canyon, so you sort that all out before you take off. Perhaps the ideology of that lesson, or that observation, is really the drive-in. We were at the top so we could see the problems: labor, which was the first one; employment taxes; and not managing your inventory. So maybe that was my beginning of going to the top and looking down."

Although he retired from the newspaper business and settled down five hours east of the 100th meridian, printer's ink and soil from Sheridan County still moved through John Gottschalk's veins. And, as it had been his entire life, whether crouched behind center on a football field, making decisions from the publisher's chair at a major metropolitan daily, or crafting a solution to a sticky problem as a corporate or nonprofit board leader, the filter through which everything flowed had always been Rushville.

Checking the latest edition of the *Sheridan County Star*, the family's
newspaper in Rushville, Neb. The *Star* was where John, with a
broom in the back shop, began his career as a newspaperman.

TWO

A New Life in Sidney and Old Friends

The women in our family were very involved in volunteer service. The Presbyterian Church women served the Rotary lunch, and they involved John and me in hauling out the tables for lunch. That may have been his first experience in public service—it set the hook. After he moved to Sidney, the parks director there said he needed something for the kids to do. John taught a class on how to build and fly a kite. This gave him great satisfaction. He talked afterwards about how good it made him feel.

-MIKE GOTTSCHALK

In 1968, John adopted a pattern of activity that would draw heavily on his stamina and attention for nearly a year. At 5 a.m. every Monday, the twenty-five-year-old would leave Sidney, where he was publisher and principal owner of the *Sidney Telegraph*. He would drive 136 miles north to his hometown of Rushville. There he would tend to the business of the *Sheridan County Star*, a newspaper that had been in his family for three generations. After a new owner had defaulted, the *Star* was now back under the control of John and his mother. Mary Jane's health had deteriorated. Alcoholism and a recent divorce from her husband Phil were factors in the decline. The *Star* needed a steady and sure hand, and on Mondays, John would arrive before 7 a.m. to provide it.

He would work in Rushville until Wednesday, writing, selling ads, setting type—whatever was needed to get the *Star* put to bed for Thursday publication. John would then head back to Sidney, his family—wife Carmen and infant daughter Jodi—and the *Telegraph*, which came off the press on Mondays, Wednesdays, and Fridays.

Thursdays and Fridays he spent in Sidney supervising the *Telegraph*'s operation. On Saturdays, he would drive one hundred miles to Cheyenne, Wyoming, where he would work on a community shopper he had purchased not long before. Sundays he would spend with his family back in Sidney. Early Monday he was back on the road again.

Running a newspaper was clearly in his sweet spot. Still, no one, including John, would have foreseen the frantic pace he would need to maintain as a newly-minted, twenty-five-year-old owner and publisher.

Seven years earlier John had left Rushville, graduating high school with honors, well-prepared for the academic rigors he would encounter at the University of Nebraska. He joined the Phi Gamma Delta fraternity and embraced university and fraternity life. The impact of each on him was considerable.

"When John came back from college, he was a different person," said his girlfriend at the time and future wife, Carmen Beck. She had stayed behind in Rushville to work at a law firm and earn money for college. "He was always responsible and mature, but now he was a lot more fun, too."

He and brother Mike would run the Quick Serv Drive-In in Rushville for three summers and host their Fiji fraternity brothers who came to town for summer jobs. Their days were long on laughs, enriched with the amusement college buddies can find in even the slightest pretext.

On campus, John's studies began with the intention of becoming a doctor. As a youngster, he had struggled with problems in his right eye, which necessitated many hours in an ophthalmologist's office. In the process, he acquired an interest in the health-care profession. But after a couple years of taking on more commitments with the Fiji house, he realized he was strapped for time. He also recognized the importance of getting on with his life, and years of medical training after college would take too long. The result: John switched majors to what he knew and loved—journalism.

His Phi Gamma Delta brothers elected John to a minor house office as a sophomore. He was tapped as house president for his junior year.

"In those days, the fraternity and sorority system was a lot closer to 1940 than it was to 1960," John said. The brothers dressed in coats and ties every Monday night for dinner and always escorted the housemother to the dining room, a level of formality with which John was completely comfortable because of trips he and Mike made as kids to Omaha with their Aunt Mabel Grimes. Aunt Mabel stayed at the Blackstone Hotel, where, in the formal dining room for evening meals, John and Mike learned to properly use the half-dozen utensils that lay alongside their plates. Not only did they learn the niceties of fine dining; they also became quite comfortable interacting with adults in a formal setting.

In the fraternity house of forty or fifty young men— although most were on board with the fun and the formalities of fraternity life—a few had idiosyncrasies that a house president's good example and leadership skills could usually offset.

But John had more responsibilities than simply setting a good example of dining room etiquette. There was also a housemother, a post held for forty years by the beloved "Mom" Minear. She retired during John's sophomore year, meaning he would be greeting a new housemother at the moment he was taking office as house president.

The Fijis hired Gertrude Thomas. Shortly after taking the job she fell ill and, although only in her sixties, died. As the house leader, John became the intermediary with her two sons who lived a considerable distance away. It became a tough stretch for John. The house became his to lead as a matter of position and practicality. He leaned heavily on the graciousness and good will of Nancy Schneider, the housemother at the Alpha Tau Omega fraternity next door to the Fijis, who supplied him with menus and ideas for the Fiji cooks. She was "a great help to me." He found himself setting the tone and providing an example for many of his young fraternity brothers who had never confronted death. "We had two classes that were younger than I was. Everybody was feeling bad, so I had to figure out how to deal with that," John said. Schneider provided him not only with an efficient plan to feed his brothers, but also a recipe for a unique leadership role at Phi Gamma Delta.

His fraternity experience—including spending a summer criss-crossing the state and meeting with Fiji alums to raise money for a house expansion—informed and influenced John's decision to be a lifelong, committed member on the national stage of Phi Gamma Delta.

That journey started with John becoming involved with Fijis' Omaha alumni chapter, rising to the group's presidency. Bill Martin, executive director of Phi Gamma Delta International going back to 1986, traced John's national Fiji involvement to his participation in the group's biennial convention in 1990 in Chicago. "We had done a profile of John in our magazine sometime during the previous two years. It might have been when John succeeded Harold "Andy" Andersen (also a Fiji) as publisher of the *Omaha World-Herald.* So John caught the eye of the nominations committee chairman as somebody who might be a good prospect to serve on our board of directors."

In typical John Gottschalk fashion, he jumped headlong into the task and rose to the board presidency in 1994, serving a two-year term. There, he found the directors spending an inordinate amount of time on two undergraduate challenges: alcohol and academic performance.

He foresaw an uphill battle.

"When I was board president, we finally decided to take on the matters of both the grade point average required for initiation and to absolutely get alcohol out of our houses," he said. "That was a long, long journey, but the national board took it on."

With a solid assist from Joseph Somora, a former White House fellow, John led the Phi Gamma Delta board through the process of crafting policies that banned alcohol from all its houses and raised the GPA threshold for initiation to 3.25. In order for the changes to take effect, the student delegates, who held 70 percent of the votes, had to approve them at the national convention in 1996.

Although the adult leaders did everything they could think of to promote passage, John said he feared that neither proposal would pass, thereby negating two years of hard work.

With John presiding, the votes were as surprising to him as they were gratifying. After a presentation of the two proposals, the first question was called. The hall exploded with a deep and resounding "yea!" When the call for opposing votes came, the huge room, filled with hundreds of college fraternity men, stood silent.

The vote on the second proposal was a duplicate of the first. John recalled the stunning moment: "Not a single nay. My jaw dropped."

For Bill Martin, the votes revealed not only John's leadership skills but also his ability to work with others in a leadership role. "John was a quick study, respectful of other points of view, whether from his fellow board members or from staff members. He was very conscious of the role of a board of directors, to see to the strategic direction of the organization, and to give that strategic direction to the staff and let the staff do its job."

Martin said John's style underscored his leadership as well. "I would describe it as a great combination of impatience and compassion: Impatience to want to see the organization move forward, but also compassion towards people and recognition of whatever the limitations might be. My impression of John is that when he serves on a board, he wants to feel that he's making a difference, and that the board is making a difference, and that the organization is making a difference."

The night of Lynn Gottschalk's high school graduation in 1966, her father, Phil, left Sidney and headed for Columbia, Missouri. His marriage to Mary Jane had come unraveled. She was having difficulties managing the family's newspaper business. Phil and Mary Jane were principal owners of the *Sidney Telegraph*. They had sold the *Sheridan County Star*, although the buyer's default was imminent. The Gottschalks looked to John, then twenty-three, to navigate the family through what were obviously troubled seas.

But John, who in 1964 had married his high school sweetheart, Carmen Beck, already had a busy life in Lincoln. He was a student and campus leader and worked at the Ayers Advertising Agency as a part-time production assistant. Nevertheless, when called, John returned to the Panhandle to keep the family's business affairs afloat. He settled in Sidney during the summer of 1966 as an advertising account executive at the *Telegraph*. He and Carmen moved into his parents' home where Mary Jane was also living. The arrangement allowed them to keep a wary eye on Mary Jane as her health was becoming more fragile.

Henry Osborne at his machine shop.
John sold his first newspaper ad to Henry.

Lynn remembered John's steadiness during the crisis. "My parents bought the Sidney newspaper and Dad moved to Sidney. Mom did not. Then she moved there, but it was my senior year in high school. I moved, too, but my Dad bribed me to do so by buying me a 1966 Mustang." The shiny car was no match for his eventual departure, however. Lynn called his exodus "devastating." She didn't talk to him for sixteen years.

Compounding Phil's leaving was the buyer of the *Star* defaulting, which left both the Rushville and Sidney newspapers needing leadership and management. "My parents were trying to run both newspapers," Lynn said. "But after Dad walked out, John stepped up to the plate. That's when I saw him as my best friend. He's the oldest and he's taking care of Mom and this mess, thank you very much, so I could go to college and Mike could go to law school."

John's arrival in Sidney was clearly amid roiling waters, but he settled in smoothly, taking over as the paper's business manager in 1967 and then buying 75 percent of the *Telegraph* in 1968 to become principal owner and publisher.

John made 1968 a watershed year in his newspaper career as he (with his mother) re-acquired the *Star* from Dick and Doris Wentland, who had defaulted. He also purchased Star Publications in Cheyenne—the shopper that for the next year consumed his Saturdays.

Jack Lowe was the *Telegraph*'s editor when the transition began, and John came to treasure Lowe's mentorship and his guidance. Lowe had a 25 percent stake in the newspaper, which he sold to John in 1971 when he retired. In Jack Lowe, John was blessed to work with a nimble mind, a wealth of experience, and a humility that proved to be a touchstone for John both professionally and personally. Lowe was able to show his young protégé the particulars when it came to running Sidney's community newspaper, and how to infuse the *Telegraph* with excellence while serving readers and the community. During John's tenure at the *Telegraph*, the newspaper won three national awards, including the Service to Agriculture Award from the National Newspaper Association in 1973.

As a tribute to Lowe, John established the Jack Lowe Community Journalism Fund, which ultimately led to the creation of the Nebraska Journalism Hall of Fame. (John was inducted into the Nebraska Journalism Hall of Fame in 2018.) But typical of John's style, a more personal reflection was in the offing when Lowe retired. John sent Lowe a letter, dated October 13, 1971, encapsulating his gratitude for the wise journalist's impact on his life.

Jack Lowe was a guiding force in John's career as a newspaperman.

Dear Jack,

A few years ago, the Presbyterian pastor who served our little Rushville congregation died in Colorado Springs, bringing upon me a terrible feeling of guilt. This man had been one of a handful of giants who shaped my life and my values. I hadn't even thanked him. In fact, it was too late when I recognized the impact he had upon me. I resolved then, that when I recognized men whose influence helped me grow as a man, I would never again let that help go without at least a thank you, and preferably a much more resounding tribute.

In my brief encounter with life, I have found it very gratifying to help others, as I am sure you have. That gratification is usually enough to satisfy whatever effort I may have consciously or unconsciously expended. With all the help you have given others, perhaps my present or future success will be enough of a reward for you. But for me, the occasion must not go without my deepest gratitude to you for so many things.

How vividly I recall my first day in Sidney and the circumstances which led up to it. It is a memory I will always cherish and be able to look back upon as the start of my yet unfinished journey. I was both fearful of my untested potential and, at the same time, assured that at least one man in my presence had such great talent that my awkwardness would not be so obvious.

Two men have established my newspaper philosophy. My grandfather, Bill Barnes, who taught me the meaning of moral courage and the necessity of exercising care when wielding the mighty pen. The other, Jack Lowe, made an equally significant contribution... the perception of dedication...and its impact as a newspaperman applies it to "lead" his community to greater achievements. You are the Master, Jack, at using great talent unselfishly and in a positive manner to achieve a better world for your neighbors. I suppose many people have talent of one kind or another. But it seems to me so few are able to apply it so as to have a lasting impact on mankind... and without tangible reward.

I have, in my files, four of these letters. One to my father, another to a Boy Scout leader, a third to a political science professor, and the fourth to you. Periodically, when things get confused, I reread them. They help me focus on solutions to problems each man encounters, and upon which he must search and apply his most basic principles.

As time marches by for both of us, I shall continue to reach out in my life for bigger and better things... another of my natural or acquired instincts. Thank God, as I grow older and my judgment improves, the probability of that reach exceeding the grasp diminishes.

Whether you intended it or not, you have a piece of John Gottschalk...and a significant one in his eyes, that he shall forever respect its source. If I can ever pay a dividend on your investment, there will be no distance too far, nor no cause too small.

Thank-you Jack Lowe for all that you have done, or caused to be done for John Gottschalk. With my profound best personal wishes.

John

~

John's taking of the *Telegraph*'s reins in 1968 at age twenty-five followed the deactivation and closing of the Sioux Army Depot just west of Sidney. The Army had opened the facility in 1942 as part of the war effort. According to the Nebraska State Historical Society, at its height the depot's operations "occupied 19,771 acres and included 801 ammunition storage igloos, 22 general supply warehouses, 392 support buildings, 225 family living quarters, 51 miles of railroad tracks, and 203 miles of roads. Depot personnel ranged from 625 to 2,161 civilian employees and from 4 to 57 military personnel depending on Army activity."

Sidney became a boom town during the war years and beyond. Also buoyed by the discovery of oil and natural gas in Cheyenne County, Sidney's population swelled as jobs were plentiful and businesses prospered.

As the Sioux Army Depot slowed its post-war pace and started making plans to close, Sidney felt the uneasiness of an economic boom going silent.

According to freelance writer and historian Dale Fehringer, Jimmy Phelps was the last employee to leave the depot, clocking out at 3:30 p.m., June 30, 1967. Phelps said he took the time clock off the wall, packed it, and shipped it to the government. Many of the buildings had been demolished as the phase-out gathered steam.

Western Nebraska Technical College had started classes on the depot property in the early 1960s. By the time Jimmy Phelps appropriated the time clock, the college had acquired over one thousand acres of depot land and nearly 220 of its buildings.

Still, for Sidney, the closing of the depot—and a leveling-off of area oil and gas production—put a dent in employment and probably more important, its morale.

"I wouldn't say it was incremental, the decline," John said. "By the time I got there in 1966 my sense was that it had reached the bottom and was ready to climb back up."

Certainly, Cabela's opening of a warehouse in the fifty-thousand-square-foot, four-story John Deere building in 1969 was momentous for Sidney. Dick Cabela had started the business in 1961 by sending out mail orders of fishing flies. He and his wife Mary and his brother Jim ran the business essentially from Dick and Mary's kitchen in Chappell, twenty-eight miles down the road from Sidney. As the business grew, finding enough space for their inventory became an issue. They had hunting and fishing equipment in buildings all over Chappell and needed to solve their space problems. Empty ammunition bunkers at the former depot provided part of the solution.

John had done business with the Cabelas while they were still in Chappell, printing the first editions of what would become the world-famous Cabela's Catalog. "Dick Cabela came to the *Telegraph* and said, 'We need somebody to print a catalog. I understand you have an offset press.'" Cabela's sold only via mail orders at the time, as it had no stores. The *Telegraph*'s press was key here, but so was John's sense of what the Cabela family was truly "selling"—a recognition of what those who loved hunting and fishing really wanted and needed.

It was a big job for a crew that was accustomed to printing broadsheet newspapers. John said the first catalog was laid out in a five-by-eight inch black-and-white format, which meant they basically printed a tabloid, folded it in half, and put it through the folder, so the result was closer to eight-and-a-half-by-eleven.

The length of the run was nearly twenty thousand. The *Telegraph* crew had no packaging equipment for a number that large, so they stacked the catalogs, borrowed a steel strapper and fixed them to pallets.

"Somewhere I have a picture of a forklift putting a pallet of catalogs up into the back of Jim Cabela's truck," John said.

Even before Cabela's brought what would become a world brand to Sidney, the city was bouncing back in other ways. Underpinning the progress were the constants of dry land wheat farming and the reality that, despite lulls in commerce, Sidney remained a market and retail hub for the area. At the *Telegraph*, the company enjoyed the stature of having one of only three web offset presses in the state, a two-unit Goss community press, which was in demand for printing more than simply newspapers. When he took over as owner/publisher in 1968, John was already looking for ways to maximize the potential of the *Telegraph*'s press. By the time he sold the *Telegraph* in 1974, it had become a commercial printing plant for about twenty papers in four states. Much of that was possible because in 1972 he added a four-unit Goss press in anticipation of more printing contracts. The press proved to be a major contributor to the increasing value of the business.

The *Telegraph*'s reputation as a leader in offset printing was known in western Nebraska newspaper circles, but it reached all the way across the state, too. One day an African American man showed up at the *Telegraph* with a newspaper in one hand and some pay stubs in another. He introduced himself and said he was from Omaha and was looking for someone to print his newspaper. This piqued John's curiosity.

"So I asked what brought him all the way from Omaha. This was a long way from Omaha. He looked up at me and said, 'Do you not do business with black people?' I said 'I noticed you have on a green shirt and that's what I look at.' He said, 'You're the right guy.' I was glad to take his money."

John's focus on Sidney's economic vitality crossed over into both of his leadership arenas. The Sioux Army Depot had closed but that impact required more than simply retooling a workforce. The city needed new ideas and new thinking, people to both create and carry out the results, and ways to solve the city's problems.

Sidney's population had reached ten thousand as the city rode the boom of the depot, the oil discoveries, and what John termed a "good underlying economy." As the economy of a place ebbs and flows, a big slide can replace a big boom. The slide in this case occurred when the depot closed its doors. But Sidney responded with new ideas.

Instead of waiting for someone else to do something, John immersed himself in Chamber of Commerce activities, economic activities, and city booster activities. "The Sidney Chamber of Commerce became the Cheyenne County Chamber of Commerce. I think it was the first or maybe only county-wide chamber in the state. It was a struggle coming back. It was a relatively healthy place but the prognosis was not good."

For John, Sidney's ongoing comeback was coupled with his responsibilities at the newspaper. "The Chamber was where I put most of my energy, plus I was buried in debt, working my butt off, and doing lots of things."

When he first arrived at the *Telegraph*, he handled much of the business side of the paper, including working with the newsprint supplier and other vendors. He then sold advertising, which occasionally required long hours given the idiosyncrasies of customers. "I had a client who insisted on working his ad copy at nine o'clock after he closed at night, which was on Monday, and this was for our Wednesday paper." Despite the hours, the advertising side of the newspaper was healthy. The *Telegraph* ran more ad lineage publishing just three times a week than the daily *Alliance Times-Herald*, and nearly as much as the daily *Scottsbluff Star-Herald* in a population base well over three times Sidney's.

His fortunes with one purchase did not work as well. "In my whole life I inherited a total of five grand, from my grandfather. This guy in Cheyenne had a shopper operation and he also had the contract for the Warren Air Force Base paper. I was more interested in the air base paper because that was a government contract, and we would print it and leverage our equipment. I thought we probably could also do *The Shopper*. So I poured that whole five thousand bucks into this shopper."

Manny Alvarez managed *The Shopper*, and he'd drive the made-up pages to Sidney from Cheyenne, a hundred plus miles one way. On a winter's day about a year into the operation, Manny slid off the road and wrecked the company's used van, which, John estimated, probably consumed a thousand of the five thousand dollars. Manny wound up in the Sidney hospital.

John felt responsible, but the *The Shopper* had no health insurance. Still, John picked up Manny's medical bills and fed his family until he could get back to work. Manny eventually mended, but the shopper would not survive.

"I was kind of down to short strokes on that deal," John said. "I think we'd gone as far as we could go because I was out of money. I've done fine with the money I've earned, but with the money I inherited, I lost every dime of it."

～

March 18, 1974, was an overcast Monday in Sidney, a little fog mixing with rain. According to Lianne Kershaw's mother, seventeen-year-old Lianne neither liked to drive nor was very good at it. So, the girl's presence behind the wheel on that Monday was unusual—and fatal. She died the next day from injuries sustained when the car she was driving crashed into a tree during a drag race in Greenwood Cemetery northeast of town. A passenger was seriously injured.

Lianne's death set in motion a series of events that spanned fifteen years and accounted for an odd and enigmatic conclusion.

Nearly a month after Lianne Kershaw's death, someone threw two incendiary devices through the window of the *Telegraph* in the middle of the night. The attack came ten days after a window at the newspaper had been broken, in what John surmised was an earlier attempt to damage the newspaper plant. According to an *Omaha World-Herald* story about the firebombing, one of the explosives, described as a "Molotov cocktail," landed in the newspaper's advertising department where it melted a ten-foot section of carpet. The other device landed in a hallway, exploded, and caused a fire in the *Telegraph*'s composing room. No one was injured and, despite the office's sustaining $5,000 in damages, the newspaper staff was able to continue work the following morning and publish the next day's issue. At the time, both John and the police were at a loss as to a motive, but John told the *World-Herald*, "If this firebombing was an effort to halt publication of the *Sidney Telegraph*, I will assure our readers we will not be intimidated."

Eventually the Sidney police were able to link the firebombing to Lianne Kershaw's death. Two months after the fire, they arrested three Sidney teenagers: eighteen-year-old Ray Benkusky, seventeen-year-old Roger Anderson, and sixteen-year-old Lonnie Kocontes. According to Anderson's courtroom testimony, the three were upset over the *Telegraph*'s story of Kershaw's accident and death.

The story used the same language that investigating officers gave the newspaper's reporter. Lianne Kershaw was killed as a result of a car accident precipitated by a "speed contest" in the Sidney cemetery.

"The cops said they were told that Benkusky, Anderson, and Kocontes were upset because of the way we handled that story," John said. "One of these guys or maybe all of them apparently knew the girl and thought that the story was a horrible thing to leave as her life legacy. They thought she had been terribly wronged, so these three bozos got together and thought, 'We need to get redemption for this.' That's how it happened."

All three pleaded guilty to various charges and were sent to prison. At that point the firebombing story faded, or so John thought. The *Telegraph* repaired the damage and neither its flag nor its fortunes were permanently ruffled. John, who had already stared down angry dairy farmers as a teenager when the "milk wars" had spilled into parts of Sheridan County, made it clear to readers that it would take more than some amateur flame throwers to keep the *Telegraph* from reaching its subscribers on schedule.

As fate and firebombs would have it, fifteen years later the story—or at least one of its principal players—showed up again in John's life. He was on the cusp of becoming the fifth publisher in *Omaha World-Herald* history. The *World-Herald*'s editorial page editor, Frank Partsch, had been with John in Sidney as the *Telegraph*'s editor when Benkusky, Anderson, and Kocontes had cooked up their plot to take down the newspaper.

"Frank came in one day and said, 'Take a look at this.' Here was a story about Lonnie Kocontes. He had gotten ahead. He had apparently been working in HHS." Dumbfounded, John and Frank read that Kocontes was being considered for advancement to a position working with thousands of children in the Nebraska Social Services Department.

While serving two prison sentences totaling about seven years for offenses including drug violations, Kocontes had worked on his bachelor's degree in integrated studies, graduating from the University of Nebraska in 1984. He was released from parole the next year. Several months after leaving prison, he failed to disclose his complete criminal past as he dealt with the State Bureau of Examining Boards, which certified social workers. Kocontes landed a job as a protective services worker with the Department of Social Services, later consolidated into Health and Human Services. He rose in the department and by 1989 was in line to become administrator of planning review for forty-five hundred foster children in the social services system. John knew what he had to do.

"He was about to get a big promotion and, when we saw his name, I gave the governor a call and said, 'You might want to take another look at this guy.'"

Kocontes was eventually fired from his state job for not reporting his entire criminal record on his application. But the bizarre story that started in Sidney and found its way to Lincoln was to have still more chapters. Kocontes received a law degree at the University of Texas in 1993 and was licensed to practice in California, where, as of early 2017, he was again behind bars facing charges that he murdered one ex-wife on a Mediterranean cruise and then solicited the killing of another ex-wife while he was in jail. The case ended in a mistrial, but not before it was featured on the CBS news program, *48 Hours*. While Kocontes made a dubious public splash in several states, his co-conspirators, Ray Benkusky and Roger Anderson, slipped into the inconspicuousness of obscurity after the firebombing of the *Sidney Telegraph*.

∿

Obviously, John was realizing business success with the *Telegraph* as an economic mainstay in Sidney and personally as a business leader in the community, one whose counsel was often sought on a variety of civic affairs—local, area, and statewide. In 1970, he made his position both public and official.

With the *Telegraph* humming along, John's keen sense of community moved him to consider widening his scope of leadership by running for a seat on the Sidney City Council. He believed being an advocate was one thing but pressing the button quite another. From his newspaper office he could advocate for many community issues, but he still thought Sidney needed to start pressing some buttons—especially on economic issues. "People needed to get off their butts and get in the game. It wasn't just an ordinary day; it was a call-to-action time. The world was not going to solve our problems. Let's get with it. That was certainly part of it. To have an active hand in the policymaking as opposed to being an advisor, even though it might have been spectacular advice, was different because you had to vote, too," he said.

Also in the mix was a short note from Jack Lowe.

John…
Why don't you run for city council? I'll be glad to
file for you.
JHL

He was elected in 1970 and so began a five-year stint during which John had two roles in civic leadership: one as the owner and publisher of the city's newspaper of record and a second as a member of the Sidney City Council. He served as mayor from 1972 to 1974 by virtue of having been elected president of the council, the city's charter specifying such a structure.

His dual roles as a watchdog journalist and a policy maker were not unusual in that time and place. Many small-town papers had owners and publishers who were among the leaders in their communities' political lives as well as in their civic and commercial spheres. John was to continue his relentless pursuit of service in bettering his community and his nation after he moved to Omaha. In doing so, he followed his predecessor, Harold Andersen, who was highly vested in Omaha and the state. John also set the bar high for Terry Kroeger, who was to follow him as the CEO and publisher of the *Omaha World-Herald.*

Frank Partsch, who succeeded Jack Lowe as editor of the *Telegraph* in 1972, saw first-hand the balancing act between publisher and elected official.

"I never saw a conflict between John's roles of mayor and publisher," he said. "It seemed to me that there was precedent in Sidney, and in many other small newspaper markets, for the publisher to engage in public service, including government service, beyond the walls of the newspaper office. Jack Lowe himself had served as mayor while editing the *Telegraph.*"

John recognized the perception of conflict and imbalance. "That was the first thing that crossed my mind," John said. "I felt that we had—I had, as owner of the paper and as publisher—a responsibility to shoot down the middle. I don't mean with opinion, but by being unencumbered. Before Frank got there, I was even writing the city council story. I would report, write, edit, do all that stuff, and the first thing that occurred to me was that I can't be sitting on the council and writing the story. That doesn't look right."

Even so, when Partsch simply did not have enough *Telegraph* staff to get to everything, he occasionally enlisted John to write stories about issues facing the community and its government. "The city council and the school board sometimes met on the same evening. John offered to help stretch our resources by producing a report on the city council meetings. That freed me to cover the school board. We discussed the ramifications and decided that, on balance, the paper and its readers came out ahead by accepting his offer. Remember, John had a professional's pride in what he wrote for publication—he had been writing and editing news stories for much of his life. He never gave me a story that caused me discomfort, and his dual role as mayor and city reporter was never held up to me by a reader as something that made the paper less trustworthy.

"I think I understand more now than I did then that John is unusual in that he is a whole person. The concept of wearing two hats was not part of his makeup. He has only one hat—a John Gottschalk hat. What happened under that hat was all John, not part of him working against another part, not one part conniving with the other for some extraneous purpose. John lives by the principle of avoiding criticism by discerning what is right in any situation and then doing it. His ability to make things happen is augmented by the admiration his character engenders in those around him."

As editor, Partsch was responsible for producing—with some input from John—the paper's editorial positions. The pair would later do the same thing for the *World-Herald* with John as publisher and Frank as editorial page editor. John maintains that after Frank arrived in Sidney, the *Telegraph* took Mayor Gottschalk to task twice in editorials, once over the city not addressing teens speeding on Main Street and the other about city land acquisition.

"What I always like to say is that Frank beat up on me twice, and once he was right."

While that line might get a laugh, the *Telegraph*'s editorial footprint was a serious business, one that neither man took lightly. Partsch detailed how the structure and reaction worked. "John did not assign editorial positions. I was attuned to his conversation in order to avoid situations in which the voice of his newspaper sounded out of character. On rare occasions, at my initiative, we discussed editorials pre-publication. One was an endorsement editorial for a judicial position in which we reminded readers that one of the candidates, a lawyer, had in the long-ago past been subjected to professional discipline. I wrote an editorial describing his offense and recommending the election of his opponent. John said, 'I have no stomach for this,' meaning that he was a great advocate of positive endorsements. But he offered no changes. We ran it. I learned later in Omaha, that he was a great advocate of positive election endorsement editorials. And our candidate won.

"Another conference came during the Wounded Knee siege of 1973. Sidney is less than two hundred miles from Wounded Knee. The possibility of wider violence was worrying some of our readers. Some of them wanted federal officials to move in and break the siege, no matter what the cost in blood and national angst. I wanted to avoid having our paper recommend that. I drafted an argument for the feds to stand down to avert possible loss of life and to renew the search for a nonviolent solution. John suggested a third way."

Together they crafted an editorial focused on the commitment to nonviolence inherent in the traditions of Mahatma Gandhi and Martin Luther King Jr. These leaders dramatized their grievances by accepting the rule of law, even an unjust law, with dignity. In so doing, they called attention to injustice and, with the nobility and forbearance of their response, generated support for their cause. Most important, their approach provided a path toward non-violent resolution. The editorial won first place, in its circulation class, in the next year's Nebraska Press Association judging for editorials.

~

John's public service reached beyond Sidney when he ran for University of Nebraska regent in 1974. The western district, which stretched from the Panhandle across the state to the northeast, encompassed thirty-two of Nebraska's ninety-three counties. What prompted the run was John's long-standing interest in the university and a mind-set that he had found wanting.

He contended that even with the size of the university and its thirst for taxpayer dollars, western Nebraska was in danger of settling into a "woe is me" complex—the notion that rural voices, especially voices in the west, were not being heard in Lincoln. Durward "Woody" Varner had become president of the university, which was in the early stages of transitioning into a multi-campus institution. While some Nebraskans saw the centralization as yet another layer of management, John saw it as the way to get "warring duchies" under control. He had voiced his opinion on the university's structure several times while in Lincoln on business but knew that the only body that could successfully implement such a significant change was the Board of Regents, whose members were elected.

"We had a guy in western Nebraska, Bob Simmons, who was not too keen on a corporate university system because he thought somehow that might change the world to the negative," John said. "I'll admit to being of the view that you don't have to sit around and bellyache. Why don't you just do something about it? So that was all clearly part of it."

John found encouragement to "do something" from the right place at the right time. A call came from Lincoln. Varner said he heard that John was interested in running and that he hoped that would happen. Varner told John that he would be hearing from others, too. Soon John found support for his candidacy both in western Nebraska and in Lincoln. He was in the game.

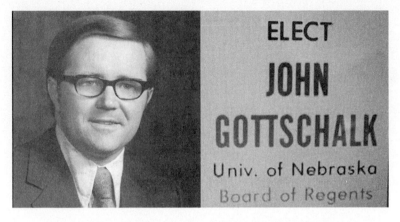

During an unsuccessful campaign for a seat on the University of
Nebraska Board of Regents, John gained insight about Nebraskans
and their values. He used that knowledge as publisher and
CEO of the "state's newspaper" for nearly twenty years.

The primary election was in May of 1974. John spent
months crisscrossing the huge district from Bushnell to
Wayne. He found campaigning to be gratifying, educational,
and occasionally exhilarating. The experience had "a profound
impact" on him even though he came in third in the primary,
which was won by Simmons.

"I ran all over this state. I'd go into a town. There were few
places where I didn't know somebody. I knew the newspaper
guy, or I knew the mayor, or I'd know somebody from business.
You wind up running into people whose responsibility it is to
make the ultimate decisions. You ask them for what I believe
is one of the most precious things they have: their opinion—
their vote."

Some voters told John he had their vote because they
were angry. Others pledged support because they wanted to
see a new, younger face on the board. He found enthusiasm
in some places, too, among people who would show up,
want to talk, and loved the contact with the candidate. John
often found himself exhausted at the end of a long day of

campaigning, which for him was almost exclusively a solo enterprise. "But you get up the next morning, have breakfast, and go again."

John knew about that.

Sometimes he was caught completely off guard, as he was in Hartington where he struck up a friendly conversation with a man at a gas station. Eventually, the talk turned to John's candidacy. The man said: "I've got only one question. Where do you stand on abortion?"

John smoothly answered that abortion was not the purview of the Board of Regents.

"The hell it isn't. You're running a hospital, aren't you?"

John said the conversation showed his lack of preparation for the question. All those days on the road, however, had not completely dulled his mental nimbleness. Somehow—he had forgotten the details—he was able to extricate himself from what was clearly one of his campaign's most awkward moments.

The third-place finish disappointed him but only because he was "young and idealistic." It did, however, put an end to campaigns for public office although he was to have, through his career as a publisher and even in retirement, plenty of offers. By then he had realized that public office was only one way to affect public policy, that a metropolitan newspaper reaching across a large midwestern state could have a huge influence on the tenor of public discourse and the direction of a city, state, and nation.

"I think if you reflected at least on the old *World-Herald*, not just because of me, but going back to its roots, it was an agenda setter," John said. "It made clear, and not infrequently, what it thought the outcome should be. But it also was what opened the door on a lot of these big discussions, and it still does. We went through kids showing up dead in the foster care system, we went through the state coroner's investigation, we went through why our roads take three years to build, we went through many big, serious stories. All that sets the agenda and people will then respond to it. Rather than running for office, I thought I could do more good for Nebraska by doing what I was doing in the newspaper business."

~

Interstate 80 stretches 455.27 miles across Nebraska, a bifurcated ribbon of concrete from Omaha to the Wyoming border carrying millions of vehicles east and west. Each day nearly seventy five hundred of them were passing Sidney's two interchanges, many of them stopping at Exit 59, the city's easternmost off ramp, where they found food, lodging, and a gateway to the Sandhills, the Badlands and Mount Rushmore via Highway 385—not to mention, for many years, the corporate offices of Cabela's. At Exit 59 alone, travelers could choose among seven hotels and motels, over a dozen restaurants, and a variety of full-service auto and truck service stations. For a place the size of Sidney, with a population just over six thousand, Exit 59 was, by the turn of the twenty-first century, a small town within a small town.

For years the interstate was unfinished at Sidney, the gap forcing traffic off the four-lane highway onto Highway 30 and, more important, directly through downtown Sidney. While a debate raged in the community whether it was better to petition the state to have one exit as opposed to two, the underlying fear for many was that the completion of I-80 would make Sidney another "drive-by" town.

Adding to the concerns—and bottom-line worries—was the town's topography. Sidney sits in the Lodgepole Creek Valley, well below the altitude of the interstate. Getting water and infrastructure up to I-80, especially on the proposed east interchange at the major north-south Highway 385, was a long shot at best and far too expensive for the tastes of those in the one-exit crowd. They preferred the lower cost and minimal commitment of Highway 19, west of the town proper and six miles from 385. Eventually, the city and state resolved the location issue, deciding on two. This left the question of development unanswered.

Moreover, to start any project on an east interchange, city leaders faced a formidable obstacle: The Union Pacific Railroad through its subsidiary, Upland Industries, owned nearly all the land along the connector road between Highway 30 and the proposed interchange. On a map today the connector is called 17J. When John "negotiated" with Upland Industries over how to obtain an easement for infrastructure development to the interchange, it could have been called Hardball Road.

He recalled a seminal moment in the back-and-forth with a mixture of irritation and delight. The U.P. had dispatched a public relations team to Sidney, a typical fence-tending move for the transportation giant in a city along the right-of-way. What had been a low-key evening of dinner, drinks, and polite conversation took an edgy turn when one of the U.P. reps wondered aloud why the government was perfectly willing to subsidize airline service to places like Sidney while never having done anything for the railroads. It was a loaded comment—*Telegraph* editorials had consistently favored subsidies for rural air service for Sidney and similar towns elsewhere.

Such talk didn't sit well with John. "The top of my head came off. I told them, 'I just bought a building that's got a four-inch thick abstract, 90 percent of which is the Union Pacific shuffling this property around, hiding the pea, to keep building the railroad. Every other section, every other township, clear across the United States was given to you by the government, you cheap bastards.'"

At stake was a water line that Sidney wanted to run across a road, so it could eventually get the water main up to the interchange. Given the easements in the area, the town would need U.P. permission to get the project done. John, surely irritated and frustrated with the railroad's refusal to discuss, finally said to its representatives, "We'd be glad to take up your challenge. If you'd rather have your land annexed so you'll be paying school taxes in Sidney, we can arrange that."

One of the railroad men protested, "You can't do that. Your own ordinances say, and the state law says, it's got to be contiguous and urban in nature."

John said, "Really? You think this isn't urban? We have houses and businesses right there. So we go across the street fifty feet. You don't think I can get away with that? You don't want to find that out."

John took the U.P.'s curveball comment, called the railroad's rep out on it, and hit it out of the park. Maybe it didn't cause the railroad to become more reasonable, but the city got its easement to run water up the hill to the interstate. It built a lift station, too, to get it to the interchange and laid pipe to get water eventually to the south side of the interchange as well. But not without some serious grumbling from downtown.

"The whole thing was four hundred thousand dollars," John said. "Man, there was wailing and gnashing of teeth. It was major grousing from major loud people. They said, 'That kid's got to be crazy. What is he thinking? Dumping four hundred thousand dollars into that? You think anybody's going to build there?'"

John was a "kid" at thirty years old, but he, and what he remembered as a solid city council, saw an opportunity to prove that if Sidney took the initiative, others would respond. Other forces would come in to play—tourism, commerce, development. They did come and, well into the twenty-first century, continued to make Exit 59 a bustling center of activity and an economic driver for Sidney and Cheyenne County.

John inspects the "Golden Link," a brass strip embedded in Interstate 80 near Sidney, with Bob Mason, Panhandle maintenance supervisor for the Nebraska Department of Roads. Working with Lodgepole banker, E.K. Yanney, John persuaded the state to embed the strip, marking the spot where Nebraska became the first state to finish its portion of Interstate 80.

John maintained that hardly anyone would use the west interchange, Exit 55, but neither was it ignored historically. A banker in nearby Lodgepole, E.K. Yanney, proposed to the Cheyenne County Chamber of Commerce that it throw a "Golden Link" celebration to commemorate Nebraska's being the first state to complete its primary interstate highway system. It would symbolically represent the meeting of east and west much as the "Golden Spike" did for the transcontinental railroad. John embraced the idea wholeheartedly, as he was later to be an enthusiastic partner in projects with E.K.'s brother, Mike Yanney.

They persuaded the State of Nebraska to embed a brass strip across the roadway to mark the point at which the east and west segments were joined. Dignitaries and civic and business leaders met at a ceremony on October 19, 1974, to mark the milestone. Nebraska Gov. J. James Exon dedicated the Golden Link at a spot near rest areas about six miles west of Sidney. Neither John nor Frank could confirm whether representatives of the Union Pacific were among the crowd that day.

John's greatest accomplishment in Sidney came neither from the publisher's chair nor with the mayor's gavel, but rather at home when, in 1967, Jodi Gottschalk arrived. Her birth changed not only the domestic landscape on 11th Street but also how John saw and approached the world. Moreover, Jodi could perhaps be the only child ever whose birth was hastened by a game of croquet.

"We wanted a child but we didn't get too serious about it until we got to Sidney," John said. "It was a considerable journey, so when Carm finally became pregnant, it was a big joyous moment. My grandfather had passed but my grandmother Ruth was still alive. My mother was there with us in Sidney, basically in our care."

Carmen's due date came and went without anything happening. The young, first-time, parents-to-be were understandably nervous. That's when Carmen decided what was needed was a Gottschalk croquet tournament. This was a sporting affair on the front lawn that John described as "brutal."

John said, "We had a lawn that rolled, so the middle hoops were always on sloping ground. When you got ready to shoot somebody out, it was necessary for others to clear out of the way—the ball was going to travel a long way."

Carmen had not been at the game long when it became clear that she needed to get to the hospital where, in those days, the fathers-to-be were unceremoniously shooed away after the check-in.

Aside from Jodi's arrival changing the obvious—"She was a joyous little thing and we were all happy to have her"—John came face to face with three factors that typically confront a new father. "The first thing is that you've got to earn some money, not that you didn't before but now you have a lot more expenses. Number two was the responsibility of raising a child, which we just didn't wander into. We were twenty-four. Third, I think there's a weight that settles down on every father. Mothers have been living with this child for nine months and have pretty much figured it out."

Years later, as a grandfather who had been able to watch his grandchildren grow and develop their own personalities, he became more convinced than ever of the critical role of parenting. That conviction extended into his civic life as many of his efforts and much of his significant financial support were directed to issues impacting K-12 education and parenting in Omaha and other parts of Nebraska. He had four grandchildren at the time of this writing: Jodi's son who was twenty-one, and daughter Christina's three who were eight, six, and four.

"Sometimes I think having children is wasted on the young," John said. "At least in my experience I pay a lot more attention to those things now than I did then. I see my grandkids a lot. I've watched them since they were born, from the time they were in the crib. There's no prejudice. There's no language. There's no color distinction that we know of. There's nothing. Everything that's going to be there has to be taught or observed and the role of parenting is to be the leader of the pack. And the kids that get (good parenting) are going to be blessed."

Carmen took to parenting and Jodi was a good baby, blessing their home in Sidney and adding a new generation and new narrative to the Gottschalk family story.

The mother who was in the same room with Carmen at the hospital was a family friend and together the pair started the New Mother's Club in Sidney, an endeavor to lend support to new parents. Their efforts morphed into an organization of young mothers in the state.

"Carm was very engaged in raising Jodi and in children's issues in general. Carm's from a really big family. To this day she enthusiastically mothers about thirty or forty nieces and nephews."

Nor did John and Carmen Gottschalk's parenting begin and end with Jodi and Christina, who arrived eight years later. Soon after adopting Christina, the Gottschalks began providing foster care for at-risk newborns through the Child Saving Institute in Omaha. They gave safety and comfort to these tiny, fragile lives brought into the world under difficult and, in some cases, life-threatening circumstances—the upshot of which was that when either John or Carmen was asked to weigh in on parenting or educational issues, their hearts and minds were filled with invaluable experience.

$\sim$

Carmen, Jodi, Christina, and John enjoying a family vacation.

In ten short years, from 1965 to 1975, John Gottschalk went from resuscitating his family's newspaper business to making it a journalistic and financial success story. He was elected to the Sidney City Council and became the city's mayor, leading Sidney through a period of growth including laying the groundwork for a spectacular project on Interstate 80 that became an economic force for the area. He was tireless in his work with the Chamber of Commerce and became a respected statewide presence both in professional press organizations and in the League of Nebraska Municipalities. He ran for Regent and, although he lost in the primary, he grew extensively through the campaign process, reaffirming both his understanding and his deep respect for Nebraskans and their values. He became a father, fully vested in the new responsibilities and absolute wonder that a child brings to a home and a family.

He would use Sidney as a training ground for even greater successes in business and civic stewardship once he arrived in Omaha and moved through the ranks of the *World-Herald*, becoming a leader in moving that city and—via leadership on national boards—the country forward.

Still, for all his leadership skills, his problem-solving abilities, his drive to move things forward for all the right reasons, John came to know the limitations and balance required of public servants, elected or otherwise. One particular moment in Sidney underscored this knowledge.

A state law provided that if 51 percent of homeowners on an unpaved street wanted it paved, a district was formed, a tax collected, and the street would be paved. Homeowners on corners were subject to taxes twice should enough of their neighbors want paving.

The night of a final reading for one particular pavement ordinance took on added meaning for John. In the audience was an elderly woman, prim and proper in a hat, a pocketbook on her arm. The question before the councilors was simple: Do you approve of this ordinance or not? The city attorney explained the details, that state law provides if 51 percent of the owners petition for pavement, the law requires that a district be formed for all the neighbors. In this case before the council, 86 percent of the people had asked for the paving. The clerk asked if anyone wished to address the council. The woman in the hat approached the podium. She reminded John of his grandmother. She spoke beautifully: "My husband, Bill, passed away. I live on Social Security. There's just no way I can stay in our house with what this tax is going to cost me because I live on a corner. Even though we don't have any debt, this ordinance will force me to have to leave the home that Bill and I lived in all of our years."

Her words brought perspective and humanity to the council chambers that night, perspective and humanity to what could have been a perfunctory public vote, one that might not consider elderly widows who live on corners. She made an impression on John.

"How were we going to vote? The law was the law. I have thought about that a hundred times and I'm thinking, that's kind of part of our deal, too," he said. "When you look at a president who makes his own laws anytime he wants, when you look at laws that are on the books that are so stupid, people just ignore them. That is fine because the cops aren't enforcing them anyhow. Then you look at this case, which was a real case, which cried out for some kind of solution. How about amending the time of the bond payments from ten years to twenty? Or letting the woman die in peace in her own house? Selling the house and paying the debt? Whatever. But no, the law said something else. In that aspect it didn't serve all the people. Maybe it never did serve all of them."

John "held his nose" and voted to form the district. The city was able to extend her payments over a longer period of time, which somewhat softened the impact on her. But this woman, so much like his grandmother, reaffirmed in him the notion that real leaders step forward, determined to find a way to solve what's before them, whether for their families, their businesses, or their neighbors. He did not recall what happened to her and her home in Sidney, but her lesson was always with him.

"I can see her to this day."

THREE

To Omaha, the *World-Herald*, and the NBA

I never met a baby I didn't love. The world
is a better place because you are in it.
Thank you for sharing your lives.

–CARMEN GOTTSCHALK

Did you see the story in the *World-Herald*
about Pete Kiewit's ultimate disposition
of his ownership to his employees?

–HAROLD ANDERSEN

When John Gottschalk reported for work at the *Omaha World-Herald* on August 18, 1975, his arrival was as natural as a stream finding its way down a mountainside. John was a third-generation newspaperman and journalist, raised to understand the news business: the substance of news, the logistics of gathering it, the proper way to write and print it, the mechanics of getting it to readers, and, perhaps most important, its impact on readers and their communities. His commitment to those readers was clear and simple.

They must be able to depend on a high-quality, accurate, meaningful newspaper—a community's singular voice—whether in mailboxes once a week in Sheridan County, or on front porches Mondays, Wednesdays, and Fridays in Sidney, or via carriers and newsstands a half dozen times a day in Omaha and far beyond.

Yet even as rivulets bend and turn to accommodate the landscape, something as small as a fallen tree or a tumbled boulder can reroute the water, in essence changing the course of nature. So it was with John. A chance meeting, a happenstance, proved providential in his finding his way to the *World-Herald*, where he was to soar during a thirty-three-year career. In Omaha, his steady and effective leadership in community affairs changed the life of a community, and many of its people, for the better. It provided a springboard to leadership in national organizations as disparate as the Boy Scouts of America, the National Benevolent Association, the United Services Organization (USO), Pheasants Forever, Phi Gamma Delta National Fraternity, and many other corporate, church, and fraternal groups.

While the Gottschalk star would have surely burned bright in any galaxy, John's life and the lives he eventually touched would have been dramatically different save for an unplanned encounter with *World-Herald* Publisher Harold Andersen.

Their paths crossed indirectly as a result of John's decision in 1974 to sell the *Sidney Telegraph*. "The company had grown, and I'd been in Sidney a long time. I was still a young man. The most graceful way to say it was that I just needed more room."

Specifically, John was looking for the challenge of owning and publishing a small daily newspaper. He was most interested in the *Kearney Hub*, a family-owned newspaper published by Bob and Jane Ayers. But they were unwilling to consider selling. The state had only about a dozen newspapers in that category and, as John found out, none for sale.

John with Harold Andersen, his predecessor as publisher and
CEO, who hired John at the *Omaha World-Herald* in 1975.

Community newspapers are those with less than thirty
thousand circulation. At the time John was looking for a paper
to acquire, the National Newspaper Association listed over
fourteen hundred daily community newspapers and another
seven thousand non-dailies such as the *Sidney Telegraph* and
what was then the *Sheridan County Star* (later renamed the
Journal Star) for a combined weekly readership of close to one
hundred fifty million. Rounding out the roster of American
newspapers were a couple hundred metropolitan dailies such
as the *Omaha World-Herald*, and a handful of newspapers
that circulated to a national audience. These included the
Wall Street Journal, the *New York Times*, the *Christian Science
Monitor*, and a few others.

While John had indications of interest from some
newspapers outside Nebraska, geography and the pull of
home narrowed his choices. "As time went on, Carm and
I started getting down to the core issue: do we want to stay
in Nebraska or not? Our conclusion was that we did want

to stay in Nebraska. That pretty much ruled out any other newspaper opportunities."

Not that John spent his days waiting by the telephone and mailbox. The sale of the *Telegraph* closed in October of 1974. John rented an office in downtown Sidney where he set about teaching himself basic computer language, surmising—rightly—that such a skill would be useful in the future. A few national headhunters inquired as to his availability and interest, but the Gottschalks were now determined to stay in Nebraska. Once it became clear that no Nebraska daily was going to be available, John turned his attention to researching small-town banks. Through his work as an owner-publisher and mayor of Sidney, John knew banks provided considerable community leadership and not simply because they were a repository for money. They were businesses that attracted solid business and community leaders. His only problem was, by his own admission, he knew very little about banks and their operation. He figured, however, that within the confines of banking regulations, a smart businessman with energy and common sense could learn the business and be successful.

His philosophy as he ventured forth looking for a bank to buy was to keep things simple. "The trick," he said, "was to take care of other people's money and give it back to them. If you're going to loan it to somebody else for a short period of time, you make sure you've got the right person and that you get paid for the risk."

The more he researched, the more he believed banking was not only an "interesting" business but also one that would afford him the opportunity to continue his goal of serving his community through civic activities and leadership.

All of which was how and why he ended up in Lincoln in the spring of 1975, picking the brains of bankers he knew at First National Bank of Lincoln. That evening, his UNL fraternity, Phi Gamma Delta, was holding a social event, so John decided to attend and renew some Fiji friendships. There he spied Harold Andersen, the president and publisher of the *Omaha World-Herald*. He knew Andersen from Nebraska Press Association gatherings, so he headed over to say hello. When the conversation quickly got around to what John was doing in Lincoln, Andersen wondered why a newspaper guy was looking for small-town banks to buy. John explained his disappointment with the tight market for purchasing newspapers and the decision by him and Carmen to stay in Nebraska. He told Andersen he had equity and was looking for ownership, not necessarily a job.

After a couple more moments of small talk, Andersen said to John, "Did you see the story in the *World-Herald* about Pete Kiewit's ultimate disposition of his ownership to his employees?"

John said, "Yeah, I think I did see that." He left it at that.

"It wasn't until after I left that place that I thought, 'Speaking of duh! It didn't even register. Here I am supposed to be this bright, alert, aggressive, hungry guy, and we kind of moved on.'"

Shortly thereafter, John, somewhat abashed, wrote Andersen saying what he realized he should have said at the Fiji function: Did the *World-Herald* have any opportunity he might explore?

While his response to Andersen's comment may have been delayed, John's timing was on the money. Andersen invited him to Omaha to "talk." That conversation took place several weeks later in Andersen's office. The publisher wanted to know everything John had done in newspapers. John recounted the experiences of his lifetime: going back to Rushville, where his lessons in the elements of newspapering were first-hand, and thereafter to the publisher's office in Sidney, where he ran a successful newspaper and central printing plant. John's curiosity was sparked by Andersen's heightened interest in John's business and production skills, as opposed to journalism skills.

John realized later that Andersen had been through a number of business managers and that this man he would come to know as "Andy," may have been looking for another one.

After more conversations, Andersen offered John a position in the executive suite as an assistant to G. Woodson "Woody" Howe, the bright, capable journalist who was then a vice president and executive assistant to Andersen. The pairing of John with Woody would be the beginning of many years of working side by side. John soon realized that Andy and Woody devoted a great deal of their attention to the quality of the news product, so John's broader newspaper experience might be his best career asset.

He also realized that Woody's newsroom responsibilities were heavy, so John grew into his new role by focusing on a variety of tasks that were outside Woody's main area of expertise, from production to accounting, circulation, and the bottom line. He took on the project of changing the *World-Herald* to a digital typesetting system, so as to migrate from hot lead to a computer-driven photographic system. The project, which had been in various stages of dormancy for nearly two years, would occupy much of John's time for many months. It was a major advancement in technology that all newspapers were finding necessary to accept, sooner or later, whether or not they employed in-house the visionary leaders to make it happen.

But change never comes easy. When John arrived at the *World-Herald* in 1975, he walked through a line of pickets, part of a compositors' strike that was in its second year. Two factors fueled the strike: The first was the impending change in newspaper production and technology. The second was Harold Andersen's refusal to let any of the six unions represented at the newspaper alter the quality of the newspaper or disrupt the process by which the *World-Herald* circulated, all the way from southwest Iowa to eastern Wyoming.

"I came to the *World-Herald* at a transitory time in the industry," John said. Part of that transition was the realization by typesetters that the days of hot metal were numbered just as their union contract was coming up for renegotiation. Word that the *World-Herald* already had a half dozen workers, secreted in another area on site, learning new processes— including photographic typesetting—had filtered down to the compositors.

By contract, the International Typographical Union (ITU) had jurisdiction over the composing room. When Associated Press copy began arriving in the form of ticker tape, the old Linotypes and their human operators were no longer a necessary part of the production process: the ticker tape was fed to a mechanized printing system that spat out a clean copy of the story for use in the printing process without ITU keyboarding. Even so, compositors, because of their contractual role, were in their spare time continuing to do business the way they always had, making a typed duplicate of the copy in hot-lead type. This type, which was never used and was eventually melted down, was known as "dead horse." Negotiations on a new contract failed to produce an agreement that was satisfactory to both the union and the company.

Eventually, the union considered a strike but settled on a slowdown. When Andersen got wind of compositors dragging their feet, he immediately went to composing. "We don't have work slowdowns at the *Omaha World-Herald*," he told them. "Make a decision. If you want to work, get back to it. If not, there's the door," he said, pointing to the "back door," the exit to the outside from composing. One hundred and sixty employees left on the spot, the door locking behind them. The "back door" was always locked; nevertheless, the union, in an attempt to make its case, called Andersen's actions a "lockout." The difference between a lockout and a walkout—which was what the compositors had done—was considerable in labor strife. The propaganda of semantics swayed few and the strike continued.

Meanwhile, typesetting and composing at the paper was left to the handful of compositors who had been trained for an alternative method. Three years later John's leadership produced a totally computerized composing system.

~

During the time when a chance meeting and a series of conversations were about to chart John's future at the *Omaha World-Herald*, the phone rang in Sidney with life-altering news for all the Gottschalks.

A baby girl was available for them to adopt in Omaha.

John and Carmen, who had been in Omaha a few days earlier, turned around and drove straight through to meet Christina. "Tina," or "Short" as her father lovingly called her, was born on March 28, 1975, but spent her first couple of weeks in a foster home, placed there by the Child Saving Institute. Unbeknownst to Carmen, John, and the Child Saving Institute, Christina's first two weeks on earth would have a dramatic effect on the lives of dozens of newborns and infants over the next three decades.

The wait for Christina had been considerable for the Gottschalks. Carmen's doctor in Sidney had suggested they start the adoption process. He recommended a handful of agencies for John and Carmen to consider, which they did over a number of months, deciding finally on the Child Saving Institute.

CSI began in Omaha in 1892 when Rev. A.W. Clark recognized that poverty, disease, and the daily grind of life faced by pioneering families left many children neglected or abandoned. Clark and his wife Sarah started the Boys and Girls Aid Society, which became the Child Saving Institute. CSI became a partner of the National Benevolent Association (NBA), the health and social services ministry of the Christian Church (Disciples of Christ). Through this ministry, the NBA provides advocacy, education, and support for its partners.

While the Gottschalks would come to understand the good works of both the Child Saving Institute and the NBA, Carmen said the caseworker assigned to them was a game changer in their choice of agencies. "During the interview she was very receptive and warm. We just felt very good about it. She seemed so positive, like this was a possibility and this could happen, so we left with that attitude. All the caseworkers were very kind and loving."

Two years would pass before Christina arrived. They wanted a newborn and they wanted a girl, conditions decreasing the odds of a match and thereby lengthening the wait. Meanwhile, John, Carmen, and little Jodi got on with their lives in Sidney, with Carmen sending periodic notes to make sure CSI knew that she and John remained committed, stable, and eager to become adoptive parents at a moment's notice. And then the phone rang.

After all the waiting, Carmen remembered feeling unprepared. Friends in Sidney came to the rescue—as small-town neighbors traditionally do—sending John and Carmen on their way to Omaha with promises to prepare their home for Christina's arrival. Carmen said the journey was a blur. "I don't remember the trip. It was one of those times you're sort of in a cloud. We drove straight through and got to Omaha and there she was. All four pounds of her."

The adoption, as were nearly all adoptions in 1975, was closed. The biological maternal grandmother was able to provide some family health history. Christina was already at CSI in a bassinet when John and Carmen arrived. They "rushed" through the paperwork and the formalities because they could not wait to get on with the joy of being a family bigger by one beautiful little girl.

She was tiny, but she was full-term. The Gottschalks found her healthy, easy-going and, according to Carmen, calm. As her daughter grew into a loving and happy child, Carmen recognized how critical it was that those first few days of Christina's life had been spent with caring and positive foster parents. This imprint on Carmen proved to be deep and permanent.

John with Jodi at a community parade in Sidney.

Six months later the Gottschalks were settled in Omaha. John was well into a new career at the *World-Herald*. Jodi was in second grade, making new friends in a new school in a new city. Carmen was home with little Christina, and, by her admission, wrapped in a joyous sense of gratitude. "I guess I was just being silly, but I was overwhelmed at the moment at how wonderful this was, and we were right where we wanted to be."

Carmen decided to share her joy with her friends at the Child Saving Institute, whom she missed after two years of frequent communications. She also wanted them to know how extraordinary they had been for her—their warmth, their caring, their expertise in delivering Christina to her arms. Later on, she recalled telling the CSI people: "If there is ever anything I can do for you, I want to be able to pay back all of the things that we got from this agency. Besides having this child, we were treated so beautifully."

The caseworker on the phone replied, "Well, you know, Carmen, we can always consider foster care. We always need short-term foster care moms." Foster care in this sense was taking a child before adoption, oftentimes on short notice as many babies were relinquished without forethought on the mother's part, creating an "emergency" for the Child Saving Institute. The placements in question were usually brief but could last several months. Because of the nature of the business, the need for a placement could come at any moment of the day or night.

Carmen, never thinking twice that she had a six-month-old daughter at home, told the caseworker she would love to do it.

Two weeks later, with Christina still on one hip, Carmen accepted a newborn foster child, a "darling little boy" for whom CSI needed to find a temporary home in a hurry. Even CSI, in desperate need of a placement, wondered if Carmen could provide foster care for a newborn just two days old when she already had a six-month-old and a second-grader. "I didn't worry about it. I had most of Christina's things such as the bassinet and all the other things. So I did a complete, insane preparation for a brand new baby. I thought, 'Oh, this will be kind of fun.' Then I realized I had to sleep sometime."

Nonetheless, she would repeat this process, in more or less the same manner, over the next thirty years: baby boys, baby girls, mostly infants but an occasional toddler, too, all races and mixed races, some born with addictions, some born early, some born into desperate circumstances, but, to paraphrase Carmen, all born to be loved.

Carmen described John's initial reaction as shock mixed with being impressed that she was interested in providing what amounted to emergency foster care. The babies stayed for a couple of weeks to a couple of months before being adopted. "I hadn't really talked to John too much about it, and, when I told him this baby was coming, he sort of was overwhelmed," Carmen remembered.

Still, John got on board and stayed on board with Carmen's outreach. Carmen went to great lengths not to slight her own daughters and the time she had for them. Christina "took to" having babies around even though Carmen would occasionally have to put her down to feed an infant. She later told her mother in all the years of having foster babies in the house, she never once felt cheated out of her mother's time. Carmen cherished a picture with the first foster baby and Christina on her lap together and six-month-old Christina grabbing the little guy's hand.

For Jodi, having babies around was nothing new. "We had lots of babies at our house. It was our normal. We took turns naming them," Jodi said. When she was in her early teens, her friends liked to come over after school to meet a new arrival and throw out potential names. In later life, as a middle-school teacher, Jodi could draw a line from her parents' concern and care for babies directly to her father's work on children's and educational issues and, in turn, to her own career in the classroom.

One might also draw a line back to the orphaned Philip Anderson, taken in by his uncle and aunt, and to Phil's son, John Gottschalk, protected in a foster-care placement for the first two years of his life.

Both Carmen and John built lengthy résumés into children's issues. After twenty-five years of fostering babies, Carmen was sought by policy makers for her knowledge and experience. Governor Mike Johanns named her to the Task Force on Child Abuse to investigate, among other things, why a number of children died in state foster care placements. While wading through the horrific details, Carmen could not shed the memory of one case, that of a young Omaha girl who died after being reunited with her mother, the mother being wholly unfit for the task. "That was a tough one. That's when the task force just tore me up. I would lie awake at night thinking of those cases, thinking there's got to be some way to fix the broken system. What were we going to do? I was not in a position to fix it. I read the cases and I went to the meetings. But not really a whole lot has happened."

Sometimes the need for an immediate foster placement led to comical circumstances. Jodi told of a hurried shopping trip by Carmen to gather supplies for a baby who was en route. Frustrated by the slow-moving check-out line, Carmen, showing no indication of pregnancy, asked loudly enough for others to hear if the checkout clerk could pick up the pace because she was, "having a baby in an hour."

For Carmen, fostering babies was her service to the public, her contribution to a better community, her gift to Omaha. As the years passed and John became a bright light in Omaha through his leadership on boards and his profile in the community, Carmen's story became well known. She saw such exposure—which was all positive—as somewhat of an intrusion on her privacy because this was her personal thing, what she loved, how she made a difference.

"This was my everything," she said. "Not just my bowling team or my bridge club and all the things that women do. It was everything I liked doing, and I felt so good afterwards. I always said it was a selfish thing that I did. I didn't give of myself. I loved and took from that so much, that I never felt it was a sacrifice. People would look at me funny and ask, 'Why are you up with kids at four in the morning?' I'd say, 'But the baby was so happy, so comfortable. How important is that?' That's the most important thing." It was something Carmen Gottschalk learned the moment she first held her happy, contented Christina.

Even though she knew a baby's stay was temporary, she cried after she delivered each child to CSI for a permanent placement. On those days she purposely stayed away from home, busying herself elsewhere rather than face a house void of a baby she had come to love.

Carmen took a leave from fostering babies when Jodi's son, Austin, arrived in 1996, and she found family life growing busier. Still, she wanted her grandson to be part of the fostering experience, so when CSI called with a little girl, a newborn, she was right back at it. Then, in addition to the pictures she had of Tina on one hip and a foster baby on the other, she had photos of Austin holding a baby girl while grandma explained she'd be there only a short time. Austin was good with both the temporary stay and the holding of the baby. After that little girl was adopted, Carmen told the Child Saving Institute not to call. "Because they knew I'd say yes."

Despite her preference for privacy when it came to fostering babies, public notice grew into public recognition. In 2006, the Knights of Ak-Sar-Ben Foundation named Carmen to its Court of Honor, the foundation's most prestigious award. She was honored during the Ak-Sar-Ben Coronation Ball. Accompanying Carmen as she made her way into the mythical court to be recognized were three escorts: the first baby she had taken in, a young man then twenty-eight; her grandson, Austin; and the last baby she had fostered, then four, and beautiful in every way and, in perfect symmetry, named Christina.

Her graceful acceptance speech that evening revealed the essence of Carmen Gottschalk—and by extension and circumstance John, Jodi, and Christina Gottschalk—given of a loving home and gentle hands for all the babies born into trying times.

Carmen was honored at the Ak-Sar-Ben annual gala for her work fostering one hundred babies over thirty years. With her are two of the children she cared for. The little girl was the last foster child in the Gottschalk home.

My gratitude goes to my family for allowing me to pursue this for so many years and their willingness to help me every step of the way.

To the Child Saving Institute for starting my journey by giving me the opportunity. To the caseworkers for working closely with me to help me succeed and crying with me when it was time to say goodbye.

To the birth mothers who made the most unselfish and difficult decision they will ever make, to want the best life possible for their babies. Reaching out, then letting go.

To the wonderful adoptive parents who were eagerly waiting to carry on for the rest of these children's lives.

Finally, to the children who made it all happen, I never met a baby I didn't love. The world is a better place because you are in it.

Thank you for sharing your lives.

Among the rushing rivers of human lives, sometimes two tributaries merge to form a powerful, single force. Such was the partnership of John Gottschalk and Richard "Rick" Lance with the National Benevolent Association of the Christian Church (Disciples of Christ). They met when Lance was the organization's national president and John was an NBA board member, including a term as chairman from 1985 to 1987. Earlier Lance had a three-year stint as executive director of Omaha's Child Saving Institute, when the Gottschalks had adopted their daughter, Christina. The National Benevolent Association was the supporting ministry for the Child Saving Institute.

Rick Lance retired from the Air Force in 1974 as a colonel and deputy director of intelligence estimates at the Strategic Air Command headquarters. Electing to remain in Nebraska, he was immediately tapped to take over the reins at CSI. He was chosen three years later as executive director of the Kansas Christian Home, another NBA partner. In 1982 he became NBA president, a post he held until his retirement in 1996. During his tenure, NBA assets grew from $78 million to $305 million and the number of care-giving facilities served rose from forty-two to eighty-two. John Gottschalk played a pivotal role in the NBA's financial and ministerial success.

To understand John's role as a board member and financial supporter in the exceptional accomplishments of the NBA, his history at the Child Saving Institute would be instructive. He joined the CSI board in 1978 and stayed until 1984, so he had some overlap with his board tenure at the NBA. He served as CSI's board chairman in 1981. John drew a straight line from his and Carmen's research on adoption agencies to his work with both the NBA and Child Saving Institute.

The one-hundred-year plus history of the Child Saving Institute had seen its care model undergo changes. Iconic pictures from the thirties and forties captured darling children in rows of CSI beds, a setting akin to an orphanage. But as more "children began to have children," CSI decided to shift its care model, choosing to focus on fewer cases while addressing a broader range of problems. CSI continued to be a fulcrum for foster care and eventual adoption, but the group widened the lens of its ministry. Staff retooled programs and facilities to provide housing and training for new single mothers while assisting in the care of their new babies. The transformation was short-lived. When CSI found it was serving far fewer people and spending about the same amount of money, it went back to its old model. It had realized that while the most difficult cases surely needed extensive services, addressing the problems of a larger number of those in need was more consistent with its mission.

The return to its previous programs coincided with John's arrival on the CSI board. In 1977, after Rick Lance had moved on, Donna Hager became CSI's CEO and Creighton University professor Maxine Burch was chairman of the board. Burch liked John's record as an adoptive parent and an executive at the *World-Herald*. She invited him to become a CSI board member. He said yes. It was to be his first experience on what would become a stunning résumé of nonprofit board service in Omaha. Prior to that, Harold Andersen had tapped John to be part of a group headed by Peter Kiewit that would create a full service education center in downtown Omaha. Relationships he built on that body proved to be invaluable— and lifelong—as John began his civic journey into the city's nonprofit universe, and, ultimately, far beyond.

The CSI board was mainly populated by members of the Christian Church (Disciples of Christ). Board members were selected as couples, so when Burch called John, she was actually calling John and Carmen to join seven other couples setting policy for the Child Saving Institute. Soon, as John described it, someone noticed "that I could walk and chew gum at the same time," so, among other duties, he was asked to serve as the Child Saving Institute representative on the NBA board.

Early on, John noticed that CSI would consistently end a year of operations about $100,000 short. Burch told John the organization needed to raise money. John agreed but urged her and CSI to make sure that potential donors knew CSI's story—now that the old model had replaced the new one. Once that tale was made clear, John said to Burch, "We can raise a hundred thousand dollars every year." But bake sales were not going to cut it. They needed to raise some "real money," one million dollars in John's estimation. Even though the NBA could help, each local agency operated independently, including fundraising. Through John's work early on with Kiewit's downtown education project, he had met many community leaders he believed could "move the ball" when it came to raising funds for local projects.

Tasked with eliminating the Child Saving Institute's annual shortfall, John decided to call on Bob Daugherty, CEO of Valmont Industries. Valmont's center-pivot irrigation systems had revolutionized farming, advancing Valmont into an important international manufacturing company. In time, more than forty out of every one hundred acres of irrigated farmland used a center-pivot system or something similar. When he retired in 1996, Daugherty allocated a good portion of his wealth to establish the Robert B. Daugherty Charitable Foundation. The Daugherty Foundation's largesse helped move many Omaha and Nebraska projects to completion. In 2010 the Foundation pledged $50 million to the Global Water for Food Institute, where it is used to underwrite research and fund policy analysis on the use of water in agricultural production.

With CSI's development director, John headed to see Daugherty in his office downtown. He found Daugherty at his desk, the brilliant sun backlighting him into a shadow. After cordial greetings, Daugherty asked John what he could do for him. John told him the nature of his errand, the good work of CSI, a mission with which Daugherty agreed. John said he was trying to raise enough endowment money to plug a yearly $100,000 hole and keep it plugged.

"What do you think you'll need?" Daugherty asked.

John said to do it right, CSI would need a million dollars.

"And what do you think you need from me?"

John asked him to consider $50,000.

"Why me?"

"Bob, because you know this needs to be done, and you have the capacity to do it."

Daugherty swiveled in his chair and looked out the window for what seemed to John to be an eternity but was probably less than thirty seconds. When he turned back around, John saw a trace of moisture in his eyes.

"I'll do it," he said.

John thanked him and left, hoping not to have to scrape the development director's jaw from the floor on the way out. For John, who would spend the next four decades asking people to write big checks for worthy causes, the moment was profound, enlightening, and instructive. "I've thought about it a lot over the years. What was Bob thinking? I mean, it struck a nerve somewhere. There are things that happen in life for which you have no idea of the impact."

Nor did he ever ask Bob what filled his thoughts that day as he stared out the window. "That's just one you leave alone."

～

According to its mission, the National Benevolent Association "exists to inspire and connect the people and ministries of the Christian Church (Disciples of Christ), to accompany one another in the creation of communities of compassion and care, and to advocate for the well-being of humanity." The Child Saving Institute stood as an example and translation of such principled prose. The level of John's board commitment increased when he began serving as CSI's "unit representative" to the NBA in 1980, the onset of a decade of service with the national group. The NBA had, since 1887, been the Christian Church's social and health services outreach, providing comfort and care in housing, nursing, therapeutic services, counseling, and education for thousands of children and adults, including over one hundred partnering units, such as CSI, and forty residential facilities at partner agencies in the nation.

By 1983 John had moved from unit representative to a board member, rising to the chairmanship in 1985, where he served for two years. By the time John left the board in 1989, the NBA had grown dramatically in its financial well-being but, more important, in the number of people it could serve. That year also marked the first seven-figure gift made by John and Carmen.

At ceremonies in 1989 honoring John and Carmen with the NBA's highest national honor, the Beasley Distinguished Service Award, NBA President Rick Lance said John was the driving force behind the organization's unprecedented growth. Lance, who came to the NBA in 1982 as president, teamed with John a total of eight years.

John said the NBA national board was made up of "wonderful people" from across the face of the nation. He found them, as he did most of those serving on nonprofit boards trying to better the lives of others, equipped "with great hearts." What he brought to the NBA board, however, was not only the compassion and caring required for a seat at the table and a part of the ministry, but also a willingness to tackle the business and fundraising issues necessary to keep such a social enterprise solvent and able to meet its service demands.

His achievements with the NBA included developing a policy (with Lance's input) that zeroed in on partner agencies, which had been shuffling along financially. The Troubled Units Policy provided leadership and managerial support to pull agencies with problems out of sometimes deep ruts and to chart financial and program courses that were effective and solvent. Lance called the development of the policy "the single most important event that allowed us to pursue our goal of increasing the number of lives the NBA has the ability to touch."

While the NBA's financial health and efficiency were John's focus, especially as chairman, fundraising occupied much of his time. He and Carmen supported the NBA financially for many years, setting an example for others. They were among the leaders of the NBA's Centennial Campaign, a national effort in the mid-1980s on John's watch that increased the ministry's coffers by $20 million and, in turn, enabled entities such as CSI to serve more people.

As chairman, John oversaw the raising of money, the effectiveness of the board and the quality of the NBA's services. Sometimes the job demanded more, and he simply had to improvise.

To celebrate the Centennial Campaign and mark its one hundredth year of existence, the NBA hosted a national gathering in St. Louis at the historic Union Station Hotel. John was board chairman at that time. At a planning meeting for the celebration, someone noted that John had once hired Helen Reddy through a talent broker to sing at an event in Omaha. They thought she would be perfect for the NBA event. "They said to me, 'You've been down that road before. Would you rodeo that part?'"

John went back to the broker, who said he could book Reddy. The cost, as John recalled, was $20,000. He had also arranged for the singer to pose for photographs with NBA attendees after her performance. As the big Saturday night in St. Louis approached, however, the plans took a foreboding turn. When John arrived Saturday morning, the hotel was being picketed by union members protesting that an event in the hotel was using non-union employees backstage. The gathering NBA celebrants became apprehensive, wondering if their big night was going to be compromised and, more important, if Helen Reddy would honor the picket line. They looked to John, who was, in part, saved by a hard-nosed hotel manager who got the pickets to back off. Still, no one knew whether Helen Reddy—who had seen the commotion earlier when she arrived at the hotel from the airport—and her band would perform. John headed to her suite.

He said to her, "The (labor) matter has been resolved. We don't want to embarrass you. We don't want to embarrass ourselves. Is there anything this will change in terms of our contract?"

Reddy said, "Not at all. I want to perform for you."

Back downstairs, anxiety wafted around the grand ballroom as the NBA crowd still wasn't convinced she would show. John said as the evening wore on the event became less about the success of their campaign and more about whether Helen Reddy was going to sing. But sing she did, wowing the crowd and, true to her word, afterward faced a gauntlet of admirers who wanted to shake her hand. John escorted her through the maze of well-wishers. When they reached the end of the hallway, she turned to him and said, "Do you have the check?"

He said he didn't but knew who did and handed Reddy off to a genial NBA staffer while John went in search of the NBA treasurer. But that person had no check and no checkbook from which to write one. Without missing a beat (but surely taking a leap of faith), John went back to Reddy, handed her a personal check from his account for $20,000, assured her it was good, and called it an evening.

Indeed it had been.

~

On June 9, 1978, publisher Harold Andersen sent out a dozen invitations for a "Front-End Editing Victory Dinner." The invites were addressed to "veterans of the nearly completed planning and installation chapter of that continuing story, 'Front-End Editing at World-Herald Square and How It Grew.'" Andersen was assembling the leaders who put together the plan for the newspaper's new editing system, checked and rechecked it, tested and retested it, and finally gave it the go-ahead. So new was the system that Andersen—somewhat kiddingly—added that each of the invitees to the backyard soiree was on call in case things went south and everyone had to head to the newspaper in the middle of the party.

"Front-end" referred to the initial stages of the production of a newspaper. For many years, the front-end consisted of placing words on paper, either by hand or by typewriter. Then a compositor, like the young John Gottschalk in Rushville, keyed the words into a device—in John's case a Linotype—that reproduced the words in metal, to be inked and pressed against paper. By the 1970s, technology had provided alternatives that were cleaner, safer, and more efficient. Using these methods, the original entry of the words into a machine was also the final entry. Computers and photographic reproduction equipment took over from there. There was no intermediate step in which another human being had to make, in effect, a second copy of the words.

The *World-Herald*'s new system, selected, tested, and overseen by a team headed by John Gottschalk, moved the newspaper to the forefront of metro newspapers, which had the new electronic copy processing system. But getting there required both enormous vision and unerring attention to detail.

John brought both to the project, a skill set he flexed at the newspaper nearly three years earlier when, on his first day at World-Herald Square, he found one item in his in-basket: the cost of newsprint "waste" report from the previous week.

Grateful for something to do right away, John devoured the report, noting with some whimsy his changing perspective: newsprint waste in one week at the *World-Herald* was more than a year's worth of consumption at the *Sidney Telegraph*. He also did something that was wholly natural and second nature but proved to be of enormous value in succeeding years as he moved through the managerial ranks at the newspaper: He went downstairs to the pressroom—on Day One.

Omaha World-Herald headquarters from 1948-2006

There he introduced himself to the pressmen and asked them about the report, not in an accusatory way but rather to gather information and build relationships, key to balancing his being the new guy from the VP's office and as a nod to the time and place—and ongoing labor issues. John couldn't forget that just hours earlier, he had passed through picket lines in order to enter the *World-Herald*. Their union was protesting coming changes in the composing room that would, at the very least, alter the way the typesetters did their jobs and, at the very worst, eliminate certain jobs as they knew them.

Having grown up in the back shop of a newspaper, John was as comfortable exchanging ideas with workers next to a rolling press as he was exchanging ideas with directors in the newspaper's boardroom. He was not one to stay in his office— even though its door was perpetually open. He preferred to be on the move, talking with employees in their own spaces, where they contributed to the creation of a daily paper, from newsroom to advertising to business office to composing.

Still, the tension of labor strife was real and palpable because most *World-Herald* employees knew soft winds of the future were gathering strength, and new technologies that would change how they worked were inevitable. Change was not to come easy.

Obviously, the International Typographical Union (ITU) was aware of management's desire to move toward "cold" type and electronic photographic typesetting—a new front-end system. Many ITU members saw their world about to be flipped upside-down, and that much of the work they did was either going to change or be eliminated.

Their concerns were well-founded. Early on, Andersen had asked John to research the development and purchase of a new front-end system. The task would grow into his being tapped project leader. "(The front-end system) was my first big assignment. It was also a big deal. Going to cold type had rambled around in *World-Herald* executives' offices for at least two years, maybe more. No decision. No decision. It was interesting, challenging, and a lot of hard work, but ended up being a fun thing for me to do."

In a memo dated November 20, 1975, John summarized his research on the front-end system to Andersen. Included in the three-page, detailed report were the reductions and savings an electronic photographical typesetting system would bring. Man-hours (and jobs) would be cut and the stereotype department would be eliminated. Stereotypes were molded plate casts made from composed type and set inside rigid frames. While the essence of John's memo would bring plenty of heartburn to printers and compositors, those in the business office and executive suite were encouraged. He also found somewhere between $1.4 and $1.7 million in savings. A large part of the savings came from the elimination of typewriters and their continual maintenance (small desktop computer terminals would replace them), the removal of stereotype equipment and personnel, the reduction of time and resources spent in engraving, and manpower reductions on the press—altogether producing a more efficient application of everyone's time from the newsroom to the pressroom to the mailroom.

The *World-Herald* wasn't unique in wanting to move ahead with new technology. When the Hendrix system was up and running in the spring of 1978—a good five years after Andersen and his management team started exploring the possibility of electronic photographical typesetting—the technology was in the vanguard of changing the newspaper business. The *World-Herald* was only the second newspaper in the country to use a Hendrix system. "The industry had moved somewhat to getting cold type electronically, but that wasn't doing anything for the inputs on the front-end," John said.

By the end of 1976, the publisher, Harold Andersen, moved John from being Woody Howe's assistant to becoming Andersen's assistant when Howe became the newspaper's executive editor. The move underscored both Andersen's and Howe's preoccupation with the newsroom and enhanced the newspaper's ability to gain traction on bringing a front-end editing system to the *World-Herald*. The move freed some of John's focus, but it also revealed Andersen's recognition of John's unique experience and well-crafted skill set. Having been a successful publisher at the *Sidney Telegraph*, John displayed business sense, leadership, and decision-making skills honed over the eight years he ran the show in Nebraska's Panhandle. So when Andersen moved John to captain the team charged with bringing the *Omaha World-Herald* into the front lines of modern newspaper technology, he had read well into John's résumé.

For John, however, the task remained daunting. By the mid-1970s, IBM and Digital Equipment Corporation were offering versions of systems that approached electronic photographical typesetting, but neither had what John wanted, namely that typesetting began with the reporter at his or her computer terminal. Hendrix, a small New England software company, wanted to sell to the newspaper industry. Eventually, Hendrix reached an agreement to partner with Digital Equipment Corporation. Its software focus was to minimize keystrokes.

This was what John was looking for. "We wanted to move composition from the Linotype room to the newsroom. We'd no longer have typos. We'd have 'newsos.'" Before electronic photographic typesetting, reporters' only concern was getting their story on time to composing, somewhat oblivious to the production end of the newspaper equation. And although writers need not also be producers of the final product, they needed to understand they were part of it. So did vendors looking to sell wares to newspapers.

John, with his background in production and Linotype, understood what was at stake. "With IBM, for example, you had to type something like caret, asterisk, asterisk, 764387 at the end of each line, a code to signify the ending of one line and the start of the next. Ultimately, someone was going to figure out, and did, how to program all of those codes into one keystroke. We weren't going to build a custom system with IBM. You'd have people running computers instead of writing news stories."

To accomplish getting an individual keystroke for an individual character—and more important, to depend on it being there in the heat of deadline—John's team devised an extensive battery of tests. It based the tests on the details of the *World-Herald*'s contract with Hendrix. John led a posse of testers recruited from the newsroom and elsewhere to Hendrix headquarters in Manchester, New Hampshire. The "textbook" of tests they had devised was thick, and John's team spent several long days doing nothing but testing and retesting, a process he likened to "Sherman marching though Atlanta."

The requirement, he said, was to be detailed and complete. "We wrote our own tests. Every direct sentence in the contract, we wrote a test for it." If, for example, the contract said the QWERTY keyboard would have an upper and lower case, John's team went through every key starting with the lower-case "a" and working its way through both cases of each letter in the alphabet, on to numbers and symbols and arrows and commands. Some tests for common keystrokes were repeated numerous times. This was well before Hendrix shipped and installed its 6500 System in Omaha. After that took place, in January 1978, tests were repeated and internal training began. The system's arrival also began a long stretch for John who spent hours overseeing installation, testing, and training, what he likened to "living down there."

Once again the newspaper was served well by John's knowledge of production and its relationship to inputs in the newsroom and outputs headed for carriers and the mailroom. "I couldn't fix the software problem but I could identify what it was, where it was, and sometimes how it was. As its beta site, we could get that done quickly by Hendrix."

The *Omaha World-Herald* brought the system online in early spring of 1978. As project leader, John still responded to bugs and glitches, but by May he decided to take a well-earned and long overdue vacation with his family to Fort Robinson in northwest Nebraska, an hour from his roots in Rushville. This was well before the advent of cell phones, so John carried a beeper in case he was needed to troubleshoot problems back in Omaha. After the Gottschalks arrived in Crawford, gateway to Fort Robinson, they headed to a restaurant for a late meal before making their way to their cabin in the park. John's beeper went off. With the restaurant getting ready to shut down for the evening, his only alternative was a phone booth next to Highway 20. From there, late into the night, he talked his co-workers through whatever guidance they needed while semis, cattle trucks, and vacationers roared by in the darkness.

Eight hours to the east, the Hendrix kept humming along.

John sensed that his leadership on the front-end editing project "must have shown them something." He was right. Seven months after the celebratory party in Harold Andersen's backyard, John was promoted to vice president, in charge of the newspaper's production departments—including the installation of a new, computerized classified ad copy processing system. Andersen also made John available for special assignments, a nod to his new VP's broad range of expertise. John Gottschalk was on the move at the *Omaha World-Herald*.

FOUR

Mergers, Acquisitions, and Kiewit Troubles

John, you'd better be prepared to work. Bill Stephenson knows the game. He will have high expectations of you. He came here to mold young men like you, and he will teach you to win in all you do.

–PHIL GOTTSCHALK

When John Gottschalk became publisher and chief executive officer of the *Omaha World-Herald* in 1989, he was only the fifth person to hold the newspaper's top position. His predecessors were the newspaper's founder, Gilbert M. Hitchcock (1885-1934); Henry Doorly (1934-1955); Walter E. Christenson (1955-1966); and Harold W. Andersen (1966-1989).

Not all of his predecessors used the title "publisher." Hitchcock and Doorly went by "president of the World Publishing Company," and each designated a subordinate as publisher during at least part of his tenure: Hitchcock gave the title to his brother-in-law, William Crounse; Doorly bestowed the title on his son-in-law, Ben Cowdery. Christenson kept the additional title of "editor." In 1985, the presidency of the company was conferred on John Gottschalk while Andersen, as chairman of the board, remained the top executive until his retirement four years later.

The distinction prior to 1985 may have been moot or perhaps simply informal as to who was running the show. But when the World-Herald Co. began acquiring other newspapers and other businesses in the 1980s, the governing structure of the company needed to be in line with the type of organization it was becoming. Accordingly, the board of directors named a chairman and CEO (Harold Andersen), a president and COO (John Gottschalk), and a vice president (G. Woodson Howe). The *World-Herald* newspaper got a publisher (Andersen) and an editor (Howe). Even though the company's CEO and the newspaper's publisher may have been the same person (as Andersen was after 1985), separating the titles seemed logical when the company owned a number of newspapers. This fell in line with common corporate practices of other newspaper holding companies. A parsing and history of the term "publisher" at the *World-Herald* would be instructive, however, both in this biography and in an understanding of where the *World-Herald* was positioned in the mid-1980s and how future publisher and CEO John Gottschalk would impact the company's growth and expanded financial strength.

The newspaper's ownership resided within one extended family from 1885 until 1963, nearly eight decades. Gilbert Hitchcock, son of a U.S. senator, and later a congressman and senator in his own right, published the first edition of the *Omaha World* on August 24, 1885, using a gasoline-powered press, cutting edge technology for the late nineteenth century. He called it the "people's paper." Four years later he purchased the competing *Omaha Herald*, forming the *Omaha World-Herald*.

Hitchcock did not post his first profit until 1893. He hired William Jennings Bryan as editor in 1894. While Bryan's name on the masthead carried some weight, during his two-year stint he spent more time on his political ambitions than he did in the newsroom.

When Hitchcock was elected to the U.S. House of Representatives in 1906, his son-in-law, Henry Doorly, stepped in to handle day-to-day management duties. That same year Hitchcock elevated Harvey Newbranch from reporter to editor. Thirteen years later, after mobs lynched a black prisoner, Newbranch called for calm and an end to violence in an editorial called "Law and the Jungle." It was awarded a Pulitzer Prize.

Doorly became the company's president and added the title of publisher when Hitchcock died in 1934. The *World-Herald* acquired the *Omaha Bee-News*, which closed in 1937, ending years of bitter and personal hostility between the two papers. The demise of the *Bee-News* meant that the *World-Herald* was the last of eight daily newspapers serving metropolitan Omaha at one time or another.

Doorly was succeeded in 1955 by Walter Christenson, who had advanced through the news and editorial departments to the position of editor. Although Christenson was at its helm, the paper was still owned by Hitchcock's heirs, including members of the Doorly family. These owners differed among themselves about the direction and future of the paper. Unable to reconcile their differences, a majority of the family shareholders decided in 1962 to sell the paper to Samuel Newhouse, a New York magnate who already owned nineteen newspapers. That solution came to an impasse when negotiations stalled between Newhouse and Martha Hitchcock, widow of the *World-Herald*'s founder and first publisher.

Enter Omaha businessman Peter Kiewit, who believed strongly that the newspaper should remain under local control.

After studying the newspaper's financial records and consulting with other community leaders, Kiewit went to the newspaper's shareholders with his arguments for local ownership. With Martha Hitchcock's support and the necessary financial fitness ($300,000 above the Newhouse bid), Kiewit bought the newspaper for just over $40.4 million in a deal that became final on December 31, 1962. Martha Hitchcock had died on December 15.

The sale of the *World-Herald* to Kiewit, who headed Peter Kiewit Sons', a global construction company, ended the family-owned and operated structure of the *World-Herald*. Kiewit's vision for the *World-Herald*, however, in many ways stayed the course charted by the Hitchcock family. He wanted the *World-Herald* to remain locally-owned and locally-managed. To solidify that future for the newspaper, Kiewit's estate plan provided for the employees to purchase ownership after his death. He gave the Peter Kiewit Foundation a maximum 20 percent of the stock, and the remaining 80 percent was to be sold to *Omaha World-Herald* employee shareholders.

John Gottschalk was fresh from the success of the Hendrix System installation and the newspaper was rolling with digital type when, in 1980, the *World-Herald* acquired the Papillion Times Printing and Recorder Publishing Company. This company was the publisher of five weeklies: the *Papillion Times*, *Ralston Recorder*, *Millard Edition*, *Springfield Monitor*, and *Gretna Breeze*. The purchase would be the first foray into *World-Herald* acquisitions that would amass nearly sixty newspapers, direct mail and marketing companies, printing businesses, a voting machine company, and even the tower in downtown Omaha where the *World-Herald* was eventually to make its headquarters. John was the driver for every acquisition until his retirement in 2007, meaning he led the process of every one. Eight were made on Andersen's watch and the remainder during John's time as CEO.

The *Omaha World-Herald* newsroom circa 1980.

Process was the correct word, too. "We didn't have a formula," John said. "We had a process. We followed a checklist, but the acquisitions were not part of some grand strategic plan." What was at work was John's notion, shared by many in top management, that leftover cash (after dividend and stock payouts to employee owners, needed expenditures, and ordinary operating expenses) was best used to expand the business through investments. As evidenced by years of a nearly 20 percent return to stockholders, the philosophy proved not only sound but also lucrative to employee owners. Ironically, the monumental financial success of the *World-Herald* led to an eventual rift between the newspaper and the Peter Kiewit Foundation.

King Midas did not touch every *World-Herald* investment, though. Some deals were never made. John also admitted to making a few that he wished he hadn't. But over the eighteen-year span with John leading the charge, the *World-Herald* achieved unprecedented growth as it proceeded into the second century of its history. For those who formed the acquisition team, not only did the process work, but also the right man was at the wheel. Terry Kroeger, CEO and publisher of the *World-Herald* and John's successor, joined the team in the late 1990s after stints as publisher at other *World-Herald* papers: the *Kearney Hub* and the *Columbus Telegram* in Nebraska and the *Stockton Record* in California. He said the boss's reputation as a leader was well-known. "John could usually detect some detail that others hadn't thought of, including me. And he could make something better. He was sort of legendary for his leadership of the conversion to the Hendrix System cold type. That would have been in the seventies—I wasn't around then, but I had heard about it."

The acquisition of the Papillion Times Printing and Recorder Publishing Company signaled that the *World-Herald* was in the market for solid newspapers. But even before the owner, George Miller, signed the papers, *World-Herald* CEO Harold Andersen had tasked John with looking into the value of the *Denver Post*, the object of sale rumors in early 1979. By then, John had been promoted to vice president for general management, which included oversight for all non-news divisions and subsidiaries.

"Looking at the *Denver Post* was a big deal," John said. The *Post*'s owners, the Bonfils family, had put the paper into a trust and the trustees were looking to sell. The *Post* was hemorrhaging subscriptions, showing losses on weekdays, Saturdays, and Sundays. Its rival for metropolitan Denver readership, the *Rocky Mountain News*, would overtake the *Post* as the circulation leader on the Front Range of the Rockies in 1980.

To John's surprise, Andersen, who had heard the paper was considering offers, asked him to go to Denver to get a sense of what shape the *Post* was in and whether it would be a good investment. After two days of looking around and talking to a number of people, John concluded the paper was a mishmash of neglect and mismanagement from equipment to labor relations. With an asking price of over $100 million, John's assessment was that the *Denver Post* was not worth the cost. That's the message he conveyed to the *World-Herald* board, to which Andersen had asked him to give his brief report.

Peter Kiewit, who would die later that year, was in the room. After the report, he asked if John had ever looked into buying a paper mill, a venture that would take well more than $100 million to accomplish. He encouraged the young executive to do so. "It might be something to look into. You fellas know what you're doing. I'm not saying you should do it, but it might be worth a look."

Afterward, John confided to Andersen that he considered Kiewit's observation rather strange. Andersen said, "John, what he was really saying was that we put a lot of time in setting up employee ownership pending Pete's passing. We have millions and millions of dollars moving in a matter of days when he dies. Everything is set. Everything is fine. Don't get impatient."

Late the following year, the Times Mirror Company, owner of the *Los Angeles Times,* bought the *Denver Post* for $95 million and ultimately disposed of it seven years later for $95 million—after spending $45 million on upgrades to the *Post'*s printing presses.

~

John highly respected George Miller, owner and president of the Papillion Times Printing and Recorder Publishing Company. "George was a fine community newspaperman. He created, down in Papillion, a good newspaper. He was well thought of in newspaper circles. He was a thoughtful kind of guy."

Despite an efficient operation and solid journalistic instincts and experience, Miller most often found himself in an uphill struggle for the advertising dollar, making it increasingly more difficult to compete. For example, advertising inches for a large downtown retailer such as Brandeis department store were not going to make their way into Miller's much smaller pools of readers. Eventually, Miller decided he wanted to sell his company, a thought he conveyed to Jim Protzman, a friend of John's who passed the information along.

After thinking about it, John took a three-fold pitch to Andersen. First, he argued that, sooner or later, they would be expanding the company, not in any way that would diminish the *Omaha World-Herald* but as a way to bring added value to the company. Second, while the *World-Herald* was the paper of record in the greater Omaha area, it struggled to hold the suburbs. Finally, having never owned other newspapers or businesses, the chance to develop communication and operating systems for multiple enterprises looked like a favorable opportunity for *World-Herald* managers.

With Andersen's blessing, John moved forward, getting back to Protzman and eventually meeting with Miller. A deal was quickly struck and, shortly thereafter, Miller along with his wife, his brother, and a son met John and Bill Kernen, the *World-Herald*'s corporate treasurer, at an attorney's office to sign the legal documents and close what was a fairly straightforward business transaction. When Miller arrived, he was carrying a small box about the size of a bowling ball. He asked John if he would step out into the hallway. He opened the box and inside was the hand crank machine that produced the seal of the *Papillion Times*, used by Miller's father and grandfather before him. He asked John if he would consider excluding the machine from the sale. Having been through the selling of two family-owned newspapers, John understood the true value of what was inside the box. He said he would be happy to grant Miller his wish.

"This was a big day for them. But it's tough to walk away from your newspaper. Of course I said yes. The seal machine was the only thing he had left of that place except his years and years of toil and his great community service. It was moving to do this with his family."

The *World-Herald* kept in place the staffs of the five newspapers, sending only a publisher to the *Papillion Times*. These staffs created systems to dovetail with systems the *World-Herald* already had in place such as accounting and profit and loss reports. While adding five weeklies to the fold was a new and challenging enterprise, the *World-Herald* was clear on how it would measure success in what was now being called Suburban Newspapers Inc., a wholly-owned subsidiary of the *Omaha World-Herald*. A year later the *World-Herald* would acquire a printing company, but it would be another five years before the company would add another newspaper, one, ironically, John had tried to buy more than a decade earlier.

Mary Jane "Pug" Gottschalk, John's mother, died of respiratory failure on January 26, 1983, in Omaha. She was sixty-five. She had moved there a year earlier from Rushville, where she had actively kept the weekly rhythm of the *Sheridan County Star* beating soundly until 1982, when she sold the newspaper to Dick and Ruth Ziegler. Mary Jane's health had deteriorated over a number of years, exacerbated by alcoholism.

Newsprint and ink were in Mary Jane Gottschalk's blood, something she and Phil Gottschalk passed on to their son John. She devoted two-thirds of her life to newspapers, starting and ending with the *Sheridan County Star*, which she owned and ran with her husband Phil from 1949 to 1966. John kept close tabs on his mother, starting in Sidney where for a time she lived with John and Carmen, and then again at the end when Mary Jane lived in a convalescent home in Omaha. After the turmoil of Mary Jane's divorce from Phil in 1966 had subsided, John continued a close relationship with his father, He made at least one trip a year for a University of Missouri football

outing either to Columbia or Lincoln when the Tigers played
Nebraska. Phil eventually found himself on the wire desk at the
Columbia Tribune until his retirement in 1986.

Mary Jane was buried in Rushville, where, for nearly four
decades, she was dedicated to chronicling life there, in a place
John called "Nebraska's best little town." A week after his
mother's death, John wrote a letter to the editor of the *Sheridan
County Star*:

> *Last weekend the Gottschalk family was once again
> the recipient of the love and warmth of so many friends
> in our hometown. Although the occasion was sad, we all
> were lifted up by the wonderful folks in Rushville. We
> thank you all.*
>
> *Most families have a scrapbook and perhaps ours is
> a little thicker than most. When a loved one departs,
> memories become so important and the yellowed
> clippings from events which appeared in the pages of the
> Sheridan County Star are treasures to us.*
>
> *At rest now are two of the three generations of our
> family, who edited the columns of the* Star.
>
> *Bill Barnes's "Just Between You and Me" took many
> opportunities to boost the community and its neighbors
> in the farming and ranching community. Sometimes it
> was a vignette about a common man and sometimes
> about an extraordinarily uncommon man. But, always
> standing in equal stature as a neighbor.*
>
> *Mabel Grimes's "Swingin' Up Main" constantly
> reminded her readers that the strength of the community
> rested in the pride and enthusiasm its residents had for
> the accomplishments of one another. Her boosting of
> the RHS band was legend, as was her support for the
> town's young people generally. I re-read a number of old
> columns written by my grandfather and Aunt "Dutch"
> and realized how much they loved their community.*

Parades, celebrations, bond issues, baseball, schools, 4-H and Farmer-Rancher events all appeared as opportunities to boost the spirit of a wonderful town.

And then "Patter By Pug," appearing infrequently but with equal fervor for the good life she enjoyed with her friends for nearly 40 years in Rushville. The rough times will fade leaving only our memories of the sparkle in "her Irish eyes" as her father dubbed them in a column written in 1937 in the Hay Springs News.

She spoke frequently and forthrightly about how much Rushville meant to her and how cherished friends provided so much support for her in later years. We want to think she gave back some, too, over those 40 years— and now she rests—at home.

Mike, Lynn, and I intend to come back to visit our hometown, too. Things, which so many of your readers don't recognize, are really extraordinary in Nebraska's best little town. "Just good folks" as Mabel would say.

I'm sure when we return, we'll find more change and progress. And I hope we will always find the spirit and warmth which the Barnes family chronicled for so long. We have returned our loved one to you, her longtime friends, and on behalf of our family, I thank you for all that you've done for us.

Three months later, the Zeiglers sold the *Sheridan County Star* to a group that eventually merged it with other newspapers, ending an era in Rushville. After Mary Jane died, John, Mike, and Lynn decided that her entire estate should go to the Gottschalk Barnes Trust to be used for the betterment of Rushville and Sheridan County.

$\sim$

During the frozen Nebraska winter of early 1981, Zane Randall, president and principal owner of Rapid Printing and Lithographers Inc., had periodic business meetings at nondescript hotels booked by a man named John Edwards.

Rapid had more than doubled its business in five years. In 1980 Rapid had produced three hundred million newspaper inserts in nearly five hundred newspapers. That same year the company had addressed and sent over thirty-two million direct mail pieces and produced about fifty-five million address labels for direct mail customers. Randall was looking for a buyer with sufficient resources to assure that the printing company's expansion plans to meet increasing demand would be realized. Edwards had the solution: The *Omaha World-Herald*.

For the *World-Herald*, such a deal would allow the newspaper to expand its services, including access to specialized web offset and sheet-fed printing. Of prime interest, too, were Rapid's direct mail systems and 1.5 million addresses.

After several months of secret negotiations between Randall and Edwards, *World-Herald* CEO Harold Andersen announced on April 6, 1981, that the newspaper had acquired Rapid. As part of the announcement, Andersen revealed that John Gottschalk—a.k.a. John Edwards—had led the negotiations with Rapid.

The Rapid deal (along with the subsequent acquisition of A-1 Mailing, a direct mail firm) addressed a growing concern for the *World-Herald*: Real and potential losses of grocery store advertising revenue if the major players decided they could reach 100 percent coverage using direct mail rather than large display ads or inserts in the newspaper. As the grocers teetered on the verge of leaving the *World-Herald*, the newspaper created a weekly, four-page "product" for non-subscribers called "Midweek," which carried the same large display ads and coupons the grocers were running in the *World-Herald*. Still, even though Rapid had the printing capabilities, they weren't making money because they did not have the distribution system. The *World-Herald* had that, in spades.

"We had a distribution system that was a lot more efficient than the post office. Our circulation data base allowed us to identify non-subscriber addresses," John said, adding that the newspaper's penetration rate in the early 1980s was between 80 and 90 percent of homes in the metro area. By adding Rapid's capabilities, the *World-Herald* started to solve its looming, potential revenue stream problem.

The acquisition of Rapid Printing led to a notable and historic conflict in Omaha's newspaper market. The *Omaha Sun*, the nation's first weekly to win a Pulitzer Prize for its 1973 investigation of Boys Town fundraising practices, filed an anti-trust suit against the *Omaha World-Herald* in January of 1983. The suit asked that the *World-Herald* divest itself of two wholly-owned subsidiaries, Rapid Printing and Suburban Newspapers Inc. Among the allegations outlined in the petition was that Rapid was offering lower prices to advertisers for "marriage mail" than had previously been offered to the *Sun's* stable of weekly newspapers. Marriage mail was the practice of packaging one advertiser's piece with those of other advertisers, meaning all included pieces contribute to the total cost of delivery, thus reducing the per piece price tag to a single advertiser.

The *Sun's* owner, Chicagoan Bruce Sagan, had bought the paper from Warren Buffett in 1981 after the Berkshire Hathaway CEO sat in the owner's chair for thirteen years. Two years later, after losing money since 1981—over $350,000 in advertising revenue according to *Adweek*—Sagan asked for a sit-down with Harold Andersen, who asked John to be at the meeting. Sagan told them the *World-Herald* was putting him out of business and gave them a choice: they could either buy him out or become the target of an anti-trust action.

They declined the former and survived to tell the tale of the latter. After winning a temporary injunction in July against the *World-Herald*, the *Sun* lost on appeal. A week after the court rejected the position of the *Omaha Sun*, the newspaper published its last edition.

While the acquisition of Rapid Printing was a seminal event in the demise of the *Sun*, John argued that the foresight to see where grocery advertising was going set in motion a number of business decisions that responded to market forces and changing times. Sagan had the same opportunity. "We didn't put him out of business. The advertisers put him out of business. They're the ones who decided how they were going to distribute, not us. He had a press. Nothing kept him from doing what we were doing—except we were good at it."

John said the lawsuit made for several unpleasant months, but it turned out to be somewhat of a "life-saving experience" for the *World-Herald*, making the paper able to hold on a lot longer than most papers to a large traditional revenue source. Like many other newspapers of its size, the *World-Herald* had counted on "big, big grocery advertising."

The Rapid Printing story eventually took a rather dismal turn but not before hitting home run after home run. The *World-Herald* poured a considerable amount of capital into the business, purchasing nine new Goss presses, subsequently buying even larger and faster presses as Rapid's growth continued unabated. Company revenues went from $11 million in 1981, the year the *World-Herald* purchased it, to $20 million the next year. While these early successes benefited both Rapid and the *World-Herald*—meaning of course *World-Herald* employee owners—John began to encounter management issues soon after Zane Randall retired.

Randall's nephew, John Brown, initially took over as company president when his uncle retired. On Brown's watch Rapid kept humming along, but John eventually dismissed him.

In a professional career that spanned five-plus decades, John Gottschalk negotiated, differed, agreed, argued, cooperated, and did business with thousands of people. High among his antagonisms was disloyalty. This was never clearer than when John discovered that Brown, a New Zealand native, had begun developing his own business, building a personal printing plant on the side—in Kansas City—while still running Rapid. Essentially, he was competing with his employer.

Concerned that Brown had control of Rapid's customer database coupled with his standing in the printing community, John decided it was time to part ways with Brown. Before he left, John offered some unsolicited advice. "John, I'm doing you a favor right now. Make sure you have a lawyer with whom you can talk. You will not be able to use anything that you have ever done in our employ in your plant, whether it's systems or templates or whatever. You'll also want to be circumspect when you're dealing with customers. I'm telling you this for your own benefit. I'm not waving the red flag here but you need to know a lot more than you know."

In a subsequent discussion with Brown, John recorded the conversation thinking that the *World-Herald* might be headed for a lawsuit. That never happened. After Brown's departure, Rapid went through a series of presidents, prompting the *World-Herald* to send one of its HR pros, Lora Villarreal, to the company to address a number of leadership and employment issues. By 1992 Rapid, although a money maker for the *World-Herald*, had become what John deemed a "distraction," and the newspaper sold it to a Louisiana company.

John considered investment acquisitions such as newspapers and companies like Rapid Printing to be a process rather than a formula. He and his team followed broad strategic goals: maintaining profitability, realizing ample return to stockholders (employees), improving quality and service to readers and the public, and providing funds for further growth and capital investment. Their targets tilted in favor of companies from the Mississippi River to the Rockies, Mexico to Canada. Preference was given to companies within the widest interpretation of the communications field, with print preferable to television and radio although broadcasters were still in play. The projected rate of return from acquisitions was to match or exceed the return on the company's long-term investment portfolio, which was rocketing along at around 20 percent per annum. Finally, liquidity had to be front and center. The team avoided high-risk, long-term companies, but softening that stance if an easy, quick sale was anticipated.

From these broad strokes John developed an acquisition checklist, a detailed dive into due diligence, twelve bases that needed to be covered before moving forward with the process.

The process then called for John and his team to assemble the checklist data, analyze it, synthesize it, and make a recommendation. John became particularly skilled at spreadsheets, crunching numbers and data to arrive at a reasoned decision. His prowess with spreadsheets was storied among managers at the *World-Herald*. Terry Kroeger said, "He loved numbers, loved math. He's still probably the best Excel programmer I've ever seen. He was exceptional at that. It's pretty funny. We actually started with the old digital equipment, Rainbow Computers. John had one of those and it ran a program called Microsoft Multiplan. It evolved into Excel, which is now the standard. When that happened, in Lotus or Excel, it was Column A, Row 1; Column B, Row 2; so it's referred to in the formulas as A1 or B2 or C3 or whatever. Well, in Multiplan, it was a relative reference, so it would say C minus 3, R minus 5. So that would be 5 rows up and 3 columns back. When they moved to Excel, you could still ask for it that way and John never quit using the old way. So we'd look at that and ask: 'How does he do this?'"

The "process" allowed his individual team members to spread their wings, using experience and expertise within the confines of a project and a policy, to determine if the acquisition on the drawing board was a solid, profitable investment for the *World-Herald*. Charged with investing the money of one of the nation's few employee-owned newspapers, John felt a special sense of responsibility when considering an acquisition because the money at risk was that of his co-workers, people alongside whom he toiled every day.

Once, however, the process took on a more personal patina. In 1985, the owner of the *Kearney Hub*, Bob Ayers, indicated to CEO Andersen that he wanted to sell the *Hub* and hoped the *World-Herald* would consider buying it. The cachet of the statewide *Omaha World-Herald* was considerable. Having "Nebraska's newspaper" as owner of the hometown paper would not only provide Ayers with a willing and stable buyer, but *World-Herald* ownership would bring to *Kearney Hub* readers a certain standing by journalistic association. Ayers had actually been picking John's brain on the subject of selling for a couple of years. Andersen was already on board. He and John both liked Kearney, a city of then nearly twenty-three thousand, three hours west of Omaha on Interstate 80. Its focal point was the nine-thousand-student Kearney State College, which would become the University of Nebraska-Kearney (UNK) in 1989. As the *World-Herald* COO, John found the potential acquisition of the *Hub* squarely in his inbox. For John, irony was part of that acquisition process. The *Kearney Hub* was the newspaper John had identified he wanted to buy ten years earlier, after he sold the *Sidney Telegraph* and was looking for a daily to buy in Nebraska. Ayers wasn't interested then.

John was dispatched to exercise some diligence. "I holed up at the Ramada Inn. I'd get the books at the close of business and stay up all night going through them," John said. He returned the books to Ayers in the morning, got some sleep, and repeated the all-nighters until he had a recommendation to take back to Omaha. While he found some flaws—"the business was okay, the newspaper not so great"—he believed these were things that some attention and solid management could remedy. He recommended to Andersen that the *World-Herald* buy the Kearney Hub Publishing Company, which occurred in late 1985—but not before some executive hand holding was in order. A standoff had developed over a closing date for the transaction. John wanted to close the deal promptly or move on. Ayers equivocated. Neither wanted to lose the opportunity, but John was getting impatient. Finally he offered to fly Andersen to Kearney to break the impasse.

The meeting was brief but fruitful. "When Andy and I met with Ayers, I opened and reiterated my position on setting a particular date. Bob had the opportunity to speak his peace on what he would prefer—but at least it was a date, which I had until then been unable to get. Andy asked if he and I could step out of the room. We waited a few minutes and then we went back in and said we had discussed it and we were willing to accept Bob's position and the date that he had suggested, which was the sole reason for all of this."

Andersen's simple reassurance came after hours of John's careful scrutiny and detailed parsing of the *Hub*'s particulars, all in the middle of the night. Such was the acquisition process, in all its variations.

John was the *World-Herald* executive in charge of operations at the *Hub*, and he sent Terry Kroeger to be the newspaper's new publisher. The acquisition and management of the newspaper commenced a long and endearing connection with the *Hub* and community of Kearney for John.

"I went out there a lot," he said. The attention paid dividends according to Steve Chatelain, managing editor when the paper was purchased in 1985 and publisher starting in 1993. Immediately, the *Hub* began quarterly board meetings.

"You could tell the *World-Herald* was getting there, setting a structure as to how they would manage as a group if the plans were to buy more papers," Chatelain recalled.

The meetings bore fruit as the *Hub* grew, becoming more of a positive force in the community. Still, Chatelain said John could be an intimidating force when they gathered in the paper's second floor conference room for meetings. "He was a clear, direct communicator. He did not suffer fools gladly. He wanted to know every detail," he said. But he was also more than complimentary when a job was well-done. Even after John became CEO of the parent company in 1989, Chatelain received notes from him, many of them encouraging.

John also had a penchant for walking around the newsroom when he was at the *Hub* for meetings, a practice that led to an exchange with reporter Julie Spiers (who would later become publisher). Shortly after the *World-Herald* purchased the *Hub*, Spiers was in the break room having lunch when John walked in. After an exchange of pleasantries, she said, "Why don't you buy me a newspaper?" John, smiled and left, returning in a couple of moments with a paper from the rack in the newsroom. "Here you go," he said. Spiers said she knew then that John Gottschalk's skill set included not only strong leadership but also a sense of humor.

The *Hub* was the first of what some would call the *World-Herald's* "I-80 papers," a roster that would eventually include the *Scottsbluff Star-Herald*, the *North Platte Telegraph*, the *Kearney Hub*, the *Grand Island Independent*, and the *York News-Times*. Eventually, managers in Omaha developed those papers into a news service, bringing extra value to the *World-Herald*, but the inverse also held true. Although editorially each was free to trim its own sails and listen to its own readers, newspapers along the I-80 corridor were strengthened by a shared expertise in management, technology, and financial strategies. There were cultural considerations, too. John said the importance of the

I-80 acquisitions could not be overstated as each already served a community where the values and readers were unmistakably Nebraskan. To that end John encouraged each newspaper to be involved in the community—a staple of Gottschalk papers from Sheridan County to Sidney to Omaha. Chatelain put this sense of community and the newspaper's responsibility to it at the top of the list of John's influences on him. "He was so committed to the community, whether it was Omaha or Kearney or really anywhere in Nebraska. He believed (the newspaper) was empowered to serve the community. That's what I always understood from him. We even put it in our mission statement."

John made community a viable and natural part of a newspaper's efforts by example, too. Even three hours west of his office at World-Herald Square, he guided the *Hub* staff as the newspaper took a more prominent role in the Kearney United Way campaigns. He and Carmen personally donated the money to build the observation tower at Kearney's spectacular Yanney Park. The *Hub* built the park's boathouse. He was a strong supporter of the Museum of Nebraska Art (MONA) in downtown Kearney.

John enjoyed close relationships with Kearney's university chancellors. That came in handy for the university on one particular occasion, when John logged serious air time to help his friends in Kearney. "I was in Newport News, Virginia, at a nonprofit board meeting when I got a call from Dr. Gladys Styles Johnston, the university's chancellor. She asked if I could deliver the commencement address in Kearney—the next day, halfway across the continent. The scheduled speaker had suffered a serious health crisis the day before the event, and she needed a sub. A few years prior I had received an honorary doctorate from Kearney State College. I told her I'd refresh the old speech overnight and then use my private plane and be able to deliver the speech the next morning. The odds favored me—my first address was probably long forgotten, and second, there would not be many in the audience who were present back then anyhow."

For John and the *Omaha World-Herald*, 1994 proved to be a watershed for acquisitions. The focus fell on two major projects, the *Stockton Record* and Stauffer Communications, owner of twenty daily newspapers and eleven broadcast stations in fourteen states.

The *Stockton Record* story began when Terry Kroeger received a call from Lee Dirks, a broker from the Detroit area. He said Gannett wanted to sell the *Record* and wondered if the *Omaha World-Herald* had an interest. Kroeger was group president for Midlands Newspapers and had served as president of the Inland Press Association, so a phone call from Dirks was not unusual. Midlands Newspapers was a wholly-owned subsidiary of the Omaha World-Herald Co. It existed for the purpose of clarifying the lines of management between the *World-Herald* and other newspapers owned by the company. The president of Midlands Newspapers reported to the CEO of the World-Herald Co. Kroeger passed the question along to John who connected with Gannett CFO, Doug McCorkindale.

"The first conversation I had with McCorkindale was to see if they were selling and discuss generally what they had in mind," John said. "Doug told me of their aversion to investing more money in *Stockton* to cure a chronic production deficiency by going offset. He knew of our strong letterpress credentials." McCorkingdale made it clear that Gannett wanted to leave the market. John had been at the *World-Herald* helm for over four years, and, although as CEO he was pulled in many directions, he was still at the tiller when the newspaper considered an acquisition. He pulled the acquisition team together and headed for Stockton to look at the *Record*. Kroeger, who eventually became its publisher, described the *Record* as being "a little like an abused child who had been in an orphanage. It really needed somebody to give it a hug."

With acquisition checklist at the ready, *World-Herald* team members pored over the books, gave the press and related machinery the once and twice over, assessed the advertising market in Stockton, judged the fitness of the *Record*'s buildings, and poked and prodded and looked in whatever nook and cranny they thought would give them insight into a go/no-go decision. While they found the *Record* wanting and its facilities in various stages of disrepair, John decided that by buying it for $75 million and giving it the requisite TLC—proper management, an upgrade to its presses and technology, and general management expertise—the *World-Herald* could gain value. Eight years later the *World-Herald* sold the *Stockton Record* for nearly $150 million, doubling the price while having made money during much of the paper's tenure as a part of the Midlands Newspapers.

"We did our due diligence, then McCorkingdale and I talked again and agreed over the phone. I felt the price was reasonable and negotiable since they really seemed to want out. The deal was completed pretty quickly after that without a lot of pushing and shoving."

If the *Stockton* purchase was quick, efficient, and proved to have a touch of King Midas in the mix, the effort to buy Stauffer Communications was Sisyphean by turns. The Stauffer group owned twenty daily newspapers, eight weeklies and shoppers, seven television stations, four radio stations, and two magazines, *Grit* and *Capper's*. The sheer magnitude and geography considerably upped the due diligence ante for the *World-Herald*.

Dubbed "Project Z," Stauffer Communications put the *World-Herald* policies and process team through their paces. Mike McCarthy was on board "from day one" to help evaluate the business and figure out a way to finance it. McCarthy even had discussions with John and *World-Herald* CFO and acquisition team "captain" Bill Kernen as to how Stauffer might fit into the stable of World-Herald companies. McCarthy said he concurred with John on the pursuit of Stauffer, which was for sale at the time. He said the scope of Stauffer's newspapers and company expertise made it a "good fit" for the *World-Herald.*

John often bounced ideas and problems off his friend and fishing buddy, McCarthy, using him as a sounding board for deals and the occasional journey into philosophy. They had worked together before. McCarthy was president of The McCarthy Group, a private Omaha-based equity firm he founded in 1986. He had met John in 1982 after having been approached to sell the Kiewit Estate Ranch near North Platte, Nebraska. McCarthy was still living in Iowa, running a small construction company, and having enough success in ag real estate to warrant the offer of handling the sale of the Kiewit Ranch. His co-lister, Jim Protzman, suggested that while McCarthy was doing that bit of business in Omaha— where he was planning to move soon—he should meet with Protzman's friend, an executive from the newspaper. That turned out to be John Gottschalk. Over lunch the pair swapped ideas and visions.

"I was convinced that unless we diversified our economy, beyond production agriculture, we were going to continue to have a decimation of the Midwest," McCarthy said. "It was kind of a big, crazy idea. But John was attracted to it right away. That's how we got started." McCarthy's firm would do work for the *World-Herald,* including the acquisition of ES&S, an election service company with ballot counting machines. John and McCarthy would spend over thirty years on ES&S's board together and John would be a mainstay on the McCarthy Group's board. "John was really interested in some of the same things I was, in that I wanted to diversify the economy of the Midwest. He wanted to diversify the *World-Herald* and take it into broader areas, all around media and somewhat outside media, like the election business." The team of McCarthy and Gottschalk would spend many years buying and selling. Some of their purchases, like ES&S, fit squarely in the winner's circle. Others, such as an electronic sign business, not so much. McCarthy labeled that foray "a disaster."

While big ideas and economic diversification forged the friendship, fly fishing, to which John introduced McCarthy, permanently sealed it, giving the pair a common vocabulary they used as a metaphorical shorthand to discuss impending deals and business in general.

The Stauffer sale came down to two suitors: The *Omaha World-Herald* and Morris Communications of Augusta, Georgia. The *World-Herald* team put in hundreds of hours of work, knowing Stauffer, as John said, "better than they knew themselves." He dispatched his team to cities where Stauffer newspapers circulated. No detail went unparsed from condition of the presses to efficiency of circulation to quality of the news report to cash flows; John's personal five-page spreadsheet teemed with calculations and recalculations. Dozens of notes in a variety of colors dotted the pages. In the end, after crunched numbers, gut instincts, and analysis that bordered on the persnickety, the bid was clear: $255 million. It was more than outside analysts had projected.

McCarthy was impressed. "What was beautiful about the exercise was that John and Bill Kernen managed a ground-up analysis by putting feet on the street of every community they were looking at and getting the newspapers themselves on the table, focusing on the connectivity between the newspaper and its community. It was an extraordinarily qualitative analysis of the newspaper itself. How well was it serving its community as a driver of value?"

With no stone left unturned and a bid on the table, John and the acquisition team waited for the outcome of Project Z. A week before the final decision, McCarthy sent John an email counseling him to find equilibrium regardless of the outcome. He pointed out that since the employee-owned

Omaha World-Herald team was offering to spend its co-workers' money, clearly this was a different financial playing field from the one on which Morris stood. "Don't be distracted by the other wolves in this hunt," he wrote. "They have no limit, but they risk none of their own capital."

On July 27, 1994, Morris Communications bought Stauffer Communications Inc. for $275 million. The price was $35 million higher than the price a trusted Chicago analyst had projected the day before the sale and fourteen times Morris's 1993 cash flow. John wrote of the "loss" in an internal *World-Herald* memo:

> *The* Omaha World-Herald *had a significant interest in the possible acquisition of Stauffer. We knew the properties well since most were in the Midlands. We knew the family and its distinguished history of journalistic service to their communities.*
>
> *We were very surprised by the successful bid in view of the earnings history of the company. There apparently was enormous optimism about the future value of (Stauffer). That is great news for the selling shareholders.*
>
> *Our company will continue to seek acquisitions. As an employee-owned enterprise, we are driven to find value comparable to the risk taken. There will be other opportunities and we will eagerly pursue them.*
>
> *We believe that newspapers are vital to communities. We will continue to operate our newspapers in a manner which fulfills our considerable responsibility to the readers. We cannot pay beyond the point that would exceed our high journalistic standards.*
>
> *We welcome Billy Morris to Nebraska via his ownership of the* York News-Times *and the* Grand Island Independent.

Then, as months of painstaking, detailed work ended in a second-place finish, the leader took the thirty-plus members of the Project Z team to a local country club where they ate and drank and partied, returning to work the next day to move in the only direction John Gottschalk knew to go after a loss—or a win: forward. McCarthy remembered the party and the sentiment. "He said, 'We're never going to talk about that again. We're moving on.' John wanted to put a period at the end of that sentence, and he did."

Highly leveraged, Morris, over the next twenty-three years, would dispose of all twenty-eight newspapers it had acquired in the Stauffer deal, the last four in 2017, and all its broadcasting interests, leaving the company with only magazines, broadband services, and other smaller business concerns.

~

Deep in the DNA of a lifelong print journalist was the appreciation of a morning newspaper: part ritual, part sustenance, part dose of daily information. Even when John found himself hundreds of miles from the nearest *Omaha World-Herald* news rack, he still spent the first few hours of every day the same way he always had: reading a morning newspaper.

His love and respect for community newspapers and their commitment to real journalism led directly to his exercise of due diligence on the last newspaper acquisition in which he played a major role—four years after his retirement. The paper was the weekly *Jackson Hole News and Guide* and its daily edition, the *Jackson Hole Daily*. These are mainstays in John's beloved Jackson Hole.

As was his lifelong practice, he read the paper while skiers slept and fishermen hit the snooze button. John's routine at his Jackson Hole residence roused him at zero dark thirty, whereupon he headed for McDonald's for a caffeine-free

Diet Coke and a stop at the nearby convenience store for a newspaper. Back home in the hills facing Snow King Mountain, he read the paper with the exacting eye of someone whose life revolved around a printing press.

Obviously, John read the *Chronicle* when he was in San Francisco and the *Post* when he was in the nation's capital. As well-traveled as he was, no doubt John Gottschalk had sampled dozens of newspapers from Los Angeles to London. But reading the Jackson Hole paper was a particular pleasure because of the role he played in seeing Kevin Olson buy the *Jackson Hole News and Guide* in 2012.

Olson recalled a series of particular events, which led to his ownership. "The opportunity for me to be a publisher of a paper or maybe even own a paper was a lot more likely in Jackson than what I was doing in Southern California," Olson said. He had worked for the *Orange County Register* in Santa Ana with a daily circulation over 250,000. It was the nineteenth largest newspaper in the nation at the time.

"The dirty little secret was that I was a ski bum. I'd been skiing my whole life. So the opportunity to live, work, and raise my family in what is my favorite ski area in the United States was like a dream come true."

Michael Sellett, the longtime owner and publisher of the *News and Guide* knew of John through publisher associations to which both belonged. John remembered a conversation with Sellett in 2007. They were in Chicago for the Inland Press Association's meeting at which John received Inland's Ralph E. Casey Award. While they discussed John's remarks on keeping standards in a changing world of journalism, they also talked about Jackson, by then a true second home for the Gottschalks. The connection was enough for Sellett to pick up the phone five years later and arrange for John to meet with Kevin Olson, his associate publisher, to whom he wanted to sell the *News and Guide*.

Olson remembered the meeting well. "The context of our first meeting was that Michael was in the frame of mind that the prospect of retirement and selling the paper was imminent. I told him in April 2001 that if he was looking to sell the paper, I wanted to be his first choice as a potential buyer. Eleven years later, he set up a lunch with me and John and John's buddy, Mike McCarthy."

What happened was what Olson described as a broad conversation about "what if." What if he was able to put together a package to buy the paper? What would such a business deal look like?

"John and Mike (McCarthy) were like my uncles. We had great rapport right out of the gate. John believed deeply in community newspapers and the value they offered to a community's health and well-being. And he loved to see a paper stay in local hands."

John's affinity for local ownership and the value of community papers was in line with Michael Sellett's. The Jackson publisher knew better than anyone the price of keeping the *News and Guide* in the right hands from both a community and economic standpoint. His was an earned and experienced view, having withstood a thirty-year newspaper "war" in Jackson Hole.

According to the Wyoming State Historical Society, in the 1970s the weekly *Jackson Hole Guide* was the primary source of news for the town of then 2,688 year-round residents and any newspaper readers among the millions of vacationers who annually made their way to the valley. The *Guide* had begun in 1956, taking over for the *Jackson Hole Courier*, the town's first newspaper, which started publishing in 1900. The *Guide* enjoyed remarkable success and was clearly the paper of record in Jackson Hole. Still, it had its detractors. Two readers, Virginia Huidekoper and Ralph Gill, became dissatisfied with the *Guide* and launched the *Jackson Hole News* in April 1970, giving the town two papers, two voices. Early on, Jackson resident Marc Fischer bought out Gill's shares but, by 1973, Huidekoper and Fischer were beleaguered with the time and effort it took to publish a weekly paper and went looking for a buyer.

They found one in their own newsroom: managing editor Michael Sellett.

Sellett had made his way from Northwestern University to the *Chicago Tribune* to the *Rawlins Daily Times* in Wyoming before the *News* hired him as a reporter. He advanced to managing editor six months later. But when Huidekoper and Fischer approached him about ownership, he balked, and for good reason. He had no money. Desperate to keep the *News* open and in local hands, the pair offered to carry 90 percent of the price. Sellett was able to scrape the remaining 10 percent together through family and friends and thus began his and the *News*'s thirty-year competition for the hearts and minds of Jackson Hole newspaper readers.

Along the way the *News* won a national "Best Use of Photos" award in 1984, competing with papers of all sizes across the country including major metros. Both the *News* and the *Guide* won many awards, a quality of journalism Jackson Hole newspaper readers came to depend upon. While strategies from price to publication days came and went, the competition took a decided turn when, in 1988, the *News* began publishing a free daily six times a week. The *Guide* followed suit in 1996. A year later the *Guide*'s owner died, and his widow took over the management of the newspaper. By 2002, the *Guide*'s editor asked Sellett if he could meet in secret. The owner was considering a merger. Sellett was taken aback, considering no one at the *Guide* had given him the time of day for three decades.

The result was the *Jackson Hole News and Guide*, published once a week, and the *Jackson Hole Daily*. Under Olson's management, the *News and Guide* had a circulation of nearly seven thousand and the *Daily* ranked third in Wyoming behind only the *Star Tribune* in Casper and the *Wyoming Tribune Eagle* in Cheyenne.

This rich newspaper history was not lost on Kevin Olson, whose feel for community journalism John recognized and supported. With his newspaper career, the financing expertise of Mike McCarthy, and the paper's foundation in Mike Sellett, Olson's ship was sailing in favorable waters from the outset.

Olson especially took to John's sense of fairness. "I really appreciated John's viewpoint, approach, and advice on what it takes to be a publisher who is tough yet empathetic when people claim they were on the other side of the news and that we were not fair."

John (and Mike McCarthy when he was available) spent a good deal of time with Olson considering ways to structure a deal that would enable him to buy the paper. While the "problem" was eventually solved, the process left an indelible mark with Olson.

"We spent most of our time together thinking through how to structure a deal, of what the deal possibilities were, a deal that I would be able to finance. Between John and Mike McCarthy talking with Mike and me, everybody was transparent and forthcoming at the table, even working with our bankers. They were super instrumental coming up with a deal structure that everybody felt good about. Most important Mike (Sellett) had to feel good about it. He's the guy who ultimately had to give up some stuff to make the deal happen."

The result of combining such experience and expertise with an eye on local control was Kevin Olson owning the *Jackson News and Guide*, which, at this writing, was the only remaining family-owned newspaper in a resort town in the Rocky Mountain West. And, John Gottschalk, who had helped him realize his dream, was a continuing supporter of Olson's success, and, more important, a daily reader.

∼

The unprecedented growth of the *Omaha World-Herald* after the 1980 purchase of the Suburban Group created a "problem" that any business would be pleased to face: What to do with success. In the *World-Herald*'s case that specifically meant how to make effective use of the growth-generated cash.

The company was originally sold by Peter Kiewit to the employees at book value: the value of the assets minus the value of the liabilities. Subsequent acquisitions were not contemplated in 1975 when Peter Kiewit established the eventual employee-ownership plan. No provisions were made in corporate documents regarding anything other than book-value pricing.

Mandatory book-value pricing, however, had certain limitations for a company that was expanding by buying other companies, as the *World-Herald* began to do after 1979. Here's why: Acquisitions were priced on the basis of their desirability to the buyer and the willingness of the seller to accept the buyer's offer—in other words, how much the prospective buyer was willing to pay based on such factors as the seller's asking price, the pressure of competing bidders, and the prospects for future profitability. In many instances, these and other factors had the effect of pushing the cost of the acquisition—the so-called market value—to a level significantly higher than the book-value figure, calculated by comparing the company's brick and mortar with its outstanding debt. Market value was sometimes two or three times higher than the book value.

To illustrate his concerns, John used the example of a hypothetical *World-Herald* employee who was a shareholder at the time the company paid $75 million for the *Stockton Record* newspaper. The $75 million was a market-value figure. It represented the sum agreed upon by a willing seller (Gannett) and a willing buyer (the *World-Herald*). For the *World-Herald*, it reflected a price at which John's acquisitions team believed the Stockton paper could become a moneymaker.

For the owners of *World-Herald* stock, however, the transaction held a more ominous potential. They paid $75 million for the *Record*, lowering the *World-Herald*'s book value—and the worth of their collective stock—by that amount. But the *Record*, when converted into book value as required by the Kiewit plan, was worth significantly less than its purchase price. Thus, the shareholders took a $75 million hit that would not be fully offset until the *Record* contributed significantly to company profits or was sold at a profit.

In John's example, the hypothetical employee retired the next year. As a condition of the employee-ownership plan, this person was required to sell his stock to the company. The value of his stock at that point had been reduced by the $75 million outlay, a deflation that was only partially offset by the addition of the *Record* to the *World-Herald*'s book value. Eight years later, the *World-Herald* sold the Stockton paper for $150 million. This was a significant gain for employee stockholders, but not for those employee stockholders whose cash was used to buy Stockton and who had already retired when it was sold. Their investment provided the profits for the stockholders who remained behind.

Peter Kiewit had sold 80 percent of his stock at a favored value (book) to the employees even though he had purchased the *Omaha World-Herald* at market value. He held some stock back for the Peter Kiewit Foundation to hold in perpetuity. By instructing his trustees to never sell the Foundation stock, he effectively gave the Foundation the power to veto any future proposal to sell the newspaper.

Altering the command to use the book value for all transactions, as John suggested as part of a solution, turned out to create a most curious and damaging rift between John and the Peter Kiewit Foundation. The fallout found the *World-Herald* and John in Douglas County District Court versus the Peter Kiewit Foundation.

Peter Kiewit Jr. was the Foundation's representative on the newspaper's board of directors. What little conversation was held over a number of years of trying to address the issue was stuck. Pete Jr.'s position was that the sale to employees was a discounted price to what his father paid for it in 1963. Employee owners, he believed, were getting a bargain. The provision in the sale to maintain book value was an understandable effort to prevent employee owners from turning around and selling the newspaper to a market-priced buyer and pocketing a windfall. In Pete Jr.'s mind, the stock should continue to be valued on the book method. He never entertained serious discussion to the contrary.

Another part of the original Kiewit plan to keep the newspaper under local ownership was his requirement that the Foundation maintain ownership of a different class of stock representing up to 20 percent of the outstanding shares. The Foundation thus assumed an interest in the financial structure of the company.

John argued that the book-value directive was unfair to the employee shareholders of a company that no longer consisted solely of the *World-Herald*. He favored separating the original *World-Herald* newspaper book price from the company's market-priced assets. This would eliminate owners having to take less than full value in retiring than the value of their purchase depending on what time had elapsed between the purchase and sale of an acquisition. In a blended valuation, the *World-Herald* portion would be valued at book as Peter Kiewit directed, while other assets could be priced at market value, thereby realizing the market price gains in the formula which could, and did, raise the overall worth of the company and its shares.

John argued further that, as an organization, the company had three choices when it came to efficiently managing its accumulating cash, a significant amount of which came from the success of many acquisitions, including non-newspaper ones.

The first option was to use "virtually all" of the newspaper's earnings to give dividends to its employee stockholders and the Foundation. The second option would be placing the company's profit in passive investments. The third option was to continue to seek sound acquisitions, minimizing risk while returning profits commensurate with the goal of 20 percent growth. It was the third option, growth through acquisition, that raised the question in John's mind as to the fairness of the book-value system to the company's employee stockholders.

Soon after taking over as CEO, John broached the subject, proposing in a white paper that the board and management find a way to "allow retiring employees (shareholders) to receive market value from assets acquired at market." John's idea was that this would recognize the coming and going of shareholders rather than the constant of a perpetual static ownership. He was confident that a blended pricing formulation was best for the company's future and that it didn't conflict with Peter Kiewit's charge that the *Omaha World-Herald* be locally owned and managed. At no time did John ever suggest otherwise, nor did he ever get much pushback from the board. "Over those years, I'm talking to myself most of the time," John said.

John understood the Foundation's position rested on the fact that Peter Kiewit had sold 80 percent of the stock to the employees at book value, which was a bargain price. That bit of history was not in contention. Nonetheless, John argued that while the Foundation was part owner of the company—and obviously pleased with the returns—its situation was unlike employee owners who did not have perpetuity but rather had to leave the company at some point via retirement, relocation, or any of the other reasons one leaves one's job. And, John added, when they did leave, they were not being fully compensated, in surrendering their stock at book value when acquisitions were made based on market values.

"This fixation that we were a bunch of renegades did not sit well with me. It sat even less well with me when Pete Kiewit Jr. just arbitrarily decided to file suit—unannounced," John said.

Fueling further internal fire for John was how he learned of a temporary restraining order stopping any possibility to discuss the issue which was on the board's agenda that day: He read it in the morning edition of the *Omaha World-Herald*.

"Smoke was rolling out of my ears when (Peter Kiewit Jr.) walked into the boardroom that day, and he knew it," he said, recalling that he had talked with Kiewit the prior day with no mention of a lawsuit. "(The temporary restraining order) was a direct assault on my credibility and everything you could imagine. Somewhere near the end of the board meeting the subject came up. I said, 'If you guys want to go to war over this, just let me know. If you want to settle the thing and move on with life like we've been trying to do around here for five years, we'd better have a meeting.'"

Meetings between John and Peter Kiewit Jr. did eventually transpire, but not before John was deposed and the affidavit filed with the district court. The meetings began after a phone call between the two men, following some stonewalling. "I told him we'd better sit down and talk," John said. The incredulity that the Foundation chose to file a lawsuit to start a conversation with the newspaper's CEO remained a sore point with John, however.

In the end, they struck a compromise: all *Omaha World-Herald* newspaper holdings would remain at book value while all other company holdings would be priced at market value. While this did somewhat improve employee-owners' per-share value, it fell short of John's position as a rational solution. The company would continue to invest in and acquire properties it felt grew wealth for the shareholders—which it did successfully focusing only on acquiring non newspapers. The arrangement satisfied the Foundation and its myopic concern that John's desire to correct an inequity in the pricing formula had somehow threatened not simply local ownership of the *World-Herald* but also the very future of the newspaper. For John nothing could have been further from the truth, but, as he said, "Being pragmatic, I was able to move on."

Still, the curious and confounding approach by the Peter Kiewit Foundation left a mark. In an email to a *World-Herald* colleague just before Christmas in 1997, John wrote, "This has been the toughest, most trying year of my career here. The burden of the Kiewit Foundation suit, so misdirected and untimely, has been the worst. We have a great franchise and a great company, both of which can and should grow significantly. Getting positioned for such growth has been very tedious. I have found myself uncharacteristically short and abrupt on too many occasions at home and at work. I grew up in a newspaper environment where stewardship was a constant and urgent demand. That part I thrive on."

The lawsuit became, simply, a sorry chapter in *Omaha World-Herald* history. Stockholders continued to reap the bounty of their efforts as the company continued to grow on John's watch. But the compromise did not fully solve the valuation formula inadequacy. It did, however, end the company's acquisition of more newspapers—the Omaha World-Herald Co.'s core strength.

John had one more employee-ownership hurdle to clear before he left the newspaper.

FIVE

Employee Ownership and the Meeting

A belated thanks for the lovely note and the formal admission into the million-dollar club, John. It's hard to believe that my tenure here is approaching twenty years.... I enjoyed running the features department, but I find more serious news and the quick-breaking news in business absolutely invigorating. My personal satisfaction, however, is secondary. I'm ready to serve in whatever capacity is needed. You need only ask.

**–AN *OMAHA WORLD-HERALD*
EMPLOYEE/SHAREHOLDER**

Warren Buffett's purchase of the *Omaha World-Herald* in 2011 ended an employee-ownership plan that followed Peter Kiewit's specific instructions carried out after his death in 1979. At the time, the *World-Herald* was the largest employee-owned newspaper in the country, and the last metropolitan daily to cash out its shareholders. None of the 275 or so *World-Herald* employee owners knew what was happening when they were invited to the Holland Performing Arts Center across the street.

Some surely felt pangs of fear. Such meetings in the newspaper industry had come to be associated with bad news: layoffs, wage freezes, forced furloughs. The standing ovation Buffett received when he took the stage that morning as the paper's new owner had to be motivated in part by relief.

Buffett's ownership came with the condition that employees would no longer be shareholders. The transaction liquidated all their holdings in *World-Herald* stock. In some individual cases, that amounted to a seven-figure payout—the same thing that had happened in earlier times, individually, when a longtime employee shareholder left the company and liquidated his or her stock.

The majority of employees who found themselves with seven figures when they left the company did so during John Gottschalk's watch as CEO and publisher. John said during his tenure at the paper, one of his great joys was to welcome a co-worker into the "million-dollar club."

Even without all the zeroes, a look at John's personal files reveals dozens of thank-you notes and cards praising him and the newspaper's leadership for the care and attention in managing a truly successful employee-owner plan. The company held an annual stockholder meeting each January, a celebratory event where John delivered updates on the value of employee stock. The news was always good as the return during John's tenure in the corner office kept its remarkable average, a cause for joy among those with stock in the company.

The newspaper also helped its employees manage their wealth. It held seminars and brought in financial planners to help those about to retire plan and invest their funds wisely. John, as CEO and the company leader, got in on the act as well, but usually in a more informal setting. Employee owners from every department and at every level often brought questions to the publisher's office, from wondering about buying more stock to picking his brain about the company's future value.

He considered his stewardship of the employee-ownership program among his highest priorities.

World-Herald employee/shareholders understood. Here is a sampling. This is from a newsroom regular after a 1998 shareholders meeting held in January.

> *Thanks for the most informative meeting and for your vision and leadership. I especially appreciate that in your work you keep in mind that our investments represent not just dollars, not just numbers on ledger sheets, but people and their families. With that in mind, I mention three family anecdotes (and proceeds to give updates on his children). I tell you those stories in appreciation of what our* World-Herald *stock ownership has meant to our family. By the way, the new stock value passed a milestone for me—seven figures. Although I've seen it coming for a few years, I never would have dreamed it when I arrived at the* World-Herald. *From me and my family, thanks, again.*

This note was from a supervisor who, in 2005, wrote in part to thank John and the newspaper for bonus checks for the workers she managed plus the employee-ownership program.

> *When I delivered the bonus checks, they were surprised and extremely grateful. To a person they were inspired and committed to do better. Thank you for acknowledging their efforts and accomplishments but especially for the motivation the financial acknowledgment inspired. On a more personal note, I am humbled and speechless by the generous bonus awarded me. It was not expected. Given that bonus combined with the stock purchase opportunities and debentures you have made available to me, and I can't even begin to adequately express my appreciation and gratefulness to you for the opportunities at the* World-Herald. *I can only echo the sentiment of*

my associates with a commitment and resolve to do everything I possibly can to contribute to the World-Herald's success. Thank you, John. It is truly an honor and privilege to serve our enterprise.

Near the top of all the things John loved about his job was whenever employees came to him or dropped him a note about how the stock program had changed their lives. He reveled in the reality that behind every stockholder was a family with a story and hopes and dreams, and that giving employees a stake in their company did indeed give them a stake in their future.

The *World-Herald* employee-ownership program was straightforward. Eligible *World-Herald* employees were notified annually of their opportunity to purchase stock. Rather than a strict formula using metrics such as years of service or promotions, managers recommended to the CEO those employees who they believed had exemplified the spirit of the *World-Herald* stockholder program: Effort and talent used to create wealth. John first dropped shares into his *World-Herald* portfolio in 1975 at the invitation of Harold Andersen, who cleared the way for John's purchase at, coincidently, $19.75 a share. He continued to purchase stock during the next thirty-two years at the newspaper. While no employee was allowed to accrue more than 15 percent of the total number of shares, after more than three decades as a full and vigorous participant of the employee-ownership program, John's portfolio had grown to $30 million.

Once a year, eligible *World-Herald* employee owners declared the number of shares they wanted to buy and the method of payment they wanted to use: cash in a lump sum, payroll deduction, or leveraging the stock with a bank loan using the value of the stock as security. The *World-Herald* maintained a valuable working relationship with Omaha National Bank (later to become part of U.S. Bank) and one of its loan officers, Janelle File. She was well-versed in the details of the newspaper's stockholder program and handled all the bank loans for employee stockholders who chose that method. File's deft efficiency and program knowledge made Omaha National a trustworthy place to do business for *Omaha World-Herald* employees.

For some at the *World-Herald*, there were opportunities beyond a straight stock purchase. Employees whom managers identified as making a considerable contribution to the company's success were eligible to accelerate their stock holdings through a convertible debenture bond program. This was a three-way transaction in which the bank lent the employee money, which was then used by the employee to make what amounted to a five-year loan to the World-Herald Co. In exchange for the loan, the employee received a five-year convertible debenture, which went to the bank as security for the original loan. Each year the company made an interest payment to the employee, which helped the employee pay the interest on the loan from the bank.

At the end of five years, the loan matured. Under the terms of the debenture agreement, the employee had the option to liquidate the debenture with *World-Herald* shares valued at the price of five years earlier when the transaction was set in motion. Because the value of the shares was increasing at 20 percent a year, more or less, a $5,000 debenture, on reaching maturity, was converted into $10,000 worth of stock. The employee still owed the original $5,000 to the bank. This could be retired either by selling half the stock to the *World-Herald* or, more commonly, by arranging with the bank to roll the loan over for a second five-year term, with the employee making annual payments of principal and interest, aided by the twice-yearly dividends received on the stock.

Monetary gain was the hallmark of any employee-ownership program, but economists and others saw more than numbers.

Corey Rosen, founder and senior staff member at the National Center for Employee Ownership, said, "Clearly, feeling like a participant is critical to a worker's greater contribution to a company after it establishes an [employee-ownership program]. But it is important not to define participation too narrowly. For a worker to feel like a participant-owner, there must be a tangible financial benefit and a process of consultation, not just abstract prestige."

John's friend Mike McCarthy was also a fan of employee ownership—within limits. "It's by far the best form of ownership and probably the hardest to sustain. Sole proprietorship, which starts out with one guy and a pencil or a shovel or a computer or whatever, is the purest form of employee ownership, right? One guy owns his own business. As it grows it gets harder and harder to have shared ownership, but it can still be done very well."

McCarthy praised "the Kiewit model" of employee ownership, but cautioned that employee ownership might be better suited in some industries and businesses and not so much in others. He did not put newspapers at the top of the best-suited list. "A construction business is particularly suited because it is project-oriented. There's a beginning and an end and you can measure results. You can hold people accountable. It's tougher in the newspaper business, and ultimately, I don't think most people who are attracted to journalism and to that industry are entrepreneurial owners."

According to McCarthy's calculus, John Gottschalk might have been the exception: a journalist with enough brains and business moxie to make employee ownership work in a newspaper. But not without effort. "John felt great responsibility as a CEO to monitor that stock program, get the right people in it at the right levels. He would grind and grind and grind on those models. I think he was right, too, in making that the priority."

Many economists agreed that suitability was key, which made the annual average return for *World-Herald* employees not simply a well-earned result from their own enterprise and effort, but unusual as well. The *Milwaukee Journal Sentinel* discontinued a similar employee-ownership plan when it was purchased by Gannett in 1995.

Still, as McCarthy and others pointed out, any employee-ownership program—even though the siren call of wealth sharing can be substantial when times are good—was dependent upon new stockholders rebuying the company every fifteen to twenty years. This "churn" of ownership was critical; otherwise, the company could become top-heavy. Too many employees near retirement owning too much stock was common as older workers were often better able to afford more and greater chunks of shares through debentures or simply through buying more stock.

To entice more younger eligible employees to purchase stock, John and the board split the stock, which had the effect of making the per-share price more appealing to younger buyers. (This caused no change in the value of anyone's holdings, as the book value of the new shares was reduced proportionately to the increase in share numbers.) While the splitting (and multiplying) provided some allure, in 2011 over 90 percent of *Omaha World-Herald* stock was owned by employees over the age of forty-five. Younger staff members, perhaps wary as the landscape for media and newspaper environments continued to shift, were not jumping into the employee-ownership program as fast and as committed as their generational predecessors had been. The consequences were clear for those managing the employee-ownership program: As retirees edged their way toward the time when the newspaper would have to buy back the considerable fortune of stock they accrued over many years, younger employees eligible for stock purchases were staying out of the plan. More cash was needed to sustain the imbalance.

Also at work, starting about 2005, was an economy lurching toward an implosion. The housing market boom, fueled by hundreds of shaky financial institutions lending money for homes using inadequate standards, was about to crash. The results were as outrageous as they were predictable. New homeowners—some without any steady or reliable source of income—had signed up for balloon loan payments of hundreds of thousands of dollars. Coupled with that was expanding sales on Wall Street of derivatives, high risk bonds based on what turned out to be worthless securities, e.g., loans from the housing market. The culmination of these events closed major lending institutions and threatened to collapse the entire economy.

John retired as publisher and CEO on New Year's Eve 2007, but Terry Kroeger, his successor, asked him to stay on for another year as chairman of the board, extending his "cash out" date by at least a year. Just a few years earlier, while the return of investment had slowed, earnings for *World-Herald* employee owners remained strong. John, however, said at the end of his tenure as CEO that he had misread "how severe the situation had become for some of the banks." Foremost in his mind were words from Harold Andersen, who more than once asked John during periods of capital investments, "This isn't going to interfere with our ability to buy stock back from our retirees, is it?"

Adding to the gathering darkness in the general economy was the newspaper's payment on a revolving loan with Key Bank, coming due in November 2009.

"I was there as chairman, but I didn't lead the band. I was chairman only in name. I chaired the meetings, and I would be at the office, be available, and consult with whomever needed to be consulted with for whatever purpose. We had started early, looking at financing and the economy's slide and, in fact, I was in many of those meetings about how to formulate an extension of this loan or refinance it somewhere else and what all our options were. And here you are, not knowing you're walking towards a cliff and all of a sudden, the lights go out and you don't know where the end is."

All the while, both he and the men he had trained, mentored, and worked with knew that the newspaper had a "sizable liability to a shareholder." That liability was the money the company would owe John Gottschalk when, as the company agreed to do in the case of every retiree, the time came for him to receive cash in exchange for his stock. In John's case, the Articles of Incorporation mandated his retirement date and thus "prohibited him from holding the stock into retirement."

In 2009, at age sixty-six, John opened an office at Three Cedars, a former advertising agency in a converted mansion near 86th and Cass Streets in Omaha. He purchased Three Cedars with the goal of offering space to retired executives who continued to keep busy civic schedules or still had business holdings. He was at Three Cedars when he got a call to stop after work to meet with a few *World-Herald* executives at the law offices of Koley Jessen, along with attorneys for both the newspaper and John personally. Arriving as requested, John detected "a nervousness in the room."

They wanted to issue a special debenture bond that would defer for five years their buying back the stock that John owned, valued at $30 million, minus a few partial payments he had already received. They handed him a document to sign. He admitted that the rest of the meeting was somewhat of a blur.

He did recall suggesting that if cash was the issue to strengthen the balance sheet as the Key Bank revolver edged ever closer, he would consider swapping his stock for an asset, a building or even perhaps a non-newspaper asset. The group declined, wanting to keep assets they could liquidate quickly if necessary. So he was left with the special debenture papers already drawn up. John took a night to consider the offer, talking it over with Carmen, but also using the intervening hours to, by his own admission, let his former colleagues "twist a little."

The next day he told them what he knew he would tell them: He'd sign the deal.

He was disappointed. Not about the money because the plan was to eventually make him whole—even though he would be without the money to invest or otherwise use as he saw fit for five years. He even tried to see the situation from his former co-workers' point of view.

"I don't think it was any more palatable to those guys than it was to me. They just didn't know any other way to deal with it. Look: The *World-Herald* was not my only asset. It was my largest asset, but it was not my only asset. We certainly weren't going to starve to death, and I had planned for retirement so, if the thing would have blown up, I'm sure we probably would have come out okay. But I didn't have near the stress that those guys had."

His dismay was about the process. "I was disappointed that they worked this way," John said. "I don't know how long it took to put this together, but they could have come to my office anytime and sat down and probably decided the same thing in a matter of minutes. There was way too little transparency in this approach and, you know, I would think that they knew me well enough. It was my group of guys, you know? I spent a lot of time with these guys."

Nor did John want his personal situation to cloud what had been a widely envied program of employee ownership. The last thing he wanted was to shade its success with whatever ignominy he felt this particular process could bring about. He was understandably proud of the *Omaha World-Herald* as an employee-owned enterprise, knowing personally how it had changed the lives of people with whom he worked for over three decades.

"The newspaper. The whole effort. The whole career. The whole everything. I think about the people," he said. "I've gone through the stock list (shareholders) with all the people in there and, you know, it was a wonderful, wonderful thing. I would hate to have it be thought of as such an unpalatable process as far as I was concerned, that the good of this program wasn't amazing. And, in fact, I've thought more than once about how many hundreds of people retired after investing in that company and had great retirements. I don't remember how many of those million-dollar bills I handed out."

Nearly a year after the Koley Jessen meeting, John got a call from Kroeger late in the day. He said he needed to see John and asked if he could come by Three Cedars. He told John he wanted to give him the courtesy of letting him know what was happening. Kroeger had received a phone call from Warren Buffett earlier that morning. He wanted to talk. "So, I went up to talk to him," Kroeger said. "He wants to buy the paper. I think it's the right thing to do."

To which John said, "Well, under the circumstances, I don't know if you've got a hell of a lot of choices."

Kroeger added that the employee-ownership plan was "restrictive and limited the ability to raise capital from non-employees." That, and the newspaper also needed to repurchase stock from existing employees. Kroeger said Buffett's offer, "presented a unique opportunity to address our long-term capital needs and continue local ownership of the *Omaha World-Herald*, which is consistent with the legacy left to us by Mr. Kiewit."

As with other stockholders, John's debenture was retired when Buffett bought the *Omaha World-Herald*, the sale of which was announced on November 30, 2011. Kroeger, then CEO and publisher, said in a news release, "We have repurchased the company about seven times since the employee-ownership plan was put in place."

Several months later Buffett was speaking to the 275 employee stockholders, telling them of the new deal. It was the end of employee ownership set in motion by Peter Kiewit and Harold Andersen and nurtured into extraordinary returns by John Gottschalk, who best summed up about four decades of workers having a stake in their futures: "I mean, in the final analysis, nobody that I know of really lost anything."

SIX

Serving the USO...Twice

Because of John, I've gotten to do more than
I ever thought possible in terms of bringing
a touch of home to our men and women
in harm's way. The only things that truly
matter in life are the hearts and souls that
we touch along the way. You have touched
an awful lot of hearts and souls, John.

–WAYNE NEWTON

John Gottschalk, son of two proud World War II
veterans, spent a week with the military during the Reagan
administration. In a roundabout way, his "tour" led to two
stints on the Board of Governors of the United Service
Organizations, known to generations of military families as
the USO. As chairman of the board for seven years, he headed
an organization that serves as a connecting, supportive link
to home for military men and women and their families.

Here was how it happened: Once a year the United States
Department of Defense invited a number of Americans to get

a hands-on look at the strength and readiness of the military. To do so, the DOD rolled out the red carpet to somewhere between twenty-five and ninety business and community leaders across the nation. They became a class in the Joint Civilian Orientation Course (JCOC), the "oldest and most prestigious public liaison program in the DOD, and the only outreach program sponsored by the secretary of defense" according to its website. The first JCOC was held in 1948.

The group spent about a week on military installations, during which participants witnessed training exercises, attended briefings with senior staff, and developed— through education and observation—an understanding of the policies that guide the nation's defense and the programs that support them.

Of critical importance for the DOD was that JCOC participants "understand the challenges faced by our men and women in uniform and by the families who supported them, both on and off the battlefield. This included help in closing the military/civilian divide and assisting transitioning service members."

It was this JCOC objective that most intrigued John, given the tenor of the times as regards the country's military. "We were fresh into the all-volunteer service, so the people we were seeing were there because they wanted to be. This was on the heels of the Vietnam War. We toured all these facilities, and I think most of us were truly astonished," John said.

The caliber of service men and women impressed John and his fellow JCOC participants. Nearly all the enlistees with whom John talked wanted "bigger and better" jobs. He considered this culture and attitude a remarkable turnaround from the days of the draft and a military heavy with people in fatigues because their number had come up, not because they wanted to be there.

Foremost for John was the reality that an all-volunteer military meant special family responsibilities for the men and women who joined the nation's fighting forces. They were, in a sense, volunteering their families as well. To that end and without causing a stir with the brass, he spent a portion of his week asking the service members in the lower enlisted ranks what their family life was like: Questions such as how their kids were doing. What was the quality of the schools? How large are your kid's classes? How long does it take your wife to schedule a gynecological exam? How good was the medical care for families? He neither expected nor found much grousing from the troops, but they were candid about their experiences.

Some things John knew could be maddening for the enlisted men and women. "We were out at 29 Palms in the summer. (29 Palms was a Marine facility in California.) The temperature was 115 degrees. Congress had been at loggerheads with the DOD over golf course fees for generals. This happened periodically, but you may specifically recall that it got to be quite a big deal for a while."

He noticed that 29 Palms had thousands of enlisted people and their families, including children. The officers' club had a big, well-tended swimming pool. The facility's old swimming pool was for the enlisted families. To John's way of thinking, this pool was wholly inadequate both in size and upkeep. What's worse, it was closed.

"You've got this spat going on in Washington, the pool's shut down, the one they had for the kids, and they can't do anything about it. It became clear that the idea of a voluntary Army with families, like many ideas that may have been great, was not very well thought through. I'm not saying there were huge deficiencies. We had plenty to be proud of in our military."

Shortly after his JCOC experience, John was asked to speak on the topic to a Rotary Club gathering in Omaha. "I said something to the effect that I thought they would be mighty proud of our military, but not quite as proud of how we, as citizens, are taking care of their families. And somehow, that got back to Chuck Hagel."

Hagel had come a long way since his boyhood days in Rushville, where he spent Friday nights watching John quarterback the high school football team. The path from Sheridan County wound its way from the battlefields of Vietnam, where he was wounded and decorated, through the power corridors of Washington, where he gained notice for his ability to get things done and get them right. Following his service on Congressman McCollister's staff, he was a deputy administrator for the Veterans Administration under President Ronald Reagan. He and John had reconnected in the mid-1970s after John began his journey at the *Omaha World-Herald*. At the time Hagel got word of John's Rotary speech, he was president of the USO.

Hagel was soon on the phone with a challenge: If John really wanted to do something about the lives of service families, he should come to Washington and go to work for the USO by serving on its governing board.

"I knew John had a great understanding of issues and organizations and how to get things done," Hagel said. "He was someone I admired, and we had a good relationship. He was in a major job, president of a newspaper, but I thought he would enjoy the board and meeting people from all over the country, all over the world. I also thought he would do a great job and would enhance our board. When I took over as president and CEO, I was looking for new board members and I thought John would be great."

That was 1988. John served on the USO board for four years.

John and Carmen share a conversation with legendary
newsman Walter Cronkite at a USO event.

He quickly discovered that while USO shows and celebrity
entertainers—from Bob Hope to Marilyn Monroe to Robin
Williams to Wayne Newton—had often been the focal point
of the USO for the general public, the organization provided
many services to military families. As theaters of war and other
conflicts spread out across the globe, the mission of the USO
was tasked to meet the needs of troops whether they were
flight mechanics at Misawa Air Base in Sapporo, Japan, or
electronic surveillance specialists atop a mountain in Bosnia.
The diffusion and disjunction associated with modern warfare
changed not the mission of the USO in providing services
to military families, but rather challenged the status quo in
delivering those services.

John was able to see where his experiences at work and
on other boards would be useful. "The USO was the same
as almost any other organization I ever worked with. You
have the headquarters, you have the mission, you have the
culture, you have the liturgy, but the work gets done down

in the various facilities. The management of that process is no small feat. Plus, the USO is funded entirely by the American people."

The USO was the brainchild of President Franklin Roosevelt, who, in 1941, with the approach to America's entry into World War II, proposed to unify six charitable organizations to provide support and increase morale among our fighting forces and their families. These were the Salvation Army, the YMCA, the YWCA, National Catholic Community Services, National Travelers Aid Association, and the National Jewish Welfare Board. Per FDR's direction, these "united service organizations" began to live the purpose and mission of a single entity under the creed of "always being by their side."

Thousands of staff and volunteers managed and ran the USO's two-hundred-plus service centers on every continent. The USO helped families stay connected. It provided transition services for families leaving military life and re-entering civilian life, a change that came with its own set of challenges. The USO's Warrior Centers reflected the organization's "continuum of care" for wounded service members and their families. The USO provided support and travel accommodations for families of the fallen and had done so for every dignified transfer at Dover Air Force Base since March 1991.

The nature of the USO's work required a board responsive to and supportive of both the mission of the USO and breadth of its services. While USO shows and movie stars made headlines and provided fighting men and women an entertaining respite from the rigors of war and deployment, thousands of other volunteers and staff were on the front lines providing a variety of services to military families.

John saw early on that strong leadership was key in moving the USO forward to meet its day-to-day responsibilities—

including the funding of its programs, which are not supported by the federal government.

John's inaugural trip to a Board of Governors meeting in Washington D.C. provided lessons in structure, management, and culture for the new guy.

With President George W. Bush and First Lady Laura Bush in the front row, John, as chairman of the USO Board of Governors, delivers remarks at the White House.

Committee meetings took place the first afternoon when the board convened for its regular two-day session. Hagel had extended John an invitation to sit in on the executive board meeting for a glimpse of the inner workings of the leadership. (The chairs of the committees largely made up the executive committee.) These executive sessions would "clear the decks" and prepare for the full board to meet the next day. John's first foray into the executive committee revealed a fascinating dynamic—as well as Hagel's coolness under pointed and occasionally heated questions—as the board went after Hagel about the closing of a USO facility in Haifa, home to a large naval installation.

"This was my first day, so I didn't know what this was really all about. However, there was a sizable explosion at that executive meeting which made me know I was in the right place and made me know that Hagel ought to be the secretary of defense," John said.

Many on the executive board, about half of whom were retired military flag officers, wanted to know why Hagel had shut down a major USO facility without consulting them. As John saw it, their concerns were not about the efficacy of Hagel's decision but rather about the process. John watched intently as Hagel and the board chairman, retired General Bernard Rogers, listened to every board member, some of whom were demanding rather than seeking answers.

"Apparently, Hagel had made a trip down to Haifa because he'd caught wind that there were some financial problems. And, when he got done in Haifa, he closed the place and came back," John said.

But around the table the generals and others on the board insisted they should have been advised before a sergeant, Hagel, went down there and did something. They all had their say about Haifa.

General Rogers, who had served as the Army Chief of Staff and run NATO before his stint on the USO board, supervised the discussion, which John described as not being "super confrontational" but with enough temperature for John to conclude that everyone "wanted a piece" of Hagel.

"(Rogers) was a terrific guy and a really good chairman. And Chuck was good, too. I didn't see any smoke coming out of his ears, but I came to know Hagel well enough that I know there was smoke."

When the questioning abated, Hagel spoke, telling the board that he knew there was a problem in Haifa, but after he arrived there he realized that "we had a bigger problem than we thought." John said that Hagel met the grumbling with this:

"I felt it was a situation that was going to impinge upon the status of the USO as a trustworthy organization. So I made that decision. You guys hired me to clean this place up. If you want it cleaned up, I'm more than happy to do it. If you don't want it cleaned up, I'm more than happy to leave. What's your choice?"

The answer was on Chuck Hagel's résumé: president and CEO of the USO from 1987 to 1990.

Hagel's tenure would include two years of John's first stay on the board, lasting from 1988 to 1992, a time he found satisfying and productive because of Hagel's leadership and a strong board. John found himself setting USO policy and making decisions with some of the nation's Fortune 500 CEOs, including George Steinbrenner, a treat for a kid from Rushville who grew up a Yankees fan.

When John left the board in 1992, the USO was under new leadership and moving smartly forward. John had no idea of the path the organization would take over the next seven years—not until he took a phone call in 1999 from retired Admiral Henry G. "Hank" Chiles, a onetime commander of the Nebraska-based U.S. Strategic Command. He knew Admiral Chiles from his Omaha days but hadn't heard from him in several years. Chiles came right to the point: the subject was the USO, and "We need to come out and see you."

John agreed to a meeting, and a handful of men showed up a few days later. "So out they come, these guys, laden with intentions, good hearts, a lot of experience and protectiveness but not a lot of nonprofit organization experience. We sat down at the round table and I said, 'You know, you guys have gone through a lot of trouble to get out here to see me. And I don't want to disappoint you. So, I think I need to ask this—how bad is it?'"

Quite bad, apparently. A decided mess had developed over the years. Serious financial problems were clear, but underneath it all were leadership failures. While retired Marine Commandant General Carl Mundy had been gracious enough to hold the fort, his was a temporary assignment. He wanted and deserved to enjoy his retirement. The group wanted John to accept the board chairmanship to lead the USO out of rough financial seas and find a willing and qualified CEO who could keep a permanent, steady hand on the leadership tiller.

"I told them what I've told everybody, and, as soon as I tell them, I want to slap myself in the face. But I said, 'You know I think the USO's important.' I mean, there are things worth doing, and I try to be helpful. So, I go."

Seven years later that help was reflected in a solvent USO with a capable and committed leader in the CEO's office, a vibrant and willing board, and the organization's profile rising once again.

But the road to solvency and solid leadership was at turns bumpy, narrow, and poorly maintained.

John's first order of business was to find a CEO and let General Mundy, who had stayed on a couple of weeks to introduce John around, get on with his retirement. According to John, however, the word was out, so he was working against a cultural undercurrent in Washington that said, "You don't want to be around the USO." He also believed that the commitment and energy on the board had faded, either from the downward spiral of compounding problems or simply the passage of time and interest. Moreover, such challenges were reflected in the staff, whose day-to-day work John described as being on auto-pilot: serviceable but not enough to put the organization on an effective path upward.

The result: John found the individuals to whom he broached the idea of moving into the USO's corner office to be exceedingly polite but, to a person, resistant to the idea of taking over as CEO. That was also about the time former Army Vice Chief of Staff John Tilleli, a four-star general, was stepping down as commander of Combined Forces Command in Korea. The timing would—at least initially—work in the favor of the USO.

When John approached him about a temporary stint at the USO, he said he'd never raised money. John assured him that what the USO needed was an organizational leader, and that John and the board would deal with fundraising. "Certainly, we were candid with him. I think we gave him the financials and the whole thing. And, somehow, he took a shine to me and he said, 'I'll do my damn best,'" John said.

Six months into Tilleli's leadership, the board met in San Diego. The CEO pulled John aside. It was early fall of 2001.

"I want to have dinner with you," he said to John the night before the meetings began. John didn't think too deeply about the request, but already knew Tilleli had figured out his staff wasn't moving fast enough toward recapturing the USO's stride, so frustration was surely afoot.

At dinner he said to John, "I've got to resign. I don't function well if I'm not moving the ball. We're not making the kind of progress we need. The USO's too important. I just don't have the skill set that's needed to do this."

John, disappointed and frustrated with Tilleli's decision, found himself back at square one: Trying to stay afloat as finances dwindled, needing an infusion of new blood on the board, and hoping to hire a CEO who could hire and train a staff responsive to the needs of the men and women in uniform and their families. It was an interwoven trifecta of necessities, none of which could be ignored in order to focus completely on the other two.

With Tilleli's days now numbered and the USO encountering obstacles at every turn, a director from the Board of Governors just happened to pass along a story to John that proved to be a game changer. She had been at a Veterans Administration function when Ned Powell, the department's former CFO, delivered a note-free, inspiring speech saying all the right things in all the right places. She was astonished. She handed John a cassette of the speech at about the time a new ad for CEO of the USO had gone to print.

Powell called himself a Rockefeller Republican or a George H.W. Bush Republican but added, "The species doesn't exist anymore." He later became a Clinton appointee to the VA and then a Democrat after enjoying a "remarkable experience" working in the Clinton administration, a position from which he retired in 2000. Powell's party affiliation wasn't important to John, but rather his talents and drive and vision.

While his speech might have put him on John's radar, his wife, Diane Powell, put him on the path to the USO's leadership. The Powells were at their home in Telluride, Colorado, when Diane came across a job opening in the Sunday *Washington Post*.

"My wife, for whatever reason, was looking at the employment section. I don't know why." She told him she had found the "perfect" job for him.

"I told her 'What perfect job? I'm happy being retired, again.' My golf handicap was coming down, we were getting ready to go skiing, and life was good."

She said the USO was looking for a new CEO, followed by, "You know, I married you for better or for worse, but not for lunch. It's been a year. Get your butt back to work. I'm tired of you being around the house."

Ned Powell went downstairs, emailed his résumé, and went to church with his wife.

Shortly afterward he Googled the board and felt good about knowing and respecting several of its members. He connected with John via telephone—coincidentally as he and Diane were traveling through Nebraska on their way back to Washington—and was soon hired.

Life in the nation's capital was never without drama, however. A young woman in the USO's entertainment department had been dragging her feet, not getting the job done. She was backstopped by her mother, who was married to an influential congressman. Not long after she was let go, the USO found itself the target of a government audit.

John was not amused. "Horrible. In the first place, a GSA audit just shuts you down. I mean, who is going to send you money, you know? We're naked and broke anyhow. But we worked through all that, and, of course, it was just politics in Washington. The audit found nothing wrong, and life went on."

Another time, John headed off an attempt by a board member, who was married to a high official in the Department of Defense, to co-opt the USO brand with a competitive entertainment tour. His defense of the organization's most important public persona was met with a gratifying silence from the Washington power structure. John read that silence as an endorsement.

Over the six years following Powell's arrival (John left as chairman of the Board of Governors in 2006 but stayed on to chair the USO Foundation board), the team of Gottschalk and Powell built a staff and board that not only righted the USO ship but trimmed its sails with eye-popping numbers. During that time, the USO went from a $40 million organization with $3.5 million in the bank to a $250 million dollar operation with $100 million in the bank including the endowment.

Each tended to pin the success on the other. "You know, it was Washington, and I got a lot of credit for making all this happen," John said. "I can tell you there wasn't a single time where that was done in public and I didn't say the most important person in rebuilding the USO was Ned Powell."

For his part Powell called John "a very good manager of the board," a skill he said many chairmen struggle to attain. This was especially clear to him as John was preparing to rearrange the board and infuse it with new energy—which he did. Together they instituted term limits, as well, assuring new ideas and perspectives regularly. John also delineated his and Powell's roles, so staff reorganization fell to Powell and board restructure to John.

"We worked very well together with that understanding," Powell said. "John was as hands-on as I needed him to be. That may sound a little funny, but the truth of the matter is John hired me because he respected my ability to do what I needed to do, what the organization needed. We discussed what we were going to do at length. I had an agenda when I was hired. I put together a list of goals. We talked at length about how I was going to proceed to accomplish them, and we talked about the status of what we were doing as we were going along. By and large, he let me go do it. If I ran into trouble or I ran into a problem, John was there to support me and back me up."

Even though the "bad," which John's office visitors had talked about many years earlier was now being transformed into "good," Powell speculated that the general public more than likely still believed the USO's primary purpose was to provide entertainment for troops abroad. "Entertainment is what people think about, but it's really a much smaller component of what's done every day," he said. "It's supporting the troops where they live and travel, and while they are away from home. It's a much more significant endeavor."

Military families whose lives had been buoyed by the USO know that, but most Americans thought of the USO as Bob Hope followed by Wayne Newton.

While the mission was clear at the USO, its entertainment tours studded with celebrity and fun still played a vital role in troop morale and connecting service men and women to home. But they, too, suffered in number and quality as dark days fell on the USO, potentially compromising the organization's brand and public image, both of which were vital to its continued existence. The depth of such a problem made John's relationship with Newton—the face of the USO—key to rebuilding an organization so necessary to the support and experience of military families deployed in war zones and overseas.

It was Newton who relit the fires that kept the USO's "entertainment division" in a positive light while John and Ned Powell were putting the rest of the house in order. In John's view, Newton's contribution was part of a life-long commitment.

Robin Williams, John Elway, Leann Tweeden, Joint Chiefs Chairman Richard Myers, and USO CEO Ned Powell break ground on the Pat Tillman USO Center in Afghanistan.

"At the time Wayne stepped forward, we desperately needed his stature to get us back on the road. I can say a lot of nice things about him because he was sincere. He goes back to when he was just a kid, singing 'Danke Schoen.' He's been doing USO shows since he was a teenager. And he's developed, over a long period of time, a great affection for our military and they have responded by inviting him to come to places and entertain them. He's not a Johnny-come-lately to support for our troops."

John's commitment to resuscitating the USO did not go unnoticed by its most eponymous name. At John's retirement dinner, Newton, via video feed, said, "John has always been my hero. When you talk about John, when you think about all he's contributed to our men and women in uniform throughout the world, John stood up and was counted. Because of John, I've gotten to do more than I ever thought possible in terms of bringing a touch of home to our men and women in harm's way. The only things that truly matter in life are the hearts and souls that we touch along the way. You have touched an awful lot of hearts and souls, John, and I want you to know that the world is a better place because you're in it. And I want you to know I'm a better man because I met you. I will always treasure our friendship and I thank you for yours."

SEVEN

On His Honor, Doing His Best

It was the best thirty-six hours, I think, of my whole life, sitting on the porch of his house with my three-ring binder and my five tabs with the things I was really concerned about, and wanted to make a real impact on, in terms of changing the course of where we were going. He was the most gracious mentor I could ever imagine. By the time we left there, we had a game plan for all five things. He was so gracious about it, too.

–BOB MAZZUCA

Boy Scout Oath

On my honor I will do my best

To do my duty to God and my country and to obey the Scout Law;

To help other people at all times;

To keep myself physically strong, mentally awake, and morally straight.

Boy Scout Law
A Scout is trustworthy, loyal, helpful, friendly, courteous, kind, obedient, cheerful, thrifty, brave, clean, and reverent.

Boy Scout Motto
Be Prepared

Boy Scout Slogan
Do a Good Turn Daily

The 1957 National Scout Jamboree in Valley Forge, Pennsylvania, was the Boy Scouts of America's largest national gathering up to that time, with 52,580 scouts from sixty-two countries in attendance. The Jamboree's theme was "Onward for God and My Country."

Olan Draper, a scout from Odessa, Texas, captured the spirit and soul of the Jamboree when later he wrote about the last evening in Valley Forge:

On the final night of the Jamboree, the story of Baden Powell, the great Englishman who founded scouting so many years ago, was told. Each scout had a candle, and when the lights were turned off, some 52,000 candles flamed up to light the huge area. It was a moment that everyone who was there will always remember. And then the Jamboree was over, the tents came down, and a city vanished before your eyes. The scouts boarded their buses, planes, and trains and left Valley Forge.

A National Scout Jamboree was and is a life-altering event for the thousands of scouts who make the trek. In 1957 fourteen-year-old John Gottschalk from Rushville, Nebraska, nearly missed it.

With his mother, Mary Jane (Pug), in 1957 in the Gottschalk backyard as
John prepared for the Boy Scout Jamboree in Valley Forge, Pennsylvania.

John had paid his fifty dollars and headed by rail for Valley
Forge. He soon found himself in the company of his bunkmate,
a scout from Torrington, Wyoming, named Max. The pair
arrived in New York City to spend the night in a hotel before
the last leg of their journey.

To their horror, John and Max awoke late. They raced
downstairs, found a cab, and headed to Grand Central Station.
Compounding their plight, they were told the train for Valley
Forge was leaving from Penn Station. A second mad dash
ensued but to no avail. The train to the Jamboree had left the
station thirty minutes earlier. Crestfallen and a little scared,
the pair was directed to a room on the second floor of Penn
Station. There they found about three hundred other scouts, all
of whom had missed the train to Valley Forge. Another train
eventually arrived to ferry them to the Jamboree. They were
assigned KP for a couple of days—a punishment John gladly
embraced because the Jamboree proved to be "one of the most
important things in my life."

Forty-four years later, at Fort A.P. Hill in Virginia, John not only made it to the Jamboree on time; he was in charge of the National Scout Jamboree, essentially a city of nearly forty-two thousand scouts, scout leaders, and staff. He could trace his ascension in scouting to the men who mentored and led him in Rushville, his scout treks to the Tetons, and his membership in the Order of the Arrow—the Boy Scout's "honor society" composed of scouts who daily embodied the Scout Oath and Law and carried on the scouting tradition of survival in the outdoors. Those, however, were the details of a life in scouting. Spirit and soul were always part of John's personal infrastructure and character, principles he both believed in and acted on his entire life.

John moved from a successful stint as the 2001 Jamboree chairman to vice president for administration of the BSA National Council in 2002 to executive vice president of the BSA National Council to the president of the BSA in 2008, a post he held into 2010, the hundredth anniversary of the Boy Scouts of America.

His journey into BSA leadership began with a meeting.

"When I moved to Omaha in 1975, one of the first people I met was Jim Protzman," John said. Protzman, a banker from western Iowa, was active in the Boy Scouts of America. John's history in scouting and his belief in its potential for both individual scouts and society as a whole gave him and Protzman plenty to talk about.

Protzman planted a seed, saying to John, "You should be part of the Boy Scouts."

The Boy Scouts Mid-America Council comprised fifty-eight counties in Nebraska, Iowa, and South Dakota, including Douglas County and the city of Omaha. The organization's structure called for a large group of trustees. In 1987, John took Protzman up on his suggestion, becoming a trustee, which was essentially a member of the council's board of directors.

The council executive at that time, Bob Fee, told John that he hoped at some point John would assume a leadership role, chairing one of the committees. Not long afterward, the chairman of the Relationship Committee needed to step aside. The chair became John's. "This committee developed and maintained relationships with supportive groups, especially churches where scouts often gathered to meet," John said.

His ascent to national president was long and deliberate. Rising through the ranks at the *Omaha World-Herald* and tackling major projects, John stayed involved with the Mid-America Council but did not became council chairman until 1994, a move that thrust him further into scouting leadership.

The BSA divided itself into four geographic regions: the East, Southeast, Central, and West. When John became the Mid-America Council chairman, part of his duties was to represent the council at the Central Region, which encompassed Iowa, Illinois, Kansas, Michigan, Minnesota, Missouri, North Dakota, Ohio, Wisconsin, and parts of Indiana, Kentucky, Montana, Nebraska, South Dakota, Virginia, and West Virginia. For purposes of administration and structure, the Central Region was divided into seven areas and was home to sixty-eight councils.

At John's first regional meeting, he met Ron Hegwood, then Central Region director and in his fortieth year in BSA leadership, including a stint as the national director of personnel. The connection would prove fortuitous. Hegwood recognized in John the kind of leadership that could move the Central Region forward. Aside from the scouting connection, Hegwood became a close and treasured friend of John's. Letters, emails, and handwritten notes from Hegwood were plentiful in John's personal file of correspondence, even after John left the BSA in 2012.

Hegwood was a scouting "lifer." His personal commitment to scouting and service to young people were on full display in this piece he wrote for the *Monday Memo*, a weekly newsletter from California's Inland Empire Council.

"Retirement worked... for five years. Then I became restless. Finally I gave in to a gnawing need to serve somewhere. It was a logical move to get active in volunteer scouting. In fact, I decided to become a scoutmaster. In January of '08, I organized Troop 50 at Aldersgate Mission in Hattiesburg, Mississippi. Aldersgate is sponsored by our church, Main Street Methodist. Troop 50 membership ranges from fifteen to twenty scouts. With one exception, all of the boys came from homes headed by a single mother."

What Hegwood failed to mention was that he started as a scout executive forty-seven years earlier in the exact same place: Hattiesburg, Mississippi.

With Ron Hegwood already in his corner, John was elected regional president at his second regional meeting and began his duties in 1996. That position put John on the national scouting stage. The next year he was asked to be the chairman for the 2001 National Scout Jamboree, scheduled for Fort A.P. Hill in Virginia. He had four years to put together a team, plan a million details, and then oversee forty-two thousand scouts during the Jamboree. He was up for the task.

~

"I can't do this," John told about twenty national scouting leaders in 1997 as they gathered to begin planning the 2001 Jamboree.

"But *we* can."

His real message was that each of them was responsible for an area. To guide their decision-making and effort, he gave them a standard.

"Our mission is to provide a once-in-a-lifetime experience for our scouts and return each of them home safely," he told his team. "As each of you go about your responsibilities, when it comes time to make an important decision, weigh it by this standard. If it contributes to our mission, do it—and if it doesn't, don't do it."

John's charge to them surely sprang from years as a CEO and publisher of a major metropolitan newspaper, stints on other national boards, and years in scouting leadership. But nothing underpinned his standard and his vision quite like Valley Forge in 1957, an experience that remained "one of the most important things in my life."

The theme for the 2001 National Jamboree, the fifteenth version of the world-famous event and the first of the twenty-first century, was "Strong Values, Strong Leaders... Character Counts." No one considered a sub-theme regarding the weather, but as the Jamboree played out, it would have been appropriate. Nevertheless, the scouting motto "Be Prepared" swung into action as thunderstorms appeared at precisely the wrong time.

John led the Boy Scout Jamboree in 2001. He was the
BSA's national president from 2008-2010.

Tradition called for the president of the United States to address the Boy Scouts at the Jamboree. The precedent was set in 1937 by Franklin Roosevelt and solidified when Harry Truman showed up at Valley Forge in 1950. With the country's wounds from World War II still fresh, Truman appealed to the scouts to be in the vanguard of "the march toward peace."

On John's watch in 2001, George W. Bush was scheduled to speak to the Jamboree on July 30, but a gathering storm required a decision from John. The president's helicopter would not make the trip into the building thunderheads, so John arranged for the president to speak by video to the scouts. (Bush would appear in person four years later on a more temperate summer day.)

In considering his decision John said one of his staff told him, "I don't think we want the kids on the move with what's coming." That was shortly before the sky darkened, the wind blew, and the heavens opened.

"We had about fifteen thousand or twenty thousand fully soaked bedrolls. The army supplied us with two hundred thousand army blankets for the night. We used its enormous dryers. By the next morning, dry bed rolls were delivered throughout the camp," John said.

For John, a Jamboree veteran as a scout, being chairman of the Jamboree proved to be more than a "full circle" experience. It was rather a touchstone to the future, a bridge between generations, an assurance of continued tradition.

He said, "On the closing night, during the candle lighting ceremony, a tear came to my eye when I looked out over the thousands of scouts and thought, 'There is a kid out there who is going to run this thing someday.'"

∼

The world had changed by 2008, the year John Gottschalk —a life-long practitioner of scouting principles; a former Boy Scout himself who still had a bag of "hallowed soil" from the Valley Forge Jamboree in 1957; and an ardent believer in strength of character and its connection to the Boy Scouts— became BSA's national president.

It was a decidedly good fit. Bob Mazzuca, chief scout executive from 2007 to 2012, said, "The values of scouting are the values of John Gottschalk. On my honor, I'll do my duty. That's Gottschalk."

Change and transformation and more change were afoot in the cultural and political landscape as the Boy Scouts of America approached the hundredth anniversary of its founding.

John considered how scouting could remain a positive factor in young scouts' lives. "We were stuck in the past, in old ways," he said. "Now we had scout shirts with pockets for cell phones. We had kids wearing out their thumbs while we're trying to get them to climb a tree."

Mazzuca had risen to the post of chief scout executive in 2007. At the time John was president-elect and a member of the Executive Council, so he sat on the selection committee that hired Mazzuca. The pair would work closely together, especially during the two years of 2008 to 2010 when John was the president of the Boy Scouts.

Modesto, California, was where Mazzuca started his forty-two years with the Boy Scouts, beginning as a district executive, then working his way through the ranks. He spent two years in the national office in Dallas before moving down the hall to the chief scout executive digs. The president when Mazzuca took over was Rick Cronk, founder of Dreyer's Ice Cream. Mazzuca said, "You cut Cronk and he bleeds Boy Scout green." While the presidential term ran for two years, the commitment was actually six on the Executive Council: two years as president-elect, two as president, and two as immediate past president.

Mazzuca was particularly pleased with the timing. "(John and I) had the pleasure of working together as president and CEO for the hundredth anniversary of Boy Scouts of America. It was an incredible adventure, and John's fingerprints were all over it. It was remarkable. John and I hit the ground running. Thank God for him. I was like a loose cannon. It was a very exciting time. I was blessed to have John around."

While each individual council was its own nonprofit entity, all councils were required to operate under the charter and bylaws of the Boy Scouts of America. The national board (and its staff) was the keeper of the vision and the owner of the brand. It was also responsible for making sure there was an articulated vision toward which all scouting leaders were working.

Structurally, John saw ways to streamline the effort while keeping the vision.

"When I became president, we had 106 committees," he said. "We had an 'all hands' meeting including every paid employee. Mazzuca said he could get the number of committees to 46. I said I could get it to 7."

It was time to step into the twenty-first century. John asked each board member how many of them had not reorganized their companies in the last one hundred years.

"They trusted me," he said, noting that many highly successful business executives and other highly qualified individuals who sat on nonprofit boards often initially struggled to get their footing. The result could be top-heavy administrative structures, lumbering progress, or both.

To restructure, John needed a partner and Mazzuca proved to be the right man. John, anticipating some foot-dragging on reorganization, told him, "We got you and we got me."

For his part, Mazzuca recounted John's willingness to listen and to partner in solving problems and creating effective strategies. Much of that involved understanding what happened at both the national level and the local level.

Mazzuca said John saw the big picture, where change was needed and where it wasn't. "There're various models, some are more top-down directed," he said. "But there are several parts of the organization that maintain an integrity stream. All of the HR stuff, all the personnel rules and regulations, are governed by the national organization, not the local organization. The consistency of program delivery and program content and all of that are owned by the national organization. It works well, it really does. John understood that really well. He was pretty cool with that."

Locally, however, councils had the option to do different things as long as the end result didn't deviate from scouting nationally, either by charter or tradition. "It's like a McDonald's franchise. A Big Mac ought to taste the same in Omaha as it does in Pittsburgh. It's an interesting concept but it works well. The closer you get to your local community owning the program, the better off we are. It's worked well for over one hundred years," Mazzuca said.

To that end, Mazzuca said one of his objectives when he came on board was to take back the narrative of the Boy Scouts, a story that he felt had been hijacked in the public eye and via mass media surrounding a series of national controversies. "I thought it was time to reintroduce scouting to the American people."

But how? Mazzuca telephoned John, who was a year into his presidency. "I told him there were five things that kept me awake at night. I'd cherish an opportunity to spend some quality time with him to share those."

John asked if he could be in Jackson Hole that weekend. "I can be there tomorrow if you want," Mazzuca said. The pair spent thirty-six hours, in the shadow of the Tetons, fleshing out the future of the BSA as they saw it. Mazzuca was able to broach all five issues that were on his mind; John was able to weigh in with his experience in scouts, on national nonprofit boards, and his time in the CEO's office at the *Omaha World-Herald*. The meeting surely changed the course of the BSA, but it also was a life-changing event for Mazzuca.

"It was the best thirty-six hours, I think, of my whole life, sitting on the porch of his house with my three-ring binder and my five tabs filled with the things I was really concerned about, and wanted to make a real impact on, in terms of changing the course of where we were going. He was the most gracious mentor I could ever imagine. By the time we left there, we had a game plan for all five things. He was so gracious about it, too, 'This is your plan, but I've got your back.' In all of these things, we actually made some real progress. We had the greatest time, incredible depth, going through a kind of reinvention exercise of the organization. That wasn't new to John. He was all about reinvention."

Chief among Mazzuca's five concerns was the issue that first led to serious bumps in the road, and eventually threatened to derail scouting in America completely: Whether the BSA would allow as members and leaders those who openly embraced a gay lifestyle for themselves.

From 1972 to 1976, Catherine Pollard filled in as a Boy Scout troop leader because Troop 13 in Milford, Connecticut, could not find a man to serve in that role. In 1974, after the boys in her troop asked her, Pollard applied to become scoutmaster. Both regional and national BSA officials rejected her application. Troop 13 disbanded in 1976 because of lack of leadership. Pollard filed suit against the Boy Scouts and added a complaint with the Connecticut Commission on Human Rights and Opportunities. While the commission sided with Pollard, the Connecticut Supreme Court upheld the BSA's prohibition against female scoutmasters. At one point in the legal proceedings, which lasted nearly a dozen years, an attorney for the Boy Scouts argued that "scoutmasters have gone through the biological changes taking place in boys" rendering males more qualified for the role.

While Pollard lost in court and her troop disbanded, her fight to become a scoutmaster captured the public's eye. Eventually, criticism of scouting came from civil rights groups, and in 1988, the BSA changed its policy against women being scoutmasters. Today, about a third of all scoutmasters are female.

Pollard's fight opened the door to increased public inquiry into the membership and leadership practices of the BSA. That included questions about gay members and leaders.

From its inception, Boy Scouts had prohibited openly gay leaders and members, arguing that "(homosexuality) is inconsistent with the obligations in the Scout Oath and Scout Law to be morally straight and clean in thought, word, and deed."

Too, any close reading of the scouting principles, as they applied to gay members and leaders, revealed they were in line with many church doctrines, which were central to the lives of many individual scouts and scout groups, such as troops and councils, and the churches that sponsored scout troops.

Still, scrutiny of the Boy Scouts continued to grow regarding gay members and leaders. In 2000, the Supreme Court of the United States, in *Boy Scouts of America v. Dale*, issued a 5-4 ruling holding that, as a private organization, the BSA was permitted to set its own membership standards. The decision affirmed the Boy Scouts prohibition against openly gay scouts or gay leaders.

Between the *Dale* case and the 2010s most of the roiling waters on the issue of homosexuals being part of the BSA remained muted nationally. But clearly forces were poised to bring the situation to a head. Which is why, when Bob Mazzuca met with John Gottschalk in Jackson Hole, addressing the issue of gays in the scouts was one of the things that kept him awake.

From John's viewpoint, the landscape was becoming more difficult, but he understood as the BSA national leader that, while change was surely inevitable, maintaining the brand and value of the Boy Scouts should guide his counsel.

"We had had gay scouts in troops for years," he said. "But we were agnostic about sexual preferences. We were simply not going to have the debate then."

Instead, he suggested to Mazzuca that they form a select group to study the issue from every conceivable angle, including concerns that ranged from protecting scouts to religious doctrine. Mazzuca remembers the moment well. "I'll never forget. We sat on his porch and he said, 'I think we need to have a wise man committee.'" The committee set in motion the process—surely not fast enough for those clamoring for immediate change—that eventually made history.

Even so, after the committee had made its study, the National BSA Council in 2012, after John's term had expired, stood pat. It affirmed its previous policy, which excluded openly gay members and leaders. In doing so, the BSA reiterated its argument from the *Dale* case and underscored John's observation that agnosticism was a guiding principle for scouting leaders when it came to matters of sexuality. The 2012 statement said, "While the BSA does not proactively inquire about the sexual orientation of employees, volunteers, or members, we do not grant membership to individuals who are open or avowed homosexuals or who engage in behavior that would become a distraction to the mission of the BSA. Scouting believes same-sex attraction should be introduced and discussed outside of its program with parents, caregivers, or spiritual advisers, at the appropriate time and in the right setting. The vast majority of parents we serve value this right and do not sign their children up for scouting for it to introduce or discuss, in any way, these topics. The BSA is a voluntary, private organization that sets policies that are best for the organization. The BSA welcomes all who share its beliefs, but does not criticize or condemn those who wish to follow a different path."

The battle over this Boy Scout version of "don't ask, don't tell" was bruising. Before it was over, many friends and supporters of the BSA called upon it to reverse its membership and leadership policies or they distanced themselves from the policy but remained indirectly involved with the Boy Scouts. They included leaders from major national church denominations including the United Methodist Church and the Presbyterian Church; two U.S. senators, Sherrod Brown and Jeff Merkley, both Eagle Scouts; the Merck Foundation; the Disney Co.; *USA Today*'s editorial board; presidential candidate Mitt Romney; Bill Gates, an Eagle Scout; MLS professional soccer league; and others. Even several executive council members publicly announced their support for a policy of inclusion. The storm rolled on unabated. The Boy Scouts decided to respond.

On May 2, 2013, the Executive Council voted unanimously to accept gay members into the BSA's ranks. The Council voted to accept gay leaders two years later, on July 13, 2015. While a myriad of forces was surely at work to alter the Boy Scout's policy, the seeding for such historical change began in a meaningful and deliberate way on John Gottschalk's porch in Jackson Hole—not far from where John earned his Order of the Arrow as a youth.

The long transformation was neither smooth nor seamless. Some parents and local scout leaders left scouting as the changes took place, in line certainly with John's point that parents, not the Boy Scouts of America, were the proper authorities for some subjects.

Since 1974, when Catherine Pollard sued to become a scoutmaster, scouting's membership and leadership policies had been under scrutiny. While the most intense pressure came after John's term as president, things heated up considerably with the removal of an openly gay scoutmaster in Ohio in 2012. John was still a member of the Executive Council and Mazzuca was finishing his last year as the chief scout executive. True to his word, Mazzuca had been on the stump for some time, retelling the scouts' story even in the face of public criticism. Mazzuca said John's example—like being part of the 2010 Rose Parade, part of celebrating scouting's hundredth anniversary—was clear and inspiring.

"He was so supportive of the notion that it was time to go public again, that it was time to be proud of who we were, and tell that story and beat that drum," Mazzuca said. "He was such a great voice of reason and calm through some pretty tumultuous times. I came to absolutely respect him so much. I never, never saw him flustered. There were times he could absolutely have been throwing things. He was focused and he was grounded.

"The thing that struck me most about the decisions we made as we worked together was that every issue we addressed, first and foremost was whether or not we were doing this with integrity. Are we doing this for the right reason? He's just a very grounded guy. He was one of the most effective people I've ever seen."

While the membership and leadership wars were a painful chapter in scouting history, the groundwork laid by John and Mazzuca kept the organization intact and gave it the wherewithal to make changes many years in coming. In time, the Boy Scouts of America accepted young women into its ranks as well as transgender scouts.

One of John's more difficult journeys in scouting came after four scouts were killed and dozens injured when an EF-3 tornado descended upon the Little Sioux Scout Ranch in Iowa, sixty miles north of Omaha in the Loess Hills, on June 11, 2008. He was away and unable to get back to Omaha for several days after the tragedy.

The storm hit just after 6:30 in the evening. Ninety-three scouts and twenty-five staff members were at Little Sioux to attend Pahouk Pride National Youth Leadership Training. When the funnel appeared, the scouts ran for cover. One group took shelter in a small cabin whose brick fireplace crumbled and toppled over onto the scouts. All four deaths and many of the injuries took place in that cabin.

Hearing the awful news, John called Mazzuca, who was already on his way there from scouting headquarters in Dallas. Amid the devastation, he found stories of courage and, eventually, hope.

In the first few moments after the storm, some scouts set up triage, administered first aid to the injured, and provided a sense of comfort and safety to a chaotic scene. Two months later the BSA's Court of Honor awarded over 130 medals for heroism to scouts who acted on their training when they were needed.

For John, the response of the scouts to the Little Sioux tragedy was emblematic of scouting. Six months later he and Bob Mazzuca wrote in *Scouting Magazine*, "These young men did what they were trained to do during an emergency. They warned others, took shelter as best they could, and afterward called for help. They freed a family trapped in the rubble and performed first aid. When emergency crews arrived, scouts led them first to the most seriously injured boys. News stories emerging from this tragedy proved to Americans that our motto, 'Be Prepared,' is much more than just a slogan."

Aside from the scouts who leaped into action in the face of tragedy, scores of local, state, and national adult volunteers arrived at Little Sioux to lend support and provide a sense of comfort and balance in the chaos. John said the selflessness and care of these people from across the country set in motion a months-long, volunteer effort to make Little Sioux whole again and honor the memory of the scouts lost there. The funds to pay for the rebuilding were all raised through corporate donations. Scouting troops and supporters of scouting came from across the country to provide sweat and muscle to the project. For Mazzuca, the process renewed all that was good about scouting.

"The human spirit is so remarkable, and so was what came out of that (tragedy), the incredible love and support that came out of that," he said. "The New York folks and others came and rebuilt Little Sioux. It was a way to bring something as tragic as that to the absolute best place you could bring it to. It really brought a lot of wonderful people together, there was such an outpouring of love and affection and emotion. It really was uplifting."

John's actions in dealing with Little Sioux revealed to Mazzuca, too, a new strain of leadership and humanity, which he had sensed in his friend in stark relief after the tragedy in the Loess Hills.

"John was out of state at the time. I went immediately. We worked together, and talked all the time. We were together on how to deal with that. He was incredible. That was one of the most emotional things I've ever been involved with. John communicated with each of (the families who lost a scout). He's very close with one of the moms who lost a son at Little Sioux. She's a remarkable woman. I know John is still in touch with her, and they're still friends."

That spirit and duty John melded into scouting was the same spirit and duty he was raised with in Rushville. He once told Mazzuca, "This is what my dad would have done." The chief scout executive said he chalked that and much of John's approach to life and leadership and problem-solving to very solid, Midwestern values. "He was a 'do the right thing' sort of guy. It was just part of his DNA."

Chief Scout Bob Mazzuca's last day leading the Boy Scouts of America.

Which was why after his retirement, when Mazzuca reflected on his years at the BSA during John's time as president, he said, "He was just a visionary guy. In stormy waters, he was so very calm and taught me a lot about seeing the forest for the trees, and looking at the long view and the big picture. I cherished working with him. Nor was he ever about 'On my watch, we did it this way.' That wasn't his style. It wasn't about what he did versus what the next guy was going to do. It was about what he could contribute at whatever level he was.

"I met some wonderful people during my career (in scouting), and, obviously, I've had a chance to work with great people in every community I've been in for forty-two years. I would, without a doubt, bar none, put John in the top three of all I've had the opportunity to work with."

EIGHT

Near Death, by Rumor

This newspaper has been under pressure
to report details of the allegations and to
disclose the names of people who are rumored
to have been involved. We have resisted the
pressure. We will continue to resist it. Our
responsibility is to gather and publish the news.

–AN *OMAHA WORLD-HERALD* EDITORIAL

Shortly after 1 p.m. on November 4, 1988, agents from the National Credit Union Administration and officers of the Omaha Police Department arrived at the Franklin Community Federal Credit Union on North 33rd Street. Their purpose: closing the place. The impetus for the dramatic midday raid was an audit of the personal tax returns of Lawrence E. King Jr., the well-connected manager of Franklin, whose extravagant lifestyle bordered, in retrospect, on the preposterous.

King had taken the reins at Franklin in 1970, two years after it was established, to provide a variety of financial services—

including consumer loans and credit counseling—to residents of Omaha's minority neighborhoods.

The garrulous, flamboyant King had enjoyed considerable support from a cross-section of local leaders, including U.S. Senator Ed Zorinsky, industrialist Walter Scott, and *Omaha World-Herald* publisher Harold Andersen. King was well-known outside Omaha, too. In 1984 and 1988 he sang the national anthem at the GOP National Convention, where he was famous for throwing lavish parties for hundreds of guests.

Auditors and the feds were convinced that, while King was making nice with national political leaders and benefiting from continued professional and personal relationships in Omaha, he most certainly had his hand in the Franklin cookie jar. Investigators would discover a stunning shortfall, which they laid at the feet of King, who eventually faced federal indictments for looting the credit union of nearly $40 million dating back to 1984. He was found guilty and sentenced to nine years in federal prison.

Federal regulations assuring investors that Franklin certificates were legit were obviously lacking. At the time of the closure, Franklin's books had not been audited since 1984. Eventually, agents found that, for at least a half dozen years, Franklin sold certificates of deposit at markedly higher-than-market interest rates. Because oversight was less than stellar, King was able to maintain his opulent lifestyle *and* pay interest on deposits, balancing on a high wire until agents arrived that November afternoon in 1988.

King left a trail of excess for investigators, spending $10,000 a month on limousines, maxing out a credit card at over $1 million, and, in just over a year, running up a $146,000 bill for flowers delivered to his Omaha mansion and elsewhere. Still, at the time of his arrest, his salary as Franklin's manager was under $17,000 a year.

Critics were quick to find blame. They accused Omaha business and political leaders who supported King of failing Franklin depositors and the city's business community either by turning a blind eye to King's obvious extravagances or, for a few, by shirking their formal fiduciary responsibilities as Franklin board members.

While dramatic in and of itself, King's financial house of cards paled next to the firestorm of gossip, innuendo, and accusations touched off by a phone call from an Omaha social worker several months before Franklin's closing. Rumors related to child abuse, sexual assault, drug use, and even murder washed over the city for months on end, prompting a prominent local attorney to refer to Omaha as "the first city in history to gossip itself to death."

The phone call detailed stories the social worker said she heard from underaged patients at a mental hospital, stories of young people being flown across the country to wild parties fueled by drugs and rampant with sex—even stories of homicide. The abuse, according to the stories attributed to the young accusers, involved King and nearly twenty other prominent Omaha business and political leaders. King would deem the accusations "garbage." He blamed the accusations on racism. Prominent Omahans swept up in the accusations were incredulous.

The call had gone first to the Nebraska Foster Care Review Board, which in turn asked Omaha police officers to investigate stories of a "child prostitution ring" connected to King and the other well-known Omahans. Eventually the state attorney general and the FBI both looked into the accusations.

Neither the police nor the attorney general nor the FBI produced evidence to substantiate the stories the social worker had reported. In the spring of 1990, more than a year after the rumors began to circulate, a county grand jury was impaneled to get to the truth and, in a sense, save a city from itself.

Six months after the phone call, the Nebraska Legislature, spurred on by a handful of its members, established its own investigative committee. John DeCamp, a former state senator who kept close ties with his former legislative colleagues, wrote a memo that went public. In it he claimed that five prominent Omahans had been accused of abusing children. The memo included the five names, flinging open the gates to the rumor mill still wider, adding layers to conspiracy theories, and charging that some in the local media were covering up the misdeeds of powerful men in high places. Particularly targeted was the *Omaha World-Herald*, where Harold Andersen retired in late 1989 and turned over the reins to the man he tabbed as his successor—John Gottschalk. The Franklin scandal and its torrential gossiping awaited John on his first official day as publisher.

Taking John's lead, the newspaper kept its head down and did its job, despite the whispers and shouts. And, when appropriate, it defended itself with facts. Editor Woody Howe bristled at any notion of timidity on the part of the newspaper, telling a reporter for the *Washington Post*, "Over these sixteen or eighteen months, we've had five of the best reporters in the Midwest on this story. We've not been timid. We've run seven hundred stories and put seven thousand reporter hours into this."

He also addressed the charge that the city fathers who supported King and Franklin should have had the sense that his lavish lifestyle was telling. "If I were still a reporter, I would find it offensive if somebody said, 'Hey, there's a black man driving a Mercedes. Why don't you find out why?'" he told the *Post*.

By late 1989, Omaha was seething with rumor. The notorious memo by John DeCamp was near the center of the maelstrom. The named individuals it identified as the Franklin Five: Andersen, King, Police Chief Robert Wadman, former *Omaha World-Herald* columnist Peter Citron, and businessman Alan Baer.

As time passed, four events further fueled the rumors: the untimely death in a private plane crash of the Legislature's committee investigator; the disclosure of videotaped interviews of three teenaged "victim-witnesses," as the committee came to call them; the arrest and conviction of Citron for sexually molesting two boys; and the conviction of Baer on charges of pandering. As it turned out, Citron, a household name in Omaha, and Baer, who socialized with King, were charged for acts unrelated to the rumored Franklin crimes. (Of the others named in the memo, King was convicted of financial crimes; Andersen and Wadman were exonerated.)

The DeCamp memo said: "The most powerful and rich public personalities of the state are central figures in the investigation." When a candidate for public office got a copy of the memo and mailed it to ten thousand homes in Omaha as a campaign ploy, the city was gripped further in a gossip frenzy. To complicate matters, the host of a call-in radio show read the memo on the air, turning the volume to ten on the whispering campaign now threatening to drown out the city's most reasonable voices.

One of those voices was the *Omaha World-Herald*, which, as John became publisher in late 1989, took the brunt of criticism, accused of soft-selling or evading the truth to save Harold Andersen and others. Pickets had begun to show up outside the newspaper. Some other media, including television and radio stations, continued to report the rumors. John, troubled by being lumped in with others whose practice of news gathering he would never tolerate in the *Omaha World-Herald* newsroom, laid out his thoughts in the February 1990 edition of *Square Talk*, his monthly newsletter to all employees.

What is The Right Answer?
Square Talk, February 1990

So many questions surrounding the Franklin Credit collapse. Where did the money go? How could it happen? Why wasn't it discovered? What is taking so long?

The frustration led to a committee of the Nebraska Legislature "investigating" whether or not our elected or appointed state and municipal officials responded appropriately and thoroughly.

That frustration, fueled certainly by some political opportunists, has raised the issues of child abuse and drug abuse. Rumors have been rampant for several weeks. Most of them heard by our reporters. So what should we do?

The answer won't satisfy a few, but should satisfy the reasonable. You, as an employee of this newspaper, are entitled to know where we stand and why.

Our First Duty

It is our first duty to be accurate… to be fair and honest… and to live up to the expectations of our readers who have placed a special trust in our reliability for 105 years.

The entire Franklin issue has been the focus of lengthy attention by numerous public institutions. The Omaha Police Department, the FBI, Nebraska Attorney General, Nebraska State Patrol, Nebraska Legislature and this newspaper are among those who have spent considerable time and energy in seeking the truth.

In the 453 days since the November 4, 1988, Franklin closing, we have run over 500 news stories. I know of no relevant information we have discovered, and could confirm, which has not been reported to our readers.

The recent furor was NOT about facts. It was about rumors. It was NOT about truth and responsibility. Instead it was somehow about whether "the press" is afraid to spread unsubstantiated charges from unknown accusers.

Three unidentified "victim-witnesses," as labeled by Senator Loran Schmit of Bellwood, have given statements to the Legislature's investigating committee. We have not seen those tapes. We do not know precisely what allegations were made. Nor against whom, nor even how many people. At this writing, we do not know the identities of those accusers. If we did, we would interview them. Our requests to do so have been refused by their attorney.

The committee tapes bearing the allegations are now in the hands of the Attorney General and soon will be in the hands of the grand jury. The Attorney General had tried unsuccessfully to interview the accusers; to determine the credibility of the allegations and, through investigation, to determine whether or not criminal charges should be brought.

His task was complicated, too. An attorney for the "victim-witnesses" refuses to allow law enforcement officials to interview her clients unless they were granted immunity from charges, which might be brought as a result of something they might say to law enforcement officers.

Our readers want to know the truth. We believe the accusers and the accused deserve our most responsible reporting. We are not in the business of making judgments. We have law enforcement agencies and courts to handle that for citizens. Our job is to report the facts and we will stick to our jobs.

It is a great temptation to return the volleys from those who accuse us of cover-up or journalistic failure to pursue the story… but we are bigger than that. We have a higher regard for both truth and responsibility than those who argue we should abandon our duty to fairness.

There is no immediate answer. The institutions of government, whose responsibility it is to investigate and bring charges if warranted, will ultimately conclude this inquiry. In the meantime, we will continue to spend our resources seeking the facts, as extraordinarily difficult as that has become in this tangled web.

Protect Our Credibility

As stewards of a long-trusted and dependable institution, we must first and foremost protect our credibility with readers. We believe that if asked, they would tell us we are doing the right thing. Certainly, if we asked them what they felt our responsibility would be to them personally, should they be in similar personal circumstances, we believe their support for our continued responsibility would be overwhelming.

The integrity of this newspaper has been tested before. And surely it will be tested again. Our reputation for fairness and truth has stood fast. We must not, and will not, publish things which tarnish our most precious asset… credibility. Our reputation is entrusted to you… and each of your associates working at this newspaper.

~

Two weeks before John's *Square Talk* landed on the desks and work stations of *World-Herald* employees, editor Woody Howe and Frank Partsch, the newspaper's editorial page editor, decided that together the Franklin fiasco and the DeCamp memo had become enough of a distraction to the city that Omaha's newspaper of record needed to respond on its editorial page. "Confidence in government was being affected," Partsch said. The following editorial ran on Sunday, February 3, 1990, nearly fifteen months after the authorities shuttered Franklin Community Federal Credit Union.

What If It Were Your Name?
Rumors and Responsibility

The Midlands are awash in rumors that have been spread by individuals who have been following the Franklin Community Federal Credit Union investigation. People in our community are being associated with the ugly crimes of child abuse and drug dealing. The people rumored to be on various lists of involved persons have no opportunity to know who their accusers are or what their motivation might be.

Some of the cruel whispers and rumors have been reduced to writing in a memorandum. It has been reprinted and mailed to thousands of Omaha homes. This newspaper has been under pressure to report details of the allegations and to disclose the names of people who are rumored to have been involved.

We have resisted the pressure. We will continue to resist it.

Our responsibility is to gather and publish the news. Readers know that a good newspaper, in carrying out its responsibility to gather and publish the news, must sift fact from rumor and maintain a fundamental commitment to fairness.

Omahans should ask themselves: *How would I feel if people in bars and on street corners were linking me with a crime and I didn't know who my accusers were? Would I want my name slipped into radio talk shows, broadcast on the evening news and printed in the newspaper? Wouldn't I expect news organizations to live up to their profession's standards of fairness?*

Nothing in memory is comparable to the current situation, in which many people in a middle-size American city are obsessed with a "story" that is based on rumors.

We generally do not print names of people who are accused of illegal or immoral activity unless we are satisfied that the people have been charged or arrested, or unless our information has been gathered through first-hand observation, confirmed through the use of documents or substantiated through interviews by our reporters with credible sources.

The Legislature's Franklin committee has made nothing public from the videotaped interviews its hired detective conducted with three people who said they were victims or witnesses. The three haven't been publicly identified. Their possible motivation is unknown, as is much about their testimony and exactly what they accuse certain Nebraskans of having done. The witness-victims are being kept away from law enforcement officers who wanted to question them.

No one outside the committee and the law enforcement community, consequently, knows what the people who are the subject of the rumors are accused of. No one even knows how many people have been named on the videotapes—the memo that was mailed to Omahans listed several names with the expression "for starters," an admission by the writer of the memo, who says he hasn't seen the videotapes, that he wasn't repeating every name that he had heard.

We aren't alone in taking the position that it is wrong to let rumors masquerade as news. Leaders representing a variety of points on the political spectrum have criticized the author and the mailer of the rumor memo. Among them were U.S. Sen. Bob Kerrey, U.S. Magistrate Richard Kopf, State Sen. Jerome Warner and Marlene Cupp, executive director of the Nebraska Civil Liberties Union.

Chief U.S. District Judge Lyle Strom, the president of the Nebraska State Bar Association, said he is "generally not in favor of spreading people's names all over the press when something still is being investigated and when the credibility of witnesses still hasn't been established."

Tom White, editor of the *Lincoln Star,* defending his newspaper's decision not to print the names, wrote that "the prosecutors must press forward, not the vigilantes." White noted that there are no charges, no public documents alleging wrongdoing, "only rumors from dubious sources and of wide variation."

This is not to suggest that we have prejudged the case. Our responsibility is to find the truth and to help to right wrongs, and *World-Herald* reporters are hard at work seeking the truth in the Franklin case. Readers should understand that we have never pursued a story by shoveling unverified barroom rumors into our newspaper. And we never will pursue a story that way.

~

Four days later, P.J. Morgan, Omaha's newly-elected mayor whose name had surfaced from the accusers and then was bandied about in the churn of local gossip, sent John a note praising the editorial and commending the *World-Herald* for its "integrity... and high standard of responsible journalism."

On January 31, 1990, Nebraska Attorney General Robert Spire filed an application in district court to convene a grand jury to look into the Franklin case and potential criminal activity including child abuse. A nineteen-member grand jury was impaneled six weeks later. While the grand jury moved forward, the legislative investigation had derailed after six months over dissension in its ranks. The committee's investigator had resigned, calling its continued work a "disgrace" and declaring that the thing had "gotten completely out of hand." Two state senators on the committee followed him out the door.

On July 23, 1990, the Douglas County grand jury under the guidance of special prosecutor Samuel Van Pelt, a retired Nebraska district judge, issued its conclusions as to the Franklin Community Credit Union's closure and the subsequent charges of child abuse, drug abuse, and other felonies. The *World-Herald* printed the full transcript of the grand jury's findings the next day, a prequel to yet another chapter in the Franklin story.

The county grand jury left the financial improprieties to the purview of a federal grand jury, which eventually returned indictments against King and several others.

As to the more prurient charges, the grand jury found the stories of sex, drugs, and wild parties involving prominent Omahans to be a "carefully crafted hoax." While several of the main young accusers had recanted their stories, one went to prison for perjury. The report named names, calling out whom it deemed "rumormongers," politicians whom it said participated in a "smear campaign" for personal or political gain, and a few members of the news media whom it said went after Andersen out of "media jealousy." Despite the tough language, the sordid episode appeared to be heading toward a conclusion.

But not, apparently, in the minds of a number of Omahans. About 90 percent of the viewers calling into one local television station the day after the grand jury report was made public said they disagreed with the grand jury's findings. Omaha radio station KFAB said 72 percent of its callers remained unconvinced. Even years later and despite no official evidence to support claims tying any of the "Franklin Five" or others to the child abuse and shocking acts detailed by the self-described victims, all but one of whom recanted their stories, some Omahans (and others across the Internet) were maintaining that the stories were true. DeCamp, who died in 2017, and other activists kept the Franklin "conspiracy" tale alive in books that are still in print.

John said that the *World-Herald* did not lose subscribers over the Franklin case and, in fact, "our status and integrity increased."

He also saw the need for the city and the newspaper to move forward, devoting his August *Square Talk* to that objective while throwing in praise for the *World-Herald* newsroom.

Thanks to Our News Staff

After months of endless innuendo and rumor, a Douglas County grand jury of 19 "disinterested" citizens concluded the Franklin-related, child sex-abuse flap was a carefully crafted hoax.

Although we were the only consistently responsible news outlet throughout this outrage, the grand jury conclusions, unfortunately, will not be accepted by some of our critics.

Attacks on the credibility of our reporters and editors will probably continue in spite of the grand jury's conclusion there was no "cover-up" throughout this wildly politicized escapade.

Each of us who labor daily to bring readers a responsible and truthful news report, whether we be the authors, editors or carriers on the route, deserve to hold our heads high.

Our newsroom associates, to whom the heaviest burden of journalistic integrity falls, acted responsibly in the best traditions of fairness. I am proud of them, and I am proud of each *Omaha World-Herald* associate who persevered until the truth was revealed.

This entire Franklin episode should serve as a reaffirmation of the immensely important role a responsible newspaper plays in our complex society. Whether it be the titillating scandal of sex, or the seemingly mundane reporting of daily events, nothing can be higher on our list than the preservation and enhancement of our reliability for fair, accurate and responsible reporting.

There are those who believe the newspaper should be a megaphone for their shouting matches to get the public's attention for their particular point of view. On the rare occasions we allow ourselves to become so, we do not enhance our standing with our readership. Much work lies ahead for each of us to make sure we are not lumped with the "media" in what for many local television, radio and fringe print products was a sorry performance over these past several months.

Child abuse and neglect are a growing concern for our society. As our citizens wrestle with finding solutions for this horrible crime, it is important that they have the information necessary to distinguish fact from fiction. When armed with the facts, our democracy and its institutions can and will respond appropriately.

Those who use this issue for demagoguery or political gain should bear the shame of a cynical public when the manifestations of real abuse are not addressed by our laws and enforcement agencies.

We have often said an informed public is essential for a functioning democracy. It is our responsibility, our duty, to provide accurate and fair information. Our coverage to date of the Franklin sex-abuse scandal has met that test. Our newspaper, with outstanding leadership from Woody Howe, avoided the trap of sensationalism in the face of one the most rumor-driven assaults on public institutions to ever face our community.

I urge you all to reflect on these past few months and to critically evaluate this experience. It is in that reflection that we will improve the high standards of journalism for which we have a long and hard-earned legacy.

Thanks to all our newsroom staff for a very good job under very difficult circumstances.

As scandal and conspiracy stories often did, the Franklin story had legs—legal ones—after the grand jury filed its conclusions.

Nebraska State Senator Ernie Chambers, with DeCamp and Senator Loran Schmit, led the initial charge in the Nebraska Legislature to investigate the Franklin story. Chambers, vice-chairperson of the investigating committee, later left the panel. He eventually sued in Douglas County District Court to expunge portions of the grand jury report, arguing that the grand jury exceeded its responsibility when it criticized local and state officials, including Chambers himself, and then made the report public.

After losing in district court, Chambers appealed to the Nebraska Supreme Court, which sided with the state senator. The state high court held that, "The grand jury's report 'shall not be made public except' when it is filed with an indictment.... In the absence of a statute authorizing such, a grand jury has no right to file a report reflecting on the character or conduct of public officers or citizens, unless it is accompanied or followed by an indictment charging such individuals with a specific offense against the state."

The grand jury did not indict anyone and only "recommended an indictment of three people." The high court ordered the entire grand jury report expunged from court records. No official grand jury report of the case of the Franklin Community Federal Credit Union existed thereafter. It was in such a vacuum that the Franklin story lives on. Were it not for the *Omaha World-Herald*, which printed the full text of the grand jury report in its edition of July 24, 1990, no official account of the grand jury's findings would now exist.

NINE

Omaha 2000 and Omaha By Design

He knew we had to create a steering committee that was very expert in each one of the goals we were going to be addressing. He also knew it was a collaboration. You have people who are the pro and the con, working together so you can come up with something everybody can live with.

–CONNIE SPELLMAN

A Nation at Risk, the ominous report of America's deteriorating public schools, was released in 1983 by the Reagan Administration's National Commission on Excellence in Education. Among its more damning phrases was this oft-quoted indictment: "The educational foundations of our society are presently being eroded by a rising tide of mediocrity that threatens our very future as a nation and a people."

The data-rich findings of *A Nation at Risk* stirred national angst toward schools. Although a number of books challenged the study, it remained a benchmark in the history of American public education. The report set off warning bells for politicians and handwringing for educators, but it took some time before any concerted or strategic effort addressed the shortcomings it detailed.

In Omaha, that effort would come to be known as Omaha 2000, led by John Gottschalk and born from the ingenuity of the Chamber of Commerce president, Bob Bell.

Bell began to put together the pieces of an educational initiative after a consultant, Ross Boyle, spoke at a Chamber meeting. In an off-handed remark about the city's licking its wounds after losing a couple of big corporate relocations to other cities, Boyle landed a haymaker, at least for Bell. The consultant asked the audience if Omaha would indeed have been ready to fill the skilled labor needs had either company chosen the city for its operations. And if not, he continued, why and how do local education policies and practices affect the city's ability to attract huge economic engines on which Omaha needs to continue to develop?

The questions moved Bell to action—at about the time President George H.W. Bush was launching America 2000, an ambitious strategy to improve American education. Many saw it as a response to the findings of *A Nation at Risk*. Bush unveiled the plan and its eight goals on April 18, 1991, giving the nation nine years to meet them and, it was hoped, change the course of American education.

Bell moved quickly, putting together an educational conference in Omaha that brought in five Bush cabinet members. The confab was a show of support for America 2000 and an informational session to explain the task ahead. Bell asked John to run the event and, before John knew it, he was heading what became Omaha 2000.

Bell knew John's ability to get things done and his passion for young people and their education. He moved former high-school classroom teacher Connie Spellman, then director of the Chamber's Leadership Tomorrow program, into the position of vice president of education for the Chamber. Bell wanted her to team with John in running Omaha 2000.

Connie Spellman was John's co-leader during the
decade-long Omaha 2000 campaign.

Spellman said Bell was determined that the project have
sizable scope. He told her, "This is going to be the only way I
can get John Gottschalk on board. I know he loves education. I
know this is a big enough issue for him. Because you've got to
have big things."

John Gottschalk and Connie Spellman, whose husband Rick
was a Phi Gamma Delta fraternity brother of John years before
at the university, set about creating the structure and processes
that would be Omaha 2000. It was an undertaking that would
eventually activate nearly one thousand volunteers, hold thirty
public forums, and distribute thousands of questionnaires in
twenty school districts, 530 organizations, and 1,350 businesses
ranging from restaurants to retail stores. While the Chamber
set Omaha 2000 in motion and the Gottschalk-Spellman
team led the fifty-person steering committee and personally
conducted the forums, the broader community drove the effort
and provided the fuel.

"The community energy that went into Omaha 2000 came
from the building of consensus," John said. "I say that because
the people who were doing the heavy lifting in Omaha 2000
were not the quote 'top civic leadership.' In many cases, it was

not even the quote 'business community.' That's not to say those groups weren't engaged and they weren't interested and they weren't helpful, but the leaders who were down there in the trenches with Connie and me were everyone from parents to teachers to small business owners."

John accepted the earlier findings of *A Nation at Risk*, even though the report was not specifically mentioned in Omaha 2000's process or outcomes. He understood the nation's and Omaha's reaction to the study and worked toward a typical Gottschalk outcome. First you had to have visioning consensus.

"*A Nation at Risk* was to the creation of Omaha 2000 as a lightning strike starting a fire fifteen hundred miles from your home," John was to recall much later. "Nothing huge had happened. But, how do you get started? That's why I did this. What you have to do is build a consensus in your community on what they want to do. Stop arguing about what's right and what's wrong and let's talk about what's needed."

Clearly, too, he saw that when it came to education, there often was a lot of "yelling and screaming" but neither really brought about the critical mass necessary to find solutions. After putting together a steering committee, John and his army of change agents decided to adopt the eight national America 2000 goals, involve the entire community, and have an empirical method to measure the results of their enterprise.

To that end, Omaha 2000 followed five guiding principles steeped in solutions and designed for collaboration: the effort was non-partisan; the focus must be on productive results; perspectives, participation, and support must be community-wide; the commitment was long-term; and the initiative must include all schools—public, private, and parochial—in Douglas and Sarpy Counties.

Omaha 2000's eight goals guided the work and underscored all the decisions that were made as a result of the enormous undertaking before them.

1. All children in America will start school ready to learn.

2. The high school graduation rate will increase to at least 90 percent.

3. All students will leave grades four, eight, and twelve having demonstrated competency over challenging subject matter including English, mathematics, science, foreign languages, civics and government, economics, the arts, history, and geography. Every school in America will ensure that all students learn to use their minds well, so they may be prepared for responsible citizenship, further learning, and productive employment in our nation's modern economy.

4. United States' students will be first in the world in mathematics and science achievement.

5. Every adult American will be literate and will possess the knowledge and skills necessary to compete in a global economy and exercise the rights and responsibilities of citizenship.

6. Every school in the United States will be free of drugs, violence, and the unauthorized presence of firearms and alcohol, and will offer a disciplined environment conducive to learning.

7. The nation's teaching force will have access to programs for the continued improvement of their professional skills and the opportunity to acquire the knowledge and skills needed to instruct and prepare all American students for the next century.

8. Every school will promote partnerships that will increase parental involvement and participation to improve the social, emotional, and academic growth of children.

While principled statements and overarching goals were necessary when a group endeavors to change the world, nothing could replace shoe leather and effort when it came to achieving results—or in Omaha 2000's case, consensus.

Connie Spellman, although she had known John socially and understood his standing in the community, came away from the experience with a greater understanding not simply of the educational needs in Omaha, but also of the dynamic, unified, and participatory leadership of John Gottschalk.

"Working with John was such a pleasure," she said. "You can't go wrong. You can't fail. He knew that we had to create a steering committee that was very expert in each one of the goals that we were going to be addressing. He also knew it was a collaboration. You have people who are the pro and the con, working together so you can come up with something everybody can live with."

After putting its steering committee together, Omaha 2000 set about getting information from the community using what John called a "gargantuan survey." The survey was distributed throughout the city, touching every geographic niche. Survey questionnaires could be found in restaurants, grocery stores, libraries, schools, churches—just about anywhere the public could be found. Key to the process was that no demographic information was on the questionnaires, only the answers to 175 questions on how the respondents felt about a variety of topics. They ranged from the school calendar to the value of the eight objectives set down as goals in Omaha 2000.

While goals, such as "every child should arrive at school ready to learn," might connote a spectrum of meanings, the survey used specific questions to drill down to a respondent's beliefs and feelings: Should a child know the alphabet before starting school? Should a child be able to count to 50 before starting school? Is 180 the right number of days in a school year?

They used machines from Election Systems and Software (ES&S), owned principally at that time by the *Omaha World-Herald* and The McCarthy Group, to tabulate the results of the survey. Only John had access to the geography of any particular survey or group of surveys.

"We weren't going to parse this thing. The question was, 'You're a citizen of this community. How do you think we ought to educate all children?' I felt comfortable that this sample, at least, was geographically gathered." He emphasized that the survey was based on already established goals from America 2000 and contained no magic in its questions. He, Spellman, and the steering committee wanted only an "insider's view," a starting point they could use when they approached the second phase of Omaha 2000—leading a community conversation about education.

A couple who owned an office supply company in west Omaha told the story of a genial young man they had hired from nearby Burke High School who turned out to be a good employee and hard worker. Nevertheless, he was stymied when they put in a new computerized cash register system. After he stumbled for a time, his employers sent him home with the operator's manual and directions to study in hopes that would help. When he returned to work, he was as lost as ever.

Because he couldn't read.

The couple told the story at one of the thirty Omaha 2000 meetings throughout the greater Omaha area. The leadership team was armed with information from the surveys, but more than anything, they wanted to engage the community in a conversation about education—specifically about what, according to the surveys, the community had revealed was important when it came to its schools.

John said after a while he and Spellman began to see a trend in who made up the bulk of the get-togethers.

"The people who were coming to those meetings were interested in helping in any way they could to take action. They weren't there to be educated about how good or bad the problem was. So, they were all pre-disposed to try to be helpful.

And one of the things that these meetings did was to allow regular folks to share, at least anecdotally, some of these issues."

Educators from classroom teachers to school administrators to consultants also showed up to see where they could be helpful.

On the other hand, some of the professional educators in the meetings found it difficult not to take it personally or be defensive over an anecdote such as the office supply store owners' tale of illiteracy. John said that an occasional quibble would show up at a meeting, fostered by an educator who contended that either the survey lacked scientific rigor or a specific story was exceptional. Still, in the case of the student from Burke, the question had to be asked and John asked it after the couple told the story: "Why do we keep passing on kids who can't read?" No one had an answer. Not the educators, not the business owners, not the parents, not the citizens there to find solutions.

After the dramatic story of a non-reading high-school student and some defensiveness on the part of a couple of educators, a tall man near the back of the room slowly stood. "My name's John," he said. "I graduated from Benson High School in 1962. And, I just learned to read this year."

The room fell silent. How could you live without knowing how to read? How did you get a job? What did you do in restaurants when a menu is presented? John from Benson High explained.

"I always had a newspaper rolled up in my pocket, which made me look like a reading person. I had a job, the same job for years and years—I worked the night shift on a loading dock. I had plenty of opportunities to advance because I'm a good worker. I knew if I took a promotion, I'd have to be able to communicate with the day shift manager, and I can't write, you know, so I never advanced in the company. I told them I liked doing what I was doing and they let me do that."

The room was enthralled and surely flabbergasted that someone, without reading or writing skills, was surviving and even more so had graduated from high school in Omaha. Omaha 2000's conversation about education was drilling down to real and critical results.

"The meetings helped in a number of ways," John Gottschalk said. "Number one, people had someplace to say something about the need to do things better. Secondly, I think it was very helpful for the educators, not superintendents and maybe not even principals, who were there. I think it was really an 'aha moment' for educators. They'd been so cloistered, you know, from reality—I mean, what really happens in the town— that it was an eye-opener, a wide eye-opener to hear from the public. It also helped them understand what we were doing. We weren't out there stirring the pot or pointing fingers. We were out there trying to find some way to get through this and to isolate those things we could do something about, the ones that were most important."

Not every meeting was as dramatic, nor as smooth as the one above. Connie said she and John especially remembered an event they called the "bowling alley meeting," which tested their resolve and poise, not to mention their courage.

"We had the teacher union representative on our committee, of course, and she was great. She was really good," she said.

The union rep arranged a meeting for the Omaha 2000 leaders at a community room inside a local bowling alley. Spellman's recollection: "We got to the bowling alley and realized that she had set it up so that we could meet with teachers because they obviously were a crucial component. These people were all members of the teachers union. It just happened to be in a bowling alley because it had a meeting room. We started the presentation and we're starting to roll and all of a sudden there were zingers from the teachers. And then we started getting negative questions. They weren't buying it.

But we hung in there. It was just the two of us. We survived unscathed. But when we got outside, we were just exhausted. We weren't anticipating that. Who were we to tell them?"

When you hold thirty meetings on a controversial subject, feelings were bound to be raw from time to time. Still, Spellman said on balance, the experience was positive. "The teachers union at the bowling alley was probably one of maybe three instances where we had anyone who was really negative. They were protective of what they were doing because they believed they were doing what was right. And we understood that."

That, plus she drew on John's example. "He is an incredible communicator," she said. "He can speak to any audience and be fully understood. He's compassionate, he's smart, and he's aware of his surroundings."

In addition to thirty public meetings, the pair met with superintendents of school districts in and around Omaha. "We thought it would be interesting for us to hear what they were saying about each other because they had a propensity to smile at each other in the room and then go out and fight like hell," John said.

Actually, most of the superintendents were more interested in John's opening question at each of the informal chats, usually over coffee: "What can we do for you today?"

For Connie Spellman, it was pure Gottschalk. "John has always been able to do that kind of thing," she said. "If you've got a problem, I can help you with a solution. If you have an idea, I can help you make it better."

Early on, her observation proved prescient when she and John sat down with the superintendent of the Papillion schools. He was convinced that seniors graduating from Papillion should have completed some sort of community service as part of their high school experience. He cited research to prove his point. A requirement of community service—in hospitals, at food pantries, in day care centers—was becoming popular with many high schools as administrators and school boards looked for ways to connect their students and their schools to the outside world, shedding the image of schools as being islands unto themselves. The superintendent was convinced the district's seniors and the community would benefit from a community service program.

His school board, however, remained unconvinced. John told him they could help. In short order, John found a business executive to lobby for the superintendent's position on community service. "And, bingo, bango, bongo, he got what he needed," John said.

Not every coffee klatch with the superintendents was as tidy and productive as that one. Jealousies and competitiveness continued to be the norm between Omaha and the suburban districts because of state tax formulas, policies for funding schools, and questions related to the voluntary transfer of students out of their home districts.

While the private meetings with superintendents gave John and Spellman some perspective when measured against the public forums, being able to deliver a tangible answer to "What can we do for you today?" proved gratifying to both of them. Their roles—John Gottschalk as the publisher of the *Omaha World-Herald* and Connie Spellman as an executive with the Omaha Chamber of Commerce—were clear for all to see. Still, John said few if any of his colleagues in the newsroom of the *World-Herald* had any idea about the extent of his role with Omaha 2000.

"I saw evidence of this at the end of a story we ran about the people who had been instrumental in solving this problem. There in paragraph ninety-eight was John Gottschalk. And that's all right. I mean, I wasn't in it for publicity. If you think something needs to be done, well, go ahead and do it," he said.

∾

Eventually all the surveys were tabulated, the public forums wrapped up, and the meetings with superintendents over. The time to assess, measure, and move forward with solutions was at hand. It became clear that, while problems existed in the schools, Omaha 2000 ended up being a mechanism by which the community could not only discuss them but also consider a framework to go forward—which happened with the Early Childhood Initiative, the Omaha Work Keys, Safe and Violence-Free Schools, and an individual focus on standards, leadership and governance, school finance, and teacher education and professional development.

For John, the response of the community remained a key asset in his personal assessment of nine years' worth of work. Omaha cared about its children's education. As a practical matter, too, John Gottschalk and Connie Spellman, on point with Omaha 2000 for nearly a decade, were in demand; Omahans wanted to know what was going on in their schools.

Omaha 2000 was more than simply a long debate about school. Programs and initiatives developed during the 1990s. While some could argue that they were not always a direct result of Omaha 2000, each improved education in the area. John remained philosophical about cause and effect. "I take no credit, and I know Connie doesn't either. And I don't suggest that Omaha 2000 does. A lot of things have happened outside the purview of the business community and the Chamber of Commerce that probably were seeds planted at the time we were doing Omaha 2000. And, some of those things progressed and grew. And so, there are tentacles out there that are doing things, even though with Omaha 2000, our job was to raise the flag."

Omaha Work Keys, a collaboration among the Omaha Public Schools, ACT, and Omaha 2000, assessed students' skills for the workplace. By 1997 over fifteen thousand students had been assessed, over sixty-five entry-level positions had been profiled for students, and over two hundred teachers had completed summer internships in the business world.

Omaha 2000 had teamed with a number of agencies to present programs on drug and alcohol use as part of the Safe and Violence-Free Schools.

Omaha 2000 supported the state school board when it released its first set of academic standards in 1998. In 1997 the Nebraska Legislature recommended that all state school districts use Coopers & Lybrand's "In$ite" software accounting system. The Legislature had used the program during its interim study on school finance. Additionally, Omaha 2000 financially supported four Omaha teachers to reach national certification in their subject matter.

Of all the initiatives, however, early childhood education resonated most among Omahans and the committee. For Spellman, whose daughter had a career in elementary education both as a teacher and an administrator, it was personal. That, plus the reality that early childhood education remained a focus for educators nationwide for years, underscoring the research on which the first goal of America 2000 rested: All children will start school ready to learn.

"We spent a lot of time and money and resources on that one initiative," Spellman said. "We learned, because we always had to do research on everything that we were doing, that there weren't very many accredited childcare or early childcare programs (in Omaha). And those would just get basic accreditation. But there were so many that would just open their doors and put a sign outside. Even the accredited ones were at the bare minimum. There was so much more going on in the world that wasn't here, and we just thought we had to get ahead of the curve. We found a lot of interest between two major foundations that helped us get some additional resources to do a model, early childcare program."

The initiative took shape in 1994 when the Early Childhood Education Center opened, serving fifty children and their families throughout the city. The center was a collaboration of businesses and educators and funded through private donations and grants. It received national accreditation in 1999 and the next year moved into a $2 million center on the campus of the College of St. Mary.

The center remained on the College of St. Mary campus but became the Spellman Child Development Center, run by the Child Saving Institute, with whom John had a long and gratifying history.

Then, in 2016, John had another surprise for his Omaha 2000 partner.

"John said we were going to have a reunion of the committee because we hadn't brought them together (since Omaha 2000 ended). I said, 'Oh, wouldn't that be fun. I'll help.' So, I get there, and of course, it's a party. Everybody came. They had such respect for John. But then I go around the corner to the back and there's a big easel with pictures of the Spellman Garden at the center. I kept bugging him over the years, kept mentioning that it would be nice if we had a good outdoor play area at the center." John had made that happen and did it in Spellman's name.

In 1999 John informed the committee that he was leaving Omaha 2000, and in his wake were initiatives and child care centers and perhaps something of even more value: community conversations.

"A very broad view of the presence of Omaha 2000 was that it always talked about (education)," John said. "Not least of the reasons for this was that those discussions ultimately were significantly extended by the press. Omahans were reading about education a lot."

Still, while Omaha 2000 moved the educational meter in the city and area, John remained philosophical as to whether it actually changed minds, given, that from his vantage point, he still heard and saw "A high degree of the Lake Wobegon effect"—radio personality Garrison Keillor's mythical community in which "all the children were above average."

Nevertheless, Omaha 2000 reinforced some ideas for him, too. "We are interested in our kids," he said. "The difficulty is that these structural processes are complex, hard to understand, so even though people felt that they wanted our community to do better and they were willing to help it do better, they really didn't know how to help. The best that we could do was to help them be great teachers and great leaders of getting the job done, so that our kids can have a great life."

That's what you get, he said—borrowing a phrase from his friend Joan Squires, the President of Omaha Performing Arts—when you have a "rooted" city, a city with a sense of place, an awareness of itself as a single, unified town, and an appreciation for legacy.

For newspapers, selecting and honoring exceptional performances from local high-school students was nothing new. Stories of athletic all-staters from high schools across Nebraska—or any other state—were always well-read. In the spring of 1993, however, the *World-Herald* truly did select an all-state team from the best and the brightest in classrooms across the entire state.

The *Omaha World-Herald* Academic All-State Team was the brainchild of John Gottschalk, who believed if newspapers were paying tribute to performances on high-school athletic fields and gymnasiums, they surely should be doing the same thing for performances in high-school classes. "We had always recognized athletes as all-staters. We needed to be doing the same thing for outstanding students.

That's why we lent our good name to a program to recognize excellent scholars."

The germ of the idea came from John's work on Omaha 2000, where, he admitted, the focus, especially early in the process, centered on students who were struggling and the best way to address the problem. He wanted to develop a way to honor those students at the top of their academic "game." The OWH Academic All-State Team was born.

Principals, grouped in the state's three congressional districts as academic "regions," nominated seniors from their schools based on four criteria: class rank, test scores, rigor of classes taken, and school activities and honors. A panel gleaned primarily from teaching and academic circles then selected the winners using a completely blind judging process. The name, gender, and school were unknown to the judges.

In any given year, the number of potential nominees could be staggering. In 1998, for example, nearly 22,000 seniors' names were eligible to be forwarded. From that number, 675 students were nominated and then winnowed to 12 per region or 36 total. Nine were selected from that group to be on the Academic All-State Team. All of the 675 students were recognized in a special Sunday section of the *World-Herald* in late May. The Academic All-State students, their parents, and one teacher chosen by each all-stater were feted at a spring luncheon hosted by the *Omaha World-Herald*.

The Academic All-State Team marked its twenty-fifth year in 2018 with its usual special section and certain status that comes with getting one's name and picture printed in the *Omaha World-Herald*. That status came almost immediately. "We got a fairly significant response right away. The (Academic All-State Team) gained cachet quite quickly," John said. "It really became a wonderful thing."

~

Omaha By Design

Connie Spellman also left Omaha 2000 and retired from the Omaha Chamber of Commerce with every intention of staying retired. Her retirement became more of a hiatus because life sometimes had a symmetry no one could forecast.

"About a year into (retirement), I started getting the jeebies," she said. "I was kind of putting myself out there more, but not really looking, just listening to hear if there was anything and there wasn't. Then all of a sudden, I got a call from Del Weber, CEO of the Omaha Community Foundation. This was when John was chairman of the Foundation, and he was working with Del, the former chancellor at UNO. Del wanted to go to lunch. We went to lunch and, you know, just always be careful. There's no such thing as a free lunch."

Her instincts were spot on. Weber told her the Foundation had a new, three-year pilot program that was steeped in solving problems neighborhood by neighborhood with a heavy emphasis on urban planning and design—and that they thought she might be interested in signing on.

"'Well, I've only done startup things,' I thought. You can't fail at a startup thing, but I had no idea about urban design or planning."

She did, however, have a talent for finding people who did have talent. She said finding the right person was something she had learned from John.

By 2001, Connie Spellman was founding director of Lively Omaha, which became Omaha By Design in 2003.

John, along with Bruce Lauritzen of First National Bank and Ken Stinson of Peter Kiewit Sons', funded Lively Omaha after the Omaha Community Foundation commissioned a study about what Omaha would be like in the distant future. The study said, "No one knows for sure what Omaha will be like in the year 2099... If its rate of growth continues, Omaha will be regional, not just a city, and its population will be far more racially and ethnically diverse than today. The community's future ranking on economic, political, and livability scales will be determined by how well it has nurtured its people, solved its problems, managed its resources, and cared for its natural and built environments."

The five words from the study that Spellman and her team focused on were "vibrant, connected, distinctive, sparkling, and fun." Omaha By Design teamed with the city to encourage Omahans to consider revitalization—of things both large and small. They used the tenets and services of the Project for Public Spaces (PPS), whose mission it was to nurture and sustain public areas that maintain and build strong communities. PPS was a nonprofit organization based in New York City.

Spellman said Omaha By Design started small. "I had a little team of three people. They worked with me a lot, and we discovered the Project for Public Spaces. They were actually brought to Omaha because they were doing research for the National Park Service and PPS does things with your environment."

The process Spellman's team used was developed by a group co-chaired by Weber and Omaha's planning director, Bob Peters. By 2003 the process engaged neighborhoods to identify problems and gave them the support and resources to solve them. Those "problems" came in a variety of packages, from a particularly troublesome daily traffic snarl to the lack of green space or playgrounds for children. Resolutions "by design" reinforced planned neighborhood betterment with an eye toward the smart use of resources and the quality of life improvements brought about by focusing on a blend of practicality and aesthetics—including public art.

Omaha By Design started its process with something called Place Games workshops, brainstorming ideas among the people most affected by a neighborhood problem or an ongoing environmental annoyance. Spellman learned Place Games' particulars by training at the Project for Public Spaces, the nonprofit educational organization in New York.

She put her training to work immediately. "I came back and we instituted Place Games workshops, working with neighborhoods. They had to be involved to say, 'We have a problem here or the traffic is this or we've got this blocked or we have people that don't take care.' So, the idea is to have the neighbors go out in teams, look and see what they like, what they don't like, what they could change. They come back, and we put it all together on boards, helping them figure out where the commonalities lie. We would help them by writing up the front page of a grant application to help them go someplace to get money to solve the problem. The philosophy, though, is that the neighborhood was the expert."

Running simultaneously were community meetings to capture input from citizens about what they wanted Omaha to be in the future—the look, feel, and spirit of the city. That research coalesced in twenty-one goals that were eventually adopted unanimously by the Omaha City Council and became a blueprint for the future: the urban design element of the city master plan.

The combined power of engaged citizens in neighborhoods across the city and thoughtful planning through local ideas and professional guidance fueled Omaha By Design.

City leadership presence was crucial to Spellman. "While the neighborhoods had to do the work with our help, we also knew that Mayor Fahey (Omaha Mayor Mike Fahey was in office from June 2001 to June 2009) was a neighborhood advocate," she said. "When we went to him, he said he would give credits for people who did Place Games when they came to get a neighborhood grant. Then we would find a donor who'd say, 'That's a great idea. If they get the neighborhood grant, they can apply to us and (we can get one as well).' So, it was just a perfect kind of thing."

Spellman also said Omaha By Design worked because at its inception were strong community advocates who believed not simply in the process and the program but also in the future of Omaha. "It was with the help of John, Ken Stinson and Bruce Lauritzen, those three, they were our founding fathers."

Spellman had retired by then but not before Omaha By Design had reached over forty neighborhoods from its pilot Place Games in the Benson neighborhood in central Omaha, which experienced a rebirth of sorts both in retail outlets and as a destination for Omahans looking for entertainment, shopping, and housing.

As she considered her time with Omaha By Design, Spellman described as "energizing" the work and the process— empowering neighborhoods, affecting planning for the future, revitalizing areas of the city, and supporting art and other aesthetic improvement.

She said, "You're feeling as if you're helping people make decisions, that they just needed a little bit of context or opportunity to share their ideas. There were just so many offshoots of it all. I feel like I'm the luckiest person in the world to have done it."

And she pinned her good fortune on the lapel of John Gottschalk whose vision included the financial backing, along with his confidence that his Omaha 2000 partner could lead the charge to get it implemented.

TEN

Solving a City Divided

While I see John's fingerprints on the newspaper,
it is in the public arena of arts, education, and
environment that his character is most evident.
His intervention—personal and editorial—
in a highly contentious issue involving the
Omaha Public Schools, showed John's deep
affection for the Omaha community and its
most vulnerable members, its children. John
did what no other citizen of Nebraska could
have done. His timely intervention, persistent
participation, and steady hand led to a
successful conclusion of a most contentious
and hurtful experience in our community's life.

–FR. JOHN P. SCHLEGEL, S.J.

John's leadership in Omaha 2000 came from his passion
for education and his willingness to be helpful—not unlike
his impulse to help his classmates in Margie Hinn's third-
grade classroom in Rushville, his tilt toward a new vision for
the National Benevolent Association, or his streamlining the
bureaucracy of the Boy Scouts.

Seven years after he left Omaha 2000, however, he found himself treading where others dared not. It was a matter of his own choosing, informed by necessity and the embers of passion that still burned brightly.

The occasion was a bombshell detonated by Nebraska's largest public school system. The Omaha Public Schools had complained for years that the State of Nebraska had failed to provide enough money to address the district's unique challenges of race and poverty. Now the district's lawyers thought they had a solution: confiscate students, schools, and taxable real estate from neighboring school districts, thereby increasing operating revenues.

To propose this, they dusted off a long-forgotten Nebraska law, dating from 1891, dealing with the expansion of a city— Omaha, in this case—by means of annexing nearby territory. The law specified that the annexed territory became not only part of the city itself but also part of the city's school district. This requirement had not been followed in many decades with the result that the city limits of Omaha encircled not only most of the Omaha School District but all of the Westside Community Schools and a significant portion of the Millard Public Schools. OPS argued that proper application of the law would produce "One City, One School District" by returning those areas to the Omaha district.

This ignited a furor, particularly in the southwestern Omaha neighborhoods that had once constituted the City of Millard. When Omaha annexed Millard in 1970, the 1891 law was not implemented, meaning the Millard School District remained independent and free-standing. The prospect of being roped into the Omaha School District stirred ancient resentments over the 1970 annexation. Apprehension also surfaced in the Westside neighborhood and in nearby Elkhorn, a more recent target for annexation by the City of Omaha.

The OPS superintendent, John Mackiel, arguing for "One City, One School District," said the hodgepodge of districts within the city limits worked against the best interest of the community. "Multiple school districts in Omaha stratify our community. They create inequity, and they compromise the opportunity for a genuine sense of community."

The suburban schools, some of whose growth was surely the result of white flight, pushed back. Some suburban officials and patrons predicted that racial-balance busing, in effect in OPS from 1976 to 1999, would be revived, this time reaching into suburban school districts including Millard, Bellevue, Ralston, and Papillion-LaVista, eventually affecting, in one way or another, all the eleven school districts in Douglas and Sarpy counties.

Soon, the Nebraska Legislature and Governor Dave Heineman became involved, elevating the fight to the state level. This was a mistake, in John's mind. "Omaha was far more directly related to education issues. But then it was dragged into the *politics* of education," he said.

Heineman's meddling, some argued, had a political method and motivation: He was to face a gubernatorial primary in a few weeks against the wildly popular former Nebraska football coach, Congressman Tom Osborne. And the suburban areas around central Omaha were especially well-stocked with Republicans who would be voting in the Heineman-Osborne race. While legislators worked toward some solution, the governor clearly favored the suburban schools against OPS, casting himself as both cheerleader and protector of the status quo. Osborne preferred the middle ground, offering to wait until he was in office to weigh in on one side or the other. Heineman's behavior was called into question in an *Omaha World-Herald* editorial called "Harming, not helping":

(Editorial on following pages)

A "Governor Heineman Committee" this week mailed invitations to some Omahans announcing an opportunity to join 15 suburban school board members in honoring Heineman "for standing up for our local schools." Recipients are promised a free barbecue and information on how to "protect the future" of their schools.

By agreeing to hold that event, Gov. Dave Heineman and the school board members involved have shown an astonishing lack of judgment. They are brazenly injecting raw politics into a divisive community issue at the very time when the Omaha area needs to approach the issue with calmness and deliberation.

Consider what has transpired over the past three months. January had barely begun before it was punctuated by an uproar over a display of pro-OPS sentiment during a boys basketball game between Omaha Central and Millard South. The incident threw an embarrassing spotlight on the chasm of alienation that separates Omaha Public Schools from nearby districts hostile to the "one city, one school district" concept.

In the wake of the episode, thoughtful observers on both sides of the issue rightly noted that things were getting out of hand and that everyone needed to step back and cool off. The *World-Herald* noted editorially:

"We are all in this together. Just as this country, the United States, struggled in its early days to overcome state-centered parochialism and build a sense of national identity, so, too, the Omaha area, whether it continues to have many school districts or moves toward consolidation, should strive to create a sense of community-wide purpose."

Slowly, despite hard feelings, an important discussion had begun to move forward to encourage that goal, to move people away from ill will and toward a tentative but constructive dialogue. Discussion has moved toward positive ideas such as how to address Omaha's challenges concerning affordable housing. These efforts have been encouraging. They have shown our community at its best.

When school officials and their legislative champions testified before the Legislature's Education Committee this year, they made their cases firmly but also extended respect to the opposing camp. Although the differences in viewpoint were clear, voices were temperate and the mood constructive. People were taking the right approach.

Since then, members of the Legislature have engaged in delicate attempts at consensus-building on the issue. Just this week, a *World-Herald* article by staff writers Jeffrey Robb and Michaela Saunders described the Education Committee's negotiations on this matter as fragile. The situation would no doubt remain delicate if the committee manages to advance a bill to the full Legislature.

Whether the Legislature can find a workable approach is open to question. This newspaper has pointed out the difficulties. But thoughtful senators of varying perspectives are making a good-faith effort. And, in the present circumstances, they deserve a chance to see what they can accomplish.

The planned March 22 pep rally, led by Heineman, a sitting governor and a self-proclaimed leader, undermines this progress. The governor cannot present himself as someone seeking a solution when he promotes a political event certain to reopen wounds within this community.

The event irresponsibly encourages polarization just when people need to be coming together, and it casts the debate in a counterproductive us-vs.-them mentality at the very time when thoughtful people are trying at last to break free from it.

The timing might be wonderful for Heineman in terms of his selfish political interests (the Republican gubernatorial primary is May 9), but it could not be worse for the Omaha area and the Legislature in terms of their efforts to move forward on this issue.

Those attending the rally no doubt will be urged to remember Heineman for cheering their view of the dispute. In one regard, he and the 15 school board members should be remembered. By stooping to a political stunt, they have failed a fundamental test of civic vision and responsible leadership.

Even without the governor's involvement, the Omaha schools' question helped turn the legislative session tumultuous, part of which was the result of a proposal introduced in January, an idea that carried with it a completely new government framework for the schools.

Senator Ron Raikes from Waverly, Nebraska, introduced LB 1024, which would have kept district boundaries while requiring the suburban schools to work with OPS in a new structure called a "learning community." The districts would share, among other things, a common tax levy and a rather amorphous duty to integrate the two counties' student bodies.

While LB 1024 was far from perfect, Raikes's idea had gained some traction during the Legislature's ninety-day session. Then, in early April, Senator Ernie Chambers of Omaha, who at that time was the only African-American senator among Nebraska's forty-nine lawmakers, pulled the pin on a policy grenade and rolled it across the legislative floor.

Chambers, with majority support, added an amendment to LB 1024 to divide OPS into black, white, and Hispanic "subdistricts." Immediately an outcry went up that the plan was unconstitutional and clearly segregationist. Attorney General John Bruning sent a letter to lawmakers indicating that settling the Omaha schools' strife by trisecting OPS raised "serious risk due to the potential constitutional problems raised by LB 1024." He wrote, "The 14th Amendment bars planned segregation regardless of the validity or belief in the fraud of 'separate but equal.'"

Chambers was adamant. While some may have believed his amendment was a ploy to defeat LB1024, the senator argued on the floor—as he had previously—that local control of education decisions in his largely African-American district would be in the best interest of the students. Chambers, who believed the schools had failed the sons and daughters of his constituents, wanted more black teachers, more black administrators, and school board members who would call the shots for black students in north Omaha.

Chambers's amendment carried on a vote of thirty-three to six, a precursor to the final vote on LB 1024, which passed thirty-one to sixteen with the amendment. Governor Heineman, seeing a win, signed it, saying, "the motivation behind (the amendment) is neither separation nor segregation."

In Omaha, John Gottschalk cringed. He heard from friends and associates who shared his deep concern. He was appalled that few were stepping forward to find a solution.

∽

The consequences—especially the optics—of LB 1024 brought an unwanted spotlight on Omaha. The legislation would segregate OPS, a metropolitan school district serving fifty-six thousand students. National attention from newspapers and television networks was not far behind.

"It was a black eye on the community," John said. Although he considered himself "out of the game," he thought about the contacts he had made during the Omaha 2000 years, and the support he knew existed in the community for excellence in education. His thinking led to action.

He picked up the phone.

"I made the first call to (Westside Superintendent) Ken Bird, and merely said, 'Ken, if I can get John Mackiel to sit down with you, would you meet?' And he said 'yes.' I called John Mackiel and he said 'yes.' We would start with a meeting." John knew neither superintendent well. From experience in Omaha 2000 and his seat at the publisher's desk, however, he saw Mackiel and Bird as clearly the leaders of their respective camps, reasonable guys interested in solutions that would be best for students and the community at large. Bird knew Mackiel well, having grown up on the same street, and was more than willing to talk. But tensions had grown during the months of bickering over "One City, One School District." Bird said he agreed to the meeting with his OPS counterpart because he "explicitly trusted John Gottschalk." Bird, in a sense, became the *de facto* representative of the suburban schools, all of whom had hardened their positions on school boundaries while some partisans—without any evidence to back it up—had put out the idea that inter-district busing would be the next step in any boundary changes. And while the segregation of OPS garnered headlines around the country, it was money, taxes, and equity forming the brew of contention that fed years of hostilities locally.

None of the other superintendents or legislators, however, knew John was about to bring together OPS and the suburban schools for a conversation. There was no agenda, no expectations, no news conference, and certainly no politically-motivated pep rally.

The first meeting between Mackiel and Bird was held at Three Cedars, the stately house on North 86th near Cass Street, which had first been transformed into an adverting agency and then, after John purchased it, into offices and meeting rooms. Cedar trees and a walking path highlighted the manicured grounds adjacent to the building.

John had no presumption of success after the phone calls. "My role that day was a self-appointed—not even a mediator—but a convener on behalf of the community. I was just looking at this and thought, 'This is a mess, I think I can do something.'"

He had subscribed his entire life to an axiom his father, Phil, had taught him: war was the last extension of diplomacy. He saw that OPS could not get what it needed, and during its quest to change the map, a "war" of sorts had broken out. "Then the Chambers amendment blew everything up. The superintendents were scattered, floundering around trying to get out of it. I thought this thing needed to be solved by educators, not politicians. So I invited myself to try this," John said.

John Mackiel,
OPS Superintendent

Ken Bird,
Westside Superintendent

Unknown to the public or John's colleagues at the *World-Herald*, a series of meetings began at Three Cedars, where Mackiel and Bird were given to long walks together on the grounds. Progress was slow but it was still progress. Bird, who was acting as a go-between to superintendents in Elkhorn, Millard, and Ralston, was optimistic. "We had worked so hard and we thought we had it, we thought we had a resolution to the problems between the schools," Bird said.

Then, several months into the meetings, an advocacy group went to court to force the OPS school board to enforce the idea of "One City, One School District." Mackiel pulled out of the process. Without Mackiel, who had been at the table the entire time, Bird said he, too, was finished. Bird even made a public statement that the suburban schools would now fight it out in the courts and Legislature.

John Gottschalk had other ideas. He called Bird and said, "You're not out of this. We're going to solve this." He urged Mackiel, too, to reconsider.

To that end John stepped up his involvement in the process. He started by hosting a small dinner at his house that included Bird and his wife and Mackiel and his wife, the ground rules of which were there could be no talk of education. "We were there to get to know each other," Bird said.

After the dinner Mackiel, Bird, and John established an informal agreement that they would meet every Saturday morning. So committed to the meetings were the trio that Ken Bird made a ship-to-shore call from an anniversary cruise with his wife, Annie.

The meetings also began to include former speaker of the Nebraska Legislature Kermit Brashear, whom John asked to join the team to lend both legal and legislative expertise. Brashear also had a good working relationship with Ernie Chambers. Brashear kept Chambers informed of the group's progress, sometimes meeting the senator at his barbershop in

North Omaha and sometimes outside the State Capitol. Bird noted that Brashear's work was not pro bono, revealing the personally expensive element of John's commitment toward undoing the "mess" he saw as a result of LB 1024.

John urged the group to exercise an example of pragmatism he had heard at a public meeting in Beatrice years before, when a tall, humble farmer rose from his chair in the back of the room, coming to his full and considerable height to remind a conflicted and contentious crowd that, "There are a few things we agree on and probably a few things we don't. We'll get a lot further if we take care of the things we agree on." The eloquence of that moment had left an indelible impression on John.

"That was the mantra in my head," he said. "And, it translated into our process. What you need is a framework. We didn't need to talk about 'One City, One School District.' We didn't need to talk about half the stuff that everybody was up in arms about. We needed to talk about how to solve the fundamental problem. I also felt very comfortable with both Mackiel and Bird although I had not talked to either one of them, frankly, about anything that had transpired up to the time when I called them for that first meeting. So like everyone else, I had been watching this get worse and worse for an entire year."

With Brashear in the fold, Mackiel and Bird talking again, and John taking a more active role, potential solutions began to gather steam—only nearly to be derailed by what Bird dubbed the "Billionaires' Bus Ride."

Bird recalled, "I got a call one afternoon from David Sokol (at that time one of the top executives at Warren Buffett's Berkshire Hathaway). He said to come to his office at 4 p.m. We're going to meet with the governor and get this (LB 1024) thing fixed. Oh, boy, I thought."

Bird tried frantically to find John to "pull the plug on this." Hardly anyone knew about John's behind-the-scenes effort and the progress that was being made. Bird feared that a blowup in the Governor's Mansion could set the progress off course. Finally he made contact with John. After a few phone calls, John informed Bird that there was nothing to be done but attend the meeting and "do no harm."

Bird and Mackiel boarded the bus with Sokol, Warren Buffett, Dick Holland, Susie Buffett, and several others and headed for burgers and Cherry Cokes at the Governor's Mansion. While Bird was concerned that a meeting with the governor might undo the work he and Mackiel had been doing, he said part of the ride was a delight, listening to Warren Buffet and Holland tell stories.

Still, Bird grew tense as the bus approached Lincoln. After conferring with the non-committal Mackiel in the back of the limo-bus, Bird decided something needed to be said. "So we're getting close to Lincoln, and I pulled Sokol aside and said, 'Trust me, David. We're close to solving this thing and don't need it to blow up. I know you got a call from John Gottschalk. What's the agenda?"

Sokol said they would be meeting with the governor and Ron Raikes, chairman of the Legislature's Education Committee and author of LB 1024. He reassured Bird that everything would be okay. Sokol then told the rest of the passengers that after burgers they would give Mackiel and Bird a chance to talk and tell the governor and Raikes that they were working behind the scenes to ease tensions.

"So we went in," Bird said. "We had a little small talk, then dinner. Then the governor got up and asked, 'Why don't we go around the room and tell why each of us is here. Warren, why don't you start?'

"Warren looked up and said, 'Ron Raikes, you're an embarrassment to all of us. I travel the world telling people I was educated in the Omaha Public Schools and you're trying to ruin them.' He ripped into Ron."

Bird said things went downhill from there. He leaned over to Mackiel and told him not to say anything. Except for a brief thank you from Bird, the pair watched from the sidelines and then headed home, nary a scratch on them, their progress mostly unimpeded. But it was close. "I always cussed Gottschalk for not being able to fix that one in advance," Bird said, laughing.

Eventually, the work of Bird, Mackiel, Brashear, and John was developed into legal language and became LB 641, which Raikes introduced in the next session. Aside from repealing LB 1024 and the controversial amendment, LB 641 once again kept school boundaries intact. It also created a common levy among the eleven districts that under the statute made up a "learning community." The learning community allowed individual districts to remain autonomous and independent yet fused with other districts to better serve the one hundred thousand students in Douglas and Sarpy counties. The common levy served as a structure to share financial resources within the community. The districts also pledged to cooperate when opportunities arose to integrate schools and improve student achievement, especially in poor or underperforming schools.

For Ken Bird, "a turbulent time became much ado about nothing. A positive consequence is that it was a harsh lesson, and we've all learned to work together better going forward. I think we still have a pretty strong division in the community over this. Ernie Chambers's legislation to divide OPS probably was as strong a warning and message to OPS as there's ever been on how fragile the education environment is. His message was loud and strong."

John Gottschalk's role remained pivotal to Bird, who saw how deeply John felt that those whom the problem affected should be the ones who find the solution. "I think John, in an earnest and genuine manner, really wanted what was best for our community," Bird said. "But he wasn't going to tell people what that should be. He wanted people to come together and work on it."

ELEVEN

"Thanks a Million"

Our little chats opened the door for me to know
it is possible that a president, whether interim or
permanent, would take the time to visit with the
front desk person. Saying the front desk is an
integral part of our office is one thing, but telling
that person is a totally different thing. Believe
me, comments like that go a very long way
with me at least.... For me they last a lifetime.

–PATTI FISCHER

Dr. Pete Whitted stepped aboard an elevator on his way to a
meeting of the University of Nebraska Foundation staff. Whitted
was chairman of the Foundation's board. He had called the
meeting to introduce the staff to its new, albeit temporary, boss,
John Gottschalk. Suddenly Whitted hesitated. He had forgotten
something. He turned to John, who was with him on the elevator.
"Oh," he said. "We haven't set your compensation yet."

John smiled. "It is only two floors before you introduce me.
Think fast." Then, after a blank look from Whitted, John added,
"I don't need any money."

The elevator doors opened to a roomful of Foundation employees, board members, and university administrators.

Whitted led the way into the packed room and proceeded to introduce John, who would step in on short notice to lead the Foundation, instilling proven business practices and a culture of professionalism to assure its impeccable reputation remained strong.

He found out within a few days that he needed to be on the payroll, a technical and legal requirement for Foundation employees. John decided one dollar should cover it, but was informed a couple of weeks later that the Foundation's payroll and accounting system wouldn't process such a small figure. When he asked how much payroll "needed," he was told at least two dollars. That became his "salary" for eight months of work.

"Gee," he quipped later, "I was there less than a month and they doubled my salary."

∽

John and Carmen Gottschalk were no strangers to the work of the University of Nebraska Foundation. The Foundation had been supporting the university since 1936. The Foundation was independent from the university but like all foundations tied to a university, it was forever linked, not simply by name but also by vision and mission.

The Gottschalks were front and center as donors, financially supporting a variety of programs and more than willing to tell their story in support of the Foundation. At the time John was tapped as its interim CEO, he was already chairman of the University of Nebraska-Lincoln portion (the largest by far) of the Campaign for Nebraska, a $1.2 billion capital fundraising effort. As an alumnus and business leader in Nebraska and the region, John took seriously the university's role in providing an outstanding education to those who would lead the state and the nation during the twenty-first century. He understood the Foundation's critical responsibility was to maintain its focus.

So it got John's attention when a former Foundation board member and long-time acquaintance—who explicitly trusted John's confidence and integrity—called one afternoon. This person was concerned about the management and direction of the Foundation and sought John's advice as to how and with whom to air these concerns. John strongly advised taking them first to the University of Nebraska president and the chairman of the Foundation board, which his visitor did later that same day.

Within a few days the Foundation president abruptly resigned. As reported in both the *Omaha World-Herald* and the *Lincoln Journal Star*, a difference in management and operational philosophies was cited as the reason for the immediate and unexpected departure. The sudden void in the corner office came as the Foundation was in high gear, fundraising for the Campaign for Nebraska.

Leaders from the Foundation and the university came to Omaha to see John. Their hope was that he would become interim president while the Foundation board began a nationwide search for its next permanent president and CEO.

"They were very flattering. They said there is only one guy who can function statewide, who can work with the Legislature, who can run a business, who has proven leadership, and who is already within the campaign structure, and 'That's you, John.'"

John was retired but still busy. Nevertheless, having heard his friend's tale and weighed the precipitous departure at the Foundation, he told them, "I can't walk away, so of course I'll help." It was his nature. About a week later he was riding with Whitted up the elevator to meet his new staff.

Before that introduction could take place, he told the Foundation leadership he needed a few important items including a balance sheet, financial statements, the Foundation's charter, its governance documents, and its budget. John spent the week poring over the documents. He soon recognized that structure and management would have to change at the Foundation if it were to continue on a positive path. His management style—and what he brought to the Foundation—would differ considerably from that of his predecessor.

During the week he developed a set of objectives (which he, Whitted, and board chair-elect Tonn Ostergard would agree on). He was optimistic about changing not simply how things were done but the culture in which they were done. These were issues that related to how employees did their daily tasks: efficiency, attitude, relationships among departments and individuals, integrity, passion. He was determined to understand the agency's cultural mores and to help employees improve themselves.

To test his plan with an outsider, he called a human resources expert and asked if she could meet with him. Laying out his case for culture change—defining the problem and detailing his solution—during what would be a temporary stay, John asked her if she thought he could change culture while there.

"Not a chance!" she declared. He framed the quote and hung it in his office.

∿

When February 2, 2012, rolled around, Foundation staff members were understandably uneasy about their future and the sudden appearance of an outsider. Only a handful knew John personally, notwithstanding the fact that he was then chairing a part of the fundraising campaign. As University of Nebraska bombshells went, few dramas could compete with the hiring or firing of a football coach or a sudden change in the college football rankings. But an abrupt transition in Foundation leadership made for an uncertain time among employees, faculty, administrators, fundraising volunteers, alumni, and political leaders.

Here was what John told them that morning after Whitted introduced him: "As the days roll by, I will have a chance to get much better acquainted with you. For now, I'm here only to say that when I was approached to man the tiller of this great University of Nebraska Foundation for an interim period, I was humbled to think I might have an opportunity to repay just a fraction of what our university has given my family, employees, and state.

"My duties are temporary, while the Board of Directors seeks a new leader. However temporary my stewardship, it will not be as an observer or titular head. We are in the largest campaign in the history of the Foundation. You, as a team of professionals, have achieved remarkable and unparalleled success in leading us closer to our campaign objective. You want to win, and so do I. And we will.

"In all my business and civic experience, one constant has been that human endeavor, human energy, human talent, are the most significant ingredients of organizational success. You represent that endeavor, that energy, and that talent. Thus, you are the most important ingredient in what has been to date— and will continue to be—our success.

"I join this team to sustain your momentum and I will do my best to assist you. My job is fundamentally you—helping you succeed in your job—helping you achieve job satisfaction by helping leverage your efforts with the best management and planning we can muster.

"It doesn't pass notice that I am the first non-university, non-Foundation executive to hold this responsibility in several decades. However, I am not inexperienced in fundraising— nor in giving. I will be guided in these early days of transition to a permanent leader by your counsel, your goodwill, and your re-energized efforts.

"Dr. Whitted, Tonn, and I have established a set of objectives to be achieved during my time with you. We'll get started on these today leading up to an all-hands meeting probably on February 11 at which time we'll all get a look at opportunities gathered and presented by this management team and shared with you. No doubt there will be some changes, largely dealing with sharpening our management effectiveness, and incorporating the thoughtfulness of all employees. I am hopeful we will lay the groundwork for an actionable and forward-looking strategic direction, which my successor can polish and implement.

"It is my nature to ask a lot of questions. That is how I learn and how I most readily understand new challenges, cultures, and work environments. Don't read a lot into the questions. I have the responsibility for moving us forward and I will do it from a platform of understanding, collaboration, and accountability.

"Along the way, we will have some fun with the great exhilaration that comes from a shared endeavor producing successful results. You have moved us well along to that end. I come to continue that journey with you and to begin to prepare us for what will come after our victory.

"I'll be holding meetings starting today to get acquainted and to begin my education. I ask for your cooperation and goodwill—and you can be assured of mine. I am proud of you and your achievements, and I expect you to be proud of me as your interim leader, as well.

"I'm open for questions. Don't be bashful—I'm an open guy with a sense of humor."

So began John's next adventure, borne of his passion for the university and his instinct to run toward the fire rather than away. While he sensed change would take some time for staff, he saw the amount of work before him and wasted little time getting to it.

Work started early, too.

He arrived most days at 5:30 a.m., far ahead of anyone else. That would be his pattern for the eight months, a practice that required him to be up at 4 a.m. every day in Omaha.

His presence initially startled the receptionist, Patti Fischer, when she showed up a couple of hours later. Eight months later, with John packing to leave the Foundation, Fischer thanked him in a note for "putting us back together."

John went right to work. Within a couple of weeks, he had developed a data analytics plan for the Foundation. It was designed to "implement business methods that are used to model complicated and hard-to-measure activities, such as why people give or what conditions lead to greater employee productivity." Using what he knew from years of running *World-Herald* companies, John sought to work on the Foundation's organizational structure—it had, in his seasoned opinion, too many layers of administration, not enough worker bees.

He found, inexplicably, 151 employees shoehorned into 134 job classifications. There were 20 departments and 40 supervisors. IT was all over the place, supporting 250 users including some part-time and phone-a-thon people, 350 indirect connections, 400 laptops, PCs and iPads, and 100 iPhones.

Besides cleaning up what he referred to as this "(dis) organization" in a memo to a Blue Cross executive concerning the Foundation's employee handbook, John clarified his focus. It included plans to develop performance incentive plans for employees, put together a budget, manage the maintenance of momentum built up in the Campaign for Nebraska, hire Gallup Research to conduct a workforce engagement study, lay the groundwork for a three-year strategic plan, which a permanent CEO would have as a guide, and find time to "teach, teach, teach" with "patience, patience, patience."

He understood that "teaching with patience" would need to continue long after he left, but he was adamant about starting immediately, to grow a "culture of owning our direction, not fire fighting."

John saw the need for cultural changes in large swaths of the Foundation's operation. Within a few days he put together a series of "observations and issues," dividing them into negative or positive categories. The negatives outnumbered the positives two to one, but remarkably—and through some dedicated and experienced top Foundation fundraisers—all outward indications and images of the NU Foundation remained quite good, even strong.

He identified fifteen areas that needed to be addressed immediately. They included intraoffice communication glitches, multiple and conflicting job titles and descriptions, tedious and costly processes that diminished productivity, and a difference between professionalism (or lack thereof) practiced in the office as opposed to outside the office.

He divided both the positive and negative into four columns: symptom, manifestation, result, cause. Identifying the cause of the problems was critical if he and the staff were to start addressing solutions. His organizational "flowchart" in the beginning was a dozen three-by-five cards on which he listed the jobs in each department and identified who worked for whom. This made it possible to pinpoint areas of overlap, inefficiency, duplication, anything that would be a barrier to the NU Foundation's hitting on all cylinders. It wasn't that he sought anyone's departure. He simply wanted to know what everyone did and how their work made them better. At his first managers' meeting he asked them, and in turn those whom they managed, to jot down on a piece of paper, "What do you get paid to do? And what percentage of your time is directly spent doing it?"

He told them more, by painting, as he called it, a picture of the future. The NU Foundation needed to be run like a business. "Severe business problems," he said, "require significant changes in how we operate. We need to develop and deliver solutions."

He told them he would restructure the organization within a couple of weeks to improve communication, direction and focus, accountability, and internal responses. "People here can make a difference," he told them. "My responsibility is to clearly lay out the structure, mission, and timeline. We will change only those things that need to be changed for the better."

John preached efficiency as it related to the demands on their time such as returning emails, meetings, and drop-by chats—all of which could get in the way of productive work. He focused on the horizontal structure, with too many job titles, some of which were ill-defined, and too many departments, some of which comprised only two or three employees. He cautioned that structure at some point needed to be re-evaluated. "This is that point in time," he said.

Progress was swift and resounding. At the March 6, 2012 briefing for the board of directors, John reported the details of his headway. He'd been at the Foundation offices twenty-three days, eight of which were Saturdays or Sundays. He had met and talked with every employee. He had instituted weekly meetings for the Foundation's twenty managers. He had held weekly meetings with Whitted, Ostergard, and University President J.B. Milliken. He had reviewed departments' "dependency" on one another. He had begun the process of hiring an HR consultant. He had met with development staff on campuses in Lincoln, Omaha, and Kearney. Significantly, he had removed all the alcohol from the office—a concern among many—and went about the normal business of a CEO, including correspondence and communications, especially with donors.

He reported that most employees were "hard-working, committed, and passionate," although some were perhaps dealing with grief, fear, or even a little guilt. Some of that was to be expected with an abrupt departure, and a newcomer, a stranger, now calling the shots. Other concerns in what John deemed "people issues" included using time wisely, accountability, and some gnawing matters in a few management slots.

John also was clear about what he needed from the board, most important of which was "a clear voice—relative to its expectations and support to make the (transition) better." He emphasized that he could and would get the Foundation back on track and refocused on its mission, but that he was not a miracle worker—only someone who could help "remove the obstacles that keep people from doing their best."

Eventually a new way of doing things—management and culture—began to show. The work of the staff continued and, whether it was the fruits of change, a new view from the corner office, or an embrace of a different way of doing things, progress was real for many employees.

Whatever disarray had caused the Foundation to stumble or stagnate, its fundraising—the Campaign for Nebraska— was nevertheless redirected to reach full stride on John's watch. Despite the obvious distractions, the Foundation raised nearly $165 million, the third highest amount ever. The Foundation was able to transfer $124 million of that to the university. While John was at the helm during only a portion of that fiscal year, he understood critical collaboration and teamwork—whether in the acquisition of a new business or in raising money to support an institution of higher learning. In an email to Foundation staff, John lauded the amount and told them, "I hope your department manager has passed along how proud I am of our fundraising success this year. I extend my personal thank-you for the dedication you demonstrated to produce yet another very successful year for the Foundation and, most important, the University of Nebraska."

Sometimes, office culture can be changed with a simple conversation, whether a walk through the pressroom, a sit-down with an editor, a pat on the back of a reporter, or, as Patti Fisher said clearly in her parting note to John when he left the Foundation, making sure everyone knew the value of his or her contribution to the whole: "I always enjoyed our little chats…. (They) opened the door for me to know it is possible that a president, whether interim or permanent, would take the time to visit with the front-desk person. Saying the front desk is an integral part of our office is one thing, but telling that person is a totally different thing. Believe me, comments like that go a very long way with me at least. I do believe that recognizing people one-on-one can boost how you feel about yourself and how you feel about the job you're doing. For me it lasts a lifetime."

Not everyone was on board with the culture change, and John replaced three staff members during his time at the Foundation. Nevertheless, by any reasonable measure—fundraising, efficiencies, or employee morale and attitude—things definitely improved for the Foundation.

That happened in the late summer of 2012. The NU Foundation board of directors chose Brian Hastings, an experienced fundraiser and executive at The Ohio State University Foundation, to be the next president/CEO of the Foundation. Experienced in transitions and handing over the reins, John started to move in that direction. His last day would be September 17, 2012.

Before then a flood of emails, notes, and cards arrived at John's desk, thanking him for his stewardship, leadership, and passion. They came from university officials, board members, campus chancellors, and, in particular, Foundation staff members, some of whom surely wondered and worried during the first week of February what the future was going to hold for them and for the Foundation.

John ordered in cupcakes for everyone and gathered the staff for one final meeting during which he thanked them for their work, their passion, their professionalism, and their commitment to the Foundation and the university.

"Thanks, a million," he told them, then held up a check he was donating to the University of Nebraska Foundation—a check for one million dollars. It was earmarked for staff excellence, including training and incentives.

Not bad from a guy who worked eight months for two dollars.

Which, he later told Whitted, he never received. When reminded in jest a few years later, Whitted reached for his wallet and paid the overdue bill on the spot.

TWELVE

Brick and Mortar, Service and Community

This word "builder" is an important one. John was a builder and a completely unselfish person on one level. On the level where it matters: When you stripped away all the things. He liked getting things done. You could count on him. He cared deeply about every community in which he was involved—the baseball diamond in Rushville, for example. He's done a lot of things in Omaha. My guess is he's still doing things in Sidney. He was a reliable community builder.

–BOB KERREY

In 1975, after only a month in Omaha, John found himself sitting across from Peter Kiewit, perhaps Omaha's most influential citizen and owner of the *Omaha World-Herald*. Kiewit had taken his family's masonry contracting partnership, founded by his father and uncle in 1884, and built it into Peter Kiewit Sons' (PKS), a powerful presence in the international construction arena. Among notable PKS projects were the Livestock Exchange Building in South Omaha in 1924—the company's first million-dollar contract—the Nebraska State Capitol Tower in 1927, the High Arctic Air Force Base at Thule, Greenland, in 1951, and the James Bay Hydro Project in northern Quebec in 1974.

Harold Andersen had recommended John to Kiewit as someone who could help with the establishment of a downtown center that the city's leadership believed would spur a civic revitalization. The idea was to provide a space at which downtown workers and residents could attend classes offered by local colleges and universities as well as receive services from selected state agencies.

"So, John," Peter Kiewit said, "Andy tells me you could get this done."

The industrialist would not be disappointed. John ably represented the *World-Herald* in a group that successfully developed the Downtown Education Center, later to be named after Kiewit. The experience deepened John's familiarity with a cross-section of Omaha's political and civic leadership— people with whom he would work on many other projects in the metro area. These people enhanced quality of life, moved the city forward in architecture and technology, and infused Omaha with a spirit of progress.

Much of John's involvement in capital projects was through his board membership at Heritage Services, a private fundraising group founded in 1989 by philanthropists Walter Scott and Robert Daugherty. John was one of the original board members. In its first thirty years, Heritage Services raised $1.1 billion for projects designed to improve the lives of Omahans, the core criterion for Heritage Services to become involved.

Institutions that received Heritage Services donor funds for all or a substantial part of their construction or improvement included the Orpheum Theater, Holland Performing Arts Center, Durham Museum, the Qwest Center (later to go by different names as naming rights changed hands), TD Ameritrade Baseball Park, and Baxter Arena at UNO.

Heritage Services donors were also instrumental in the construction of the Botanical Center and Conservatory at Lauritzen Gardens, the Salvation Army Kroc Center, the Strategic Air and Space Museum, the Do Space Center, the Veterans Affairs Omaha Ambulatory Center, and the Siena Francis Homeless Shelter. Other Heritage Services beneficiaries were Joslyn Art Museum, Creighton University, Omaha South and Central High Schools, Metropolitan Community College, the Peter Kiewit Institute at the University of Nebraska-Omaha, Opera Omaha, and the Henry Doorly Zoo and Aquarium.

John's work as vice president of the Heritage Services board for twenty-one years held him in good stead when the *Omaha World-Herald*, bursting at the seams from its corporate growth in the 1980s and 1990s, began to run out of office space. In 2006, the company purchased the sixteen-story Qwest Building across the street from World-Herald Square. This made possible the consolidation of the company's operations under one roof, which John believed was vital to its success. He also considered his downtown neighbors and his community in the process.

The entrance to the John Gottschalk Freedom Center.

Since the founding of its predecessor, the *Omaha World,* in 1885, the *World-Herald* had occupied four different homes before landing in the former Qwest Building. But always the newspaper was within a couple of blocks of the First National Bank and the Union Pacific headquarters. Together, for more than a century, these Omaha mainstays had nurtured a commitment to the health of the city's core. The *World-Herald* christened a new printing plant—downtown—in 2001. Not far away, First National Bank opened its forty-five-story downtown tower in 2002 and the Union Pacific followed a few blocks away two years later. John knew staying close was critical to the growth that was occurring in downtown Omaha. The three companies' effort was a critical cog in a rebirth of the city center and adjacent neighborhoods—a rebirth that included a surge in housing, retail opportunities, and entertainment venues.

Although Heritage Services provided a vehicle and structure for John to be part of tangible improvements throughout the Omaha community, three brick-and-mortar projects—one of which eventually bore his name—were especially emblematic of John's leadership in getting things done.

The Holland Performing Arts Center and Orpheum Theater

When Omaha Performing Arts Society President Joan Squires was first recruited to head the Omaha Performing Arts Center, the facility was mostly on the drawing board. The Holland Center, as it became known, existed only in the form of preliminary drawings and, more important, a concept. Squires had never met John Gottschalk, the board chair for the Omaha Performing Arts Society (OPAS). As president and CEO of the Phoenix Symphony, she lived in a place where winter required at most a sweater or light jacket in the evenings. Squires said a woman from the search firm OPAS was using called her about a "great" job. "I really didn't think I was going to leave, so I asked, 'Where is it?' And she said, 'No, no, no, let me tell you about the job.'"

Despite her beloved climate and location, Squires felt her attention being captivated by sketches and ideas. In time, she met in Phoenix with representatives from Omaha who discussed their preliminary plans with her. "I knew the vision was here for a new organization and this new building," she said.

John figured he could sell Squires on Omaha and OPAS, but he knew it wouldn't be easy. "To be honest, this was a big reach. She was chief executive of the Phoenix Symphony," he said. "She had a great reputation. She lived in a warm climate. But we offered her a big palette to paint upon."

He was right. Said Squires, "When I learned about what was being planned for Omaha Performing Arts and the Holland Center, and then met the leadership, and especially John, I knew I wanted to be part of that."

In 2002, she and her husband Thomas Fay, a gifted musician in his own right, made the move to Omaha. Her first winter in Nebraska was mild by any measure, prompting John to tell her that the Nebraska winters weren't as harsh as she might have heard. The next winter—she liked to remind him in later years—more than offset the tameness of the first.

What awaited her in Omaha was the ongoing renovation of the Orpheum Theater and the construction of the Holland Performing Arts Center. "They knew they needed an organization that would run both facilities and book the shows and make sure the venues were taken care of," she said. "We had a board of five at the time. I got a desk, a computer, and an assistant production manager at the Orpheum and that was it. And they said, 'Go!'"

The back story that created the Omaha Performing Arts Society would make any audience cheer, but perhaps not during its early chapters.

John was on the Omaha Symphony board in 1988 when the symphony's president invited him, other board members, and patrons to meet at the old Orpheum Theater in downtown Omaha. The Orpheum had opened in 1927, when vaudeville was all the rage. Live entertainment and big names became the theater's hallmark. Over the years, its stage featured Frank Sinatra and Bing Crosby belting out favorites, Broadway shows lighting up the nights, and Jerry Lewis making audiences roar with laughter. Before the Orpheum transitioned to a movie theater, Lewis was said to have been the last known live performer in 1961.

Eventually, neglect overtook history and the Orpheum closed in 1971. It sat empty until a local civic group, the Knights of Ak-Sar-Ben, bought it and pumped $2 million into its renovation. It re-opened in 1975. Soon afterward, the Knights offered the facility to the city with the provision that it be used for live stage plays and musical theater. During the next two decades under city management, singers, dancers, and drama graced the Orpheum's stage. But once again it fell into disrepair. That was how John found it when given a tour in 1998.

The tour eventually found itself in the Orpheum's "catacombs" below the stage. "It was a pit," John said. "It was embarrassing. It was shameful. The theater's amenities were badly outdated and in poor repair. This is a theater that seats twenty-five hundred. I had seen women in line to use only three restrooms. Paint was falling off the ceiling. The symphony president said to us, 'We need to do something about this—for Omaha.'"

About a year earlier, Dick Holland, philanthropist and consummate supporter of the arts, had been talking about putting together a better venue for the symphony. He had gone as far as to have drawings of a new hall prepared. John said that Dick's intentions were good as was his commitment—he was ready to write a check as a lead gift. But, to Dick's astonishment, nobody seemed interested in following his lead. John believed the performing arts scene in Omaha needed not simply a building but a comprehensive vision and a plan to execute it. Land acquisition and building plans would take time.

The tour of the Orpheum moved some minds, however. "With the kind of guys who were sitting there, you didn't have to say another word. Once we saw that it wasn't right for Omaha, we didn't want our town to look like that," John said. "So the first thing before the meeting broke up, questions arose about the city's responsibilities. I was the strongest voice on that matter. I made it clear that I didn't know how we were going to raise money to do this when we had already rehabbed it twice, only to see it fall backwards in the city's hands."

The Orpheum not only had structural problems tracing to inadequate maintenance; it also had inefficiencies related to its management. Its booking schedule for everything from rock shows to large meetings and cooking schools tied up the stage for nearly 330 days out of 365, which often prevented Broadway shows—the big money-makers—from staying more than three days.

In addition to physical and scheduling issues, the Orpheum's acoustics were far below average, not the type of venue entertainers sought while planning national tours. The result was an ornate, historic theater in disrepair with no plans and no readily-available resources to undo the ongoing structural neglect and the withering inertia of inattention.

"You couldn't fix the Orpheum enough to make it a good symphony hall," John said. "You don't have Broadway because you don't have enough open time. So, the thing on the table that took about three nanoseconds to see was that unless we could get control from the city, we weren't going anywhere. Well, I was the one yammering about it. So I said I'd be glad to see what we could do."

John met with Mayor Hal Daub, convincing him that the governance structure was working against improvement of the Orpheum but adding that the city should remain a participant. Daub agreed to lease the building. The question was to whom? The answer to that question led to the beginning of one of Omaha's true civic success stories, the Omaha Performing Arts Society.

"We formed the Omaha Performing Arts Society just because we needed some name that sounded okay at the spur of the moment, so that's what it was. Next we needed to talk to the city council," John said.

They met with council members in groups of two or three, avoiding a quorum as this was merely a fact-finding and temperature-taking mission. The purpose was to gauge interest and commitment in OPAS managing the Orpheum and developing a plan to make Dick Holland's dream a reality. The meetings took place at the Orpheum. To get an accurate accounting, John devised a five-question test.

He started by telling the council members that OPAS was willing to address the theater's problems as well as move forward on a separate facility—an acoustically superior performance hall. The first question was, "Does the Orpheum fully serve the needs of Omaha in its present state? Yes or no?" He was looking for three "yes" responses and two negative replies. The answer to this first question was a sure no. "Is renovation going to require a significant investment of money?" (Yes.) "Does the city have the money and a desire to invest it?" (No.) "Do you want others to invest their money?" (Yes.) "Are you willing to change the governance to have this all happen?" (Amid some ambiguity, John got his third yes.)

At the time, the city had been running an annual loss of $500,000 on Orpheum operations. Its funds were insufficient to address the renovation needs. Knowing the amount of work that lay before it, OPAS put together a memorandum of understanding that would allow the council enough cover to appropriate funds to move everything along. The mayor could then mark those funds as a capital obligation. Meanwhile, OPAS had its eye on a former Campbell Soup factory, now sitting idle.

The OPAS plan: First, restore the Orpheum to its original and stunning self, using it primarily to stage Broadway shows. Then, when the theater was up and running, use the soup company property to build a performance hall with an acoustical reputation that would create a buzz among international entertainers and audiences. OPAS wanted the big booking agencies to jostle for the opportunity to add Omaha to their tours.

The first question was who was going to pay for the Orpheum's rehab and a concert hall of extraordinary sound quality and visual beauty. The city threw in $15 million, mostly for site acquisition and clearing. This left OPAS to raise, as estimated, $85 million. That privately-funded number rose to $104 million before construction started. Dick Holland, true to his word and his love of the arts, gave the lead gift.

John was convinced that raising enough money to resurrect the Orpheum one more time would be difficult, so OPAS wedded the projects in a fungible pot of money designed to respond to the question, "Do you want to solve the performing arts problem?"

"We started by getting on with the Orpheum renovation," John said. "For one thing, it carried most everything that came to Omaha, and it was booked except in the summer when you had at least a little slack time. So, you really had to get after it. Our OPAS group got together what was needed in order to go on at the Orpheum and we started there. Then Joan arrived."

Squires's arrival was a step forward for the performing arts in Omaha. She immediately began booking shows, and the new look and feel of the Orpheum did the rest, making it a must stop for national tours. Having Squires in the driver's seat proved exceptionally valuable. She had earned her own national reputation and shortly after arriving became a member of an informal Broadway business board. The Orpheum became highly successful for OPAS as well as the touring companies.

John said that later, with the Orpheum at full speed and the Holland coming on line, the touring companies were calling Omaha, just as hoped. "Joan got a call from a Broadway producer. The guy said, 'I don't know what's going on in Omaha, but you guys are doing spectacular work out there.' The Orpheum and the Holland were mainstays in the top ten or so for percentage of sellouts, and even on the world stage, they were showing up in the top twenty. So when they booked shows in here, obviously these producers were doing well. I told people that most Broadway shows arrive in three semis, except in Omaha, they bring four. One is to take the money out."

Omaha Performing Arts President Joan Squires amid the
magnificence of the Holland Performing Arts Center.

As OPAS members traveled the country looking at venues for ideas to build into the new hall, a crucial, six-word juncture occurred on a plane as John, Walter Scott, Heritage Services President Sue Morris, and a few others were flying back from Cerritos, California. The group was nearing completion of the performing arts center plan, ready to move forward, hoping that a path still lay before them.

John remembered the six words, calling them the most empowering words in Omaha. "We were traveling back on Walter's plane, and we were around a conference table and had the plan laid out. We were talking about our western swing. Walter sat back in his chair and said, 'I think we can do this.' Six words. He didn't say 'I'll give you a lot of money.' He said, 'I think we can do this.' And the eyes flashed around the table and we were in business."

For Squires, it was those six words and more. It was about leadership, particularly from John.

"John's vision was to elevate the performing arts to the next level for the community and the region," she recalled. "He had the ability to see the big picture for the city and the region and the citizens. And everything that he devoted to it was for the greater good. He knew we needed a first-class concert hall. He knew that the symphony needed the support of good acoustics. Plus there were other performances to bring in. And the fact remained that we had a responsibility to take care of the Orpheum, which had fallen into disrepair."

She said John's high standards pushed the quality of the Holland Performing Arts Center with its magnificent acoustics and beautiful architecture. He understood what it took to really be one of the best concert halls in the country.

"John had the vision—and Dick Holland's support—to have renowned architects of New York be part of the project, to make sure that everything was at the highest level, to ensure that the Orpheum was being cared for and would bring in the top performing arts and Broadway shows. I mean he always, always had a deep and abiding commitment to achieving the highest level. Coupled with that was the fiscal responsibility our organization needed to demonstrate we were responsible to our budgets, to the donors… so that we were being responsible stewards. Working with John was a tremendous opportunity. His strategic ability is unparalleled."

John liked to say acoustics was about 95 percent engineering and 5 percent luck. The brilliance of architect James Polshek and acoustician Larry Kirkegaard produced Holland's interior walls buffered with a gap between them and the main structure to arrest noise from elsewhere inside the building. Cloth banners helped control reverberation and turned down the "brightness" of the sound. Windows were thick enough to prevent any tumult from downtown Omaha invading the hall.

OPAS put sound quality at the forefront of its expectations for the Holland, and John found out early on to what extent both silence and sound had been engineered to near perfection. One afternoon he was in his office across the street from the Holland. The center was six months from completion. The phone rang. His presence was requested. "They were getting ready to test the HVAC system," he said. "Moving air is a big deal. It's noisy. And, you've got to move enough air to fill your hall. So you have to have it, in our case, underneath. So, beneath the hall is a plenum, as big as the hall above it. The air goes up. In older buildings, and not good acoustical buildings, it tends to whistle and make noise. We couldn't have that."

The idea was to allow the sound from the stage to be as spectacular in the last row of the balcony as it was in the front row of the main floor seats. John hurried across the street. Technicians had set sound-measuring devices throughout the hall. The space in the main hall was without seats and other furnishings, but the curved sidewalls, part of the acoustical engineering, were already in place.

Acousticians explain the Holland Center's sound engineering to John
during construction. The Holland's acoustics are regarded among
the best in the world, according to performers and audiences.

"The acoustician was there, the architect was there, HDR (Omaha's internationally known engineering and design firm) was there, Sue Morris and I were there. We gathered around this circular opening about the size of a campfire. In the middle was a highly, highly sophisticated device that measures sound. These guys had walkie talkies and before we could start they had to shut down one last worker hammering on the other side of the building. When at last the building fell silent we were told, 'Okay, we're ready. Please don't speak, just look at the needle.' We were riveted to this needle. And the guy says, 'Okay, turn it on.'"

That meant starting to move two hundred thousand cubic feet of air up into the building. It was a tense moment. OPAS and its donors had a $100 million stake on how little the needle would move. What seemed like an eternity, but was probably at most fifteen seconds, elapsed and the needle remained motionless. Uneasiness continued. The acoustician got back on the walkie-talkie and said, again, "Turn it on." A voice on the other end said, "It is on."

They ran many more tests including bringing in audiences to put the acoustics through their paces. Each time the sound was extraordinary in every corner of the place. By the time construction was completed in September 2005, the Holland Performing Arts Center had two halls, the Peter Kiewit Concert Hall and The Suzanne and Walter Scott Recital Hall. The Holland glimmered in the light of downtown Omaha, a spectacular new beauty awaiting only performers and audiences.

They showed up a month later on opening night, October 21, when the final acoustical exam took place, this time under the supervision of the legendary Tony Bennett, headliner for the evening.

Welcoming a packed house on opening night of
the Holland Performing Arts Center.

Bennett told the packed house, "This is a beautiful, beautiful place you've got. It's one of the finest places in the country. You know, acoustics is a wonderful thing. When artists come into a hall, they want to give you the best they've got. And they consciously try everything in their power, in my case, to project out of this mouth, the best sound I can.

And I want you to hear my best sound. So, I like to be in halls that take care of my sound on its way from me to you."

With that, Bennett asked the stage crew to shut off the sound system. He called over a guitarist. For the next five minutes the singer, accompanied only by the guitar, mesmerized two thousand sets of ears and hearts with no boost from the sound system, just the acoustical excellence of the Holland. Afterward the crowd rose and cheered, the sound engulfing the Holland. Sue Morris, who was watching the far reaches of the balcony during Bennett's song, told John, "The first people on their feet when he finished were up there."

The Holland has been packing them in ever since. Bennett was one of many artists and entertainers who travelled the globe yet continued to reach out to the Holland, hoping to make it part of their tour. To keep up, OPAS put another $20 million into the hall in the first fifteen years. It also put an additional $10 million into the Orpheum, which had been hosting Broadway shows and regularly filling its seats.

Between the two, according to Squires, the performing arts in Omaha became a staple of a vibrant city. "We continue to upgrade and invest and improve, just to ensure that the venues reflect the quality of the arts that are on the stages," she said. "We have performances that reach into all parts of this community and engage all backgrounds, ethnicities, and socioeconomics. The buildings are here for everybody. There are people who love the Orpheum, and we continue to invest in that. We celebrated the ninetieth anniversary of the Orpheum in 2018, and we will have invested over $20 million dollars in that facility since we assumed responsibility."

OPAS became the largest arts organization in the state, sponsoring the Nebraska High School Performing Arts Competition at the Holland. In its first twelve years, John said the Holland Performing Arts Center had hosted nearly four million patrons and students—one of whom had a very special audience for a brief trumpet solo.

Doc Severinsen was playing the Holland, so John, who tried in the beginning to meet with every performer and bring a bit of Nebraska hospitality to their stay, invited Severinsen to have lunch with him at the Holland's Founders Room. Joining John and Severinsen were the director of the Omaha youth symphony, one of her young musicians, and Joan Squires. During a discussion about "what was music, what was noise," Severinsen said, "If I had my way, every child at the age of six would be strapped to a chair to have them listen to Mahler's entire Fifth Symphony." Others at the table laughed.

After lunch, John and Squires walked Severinsen to the concert hall where he was scheduled to complete a microphone check. As they entered the back of the hall, they were met by the young musician standing on stage. He said, "Mr. Severinsen, I'd like to play something for you."

Severinsen said, "That would be fine."

So, without a bit of music, just trumpet in hand, plenty of air in his lungs, and enough moxie to impress an international star, he belted out the fanfare to Mahler's Fifth Symphony. John said, "Doc loved it. And the kid lit up like a Christmas tree."

Obviously, when John and OPAS unveiled their grand vision—resuscitate the Orpheum and make it profitable *and* build a concert hall with a sterling international reputation— some pushback came immediately. Not everyone held Walter Scott's six-word conviction. John remembered the naysayers' lament. It was not unlike the complaints he had heard decades earlier about a young guy wanting to build another interstate interchange in Sidney, a plan some local downtown businesses said, would surely destroy the town.

"They called it folly to think we could remodel the Orpheum, build the Holland, and create a model to use them in tandem. There's no market for this, they said. We're too small. We can't have that kind of stuff. I don't know what they were thinking down there. So we stood against the wind and kept moving."

For Squires, the Orpheum Theater and the Holland Performing Arts Center represented the best of the city she called "a deep-rooted community, (where) people wanted to make the right things happen for the greater good of the community."

She knew, too, that citizens like John Gottschalk, Walter Scott, and Dick Holland, were part of a team, and that others responded to their leadership. She especially felt that John, who led both projects, also believed in and respected the ideas of others. The results were two arts success stories.

"You know, John did have a lot of ideas," she said. "He communicated well. John's leadership style is primarily listening, not talking. But he also ran a wonderful board meeting and valued and appreciated the input from the other board members. We had a very committed board—and basically the original board members stayed with us. We've added to that board over the years. People valued and respected John's leadership. Some people don't stay with you all those years if there are challenges. Yes, John fills the space, but he also puts a great team together and understands you need a lot of people to make these organizations work."

She was clear, too, that Omaha's performing arts belonged to the community. The community and more responded in OPAS's first two decades. "We have elevated the arts community, have brought a new energy and focus to it and have had a huge impact. We reach 350,000 to 400,000 people a year.... It's extraordinary progress. We have a $40 million annual economic impact."

Dick and Mary Holland, the lead donors and namesake for the magnificent Holland Center for the Performing Arts, understood whose building it was, too. Inscribed prominently inside was their wish: "All who come here, listen, reflect, dream, cry, cheer. This hall belongs to you."

According to Squires, donors were legion and the board remained financially supportive as well. She said leadership from John and others gave those supporters a confidence that their money was getting the result for which it was given. "People contribute to organizations because they know there's a strong leader in place. John represented that. They want to know that their funds are being well used, a fiduciary responsibility is in place, and a vision exists to meet the mission and serve the community. Certainly under John's leadership we continued to keep moving into the next level." Soon after it opened, the Holland Performing Arts Center, already receiving widespread attention as an acoustical triumph, graced the pages of *Architecture Review*. The publication called it a "serious building but a welcoming one. Muscle and finesse nicely balanced, vertical and horizontal, right angle and diagonal, light and dark. And Omaha now has one of the country's best-sounding new concert halls."

On opening night, just after intermission and the second half opening piece by Branford Marsalis and the Omaha Symphony, actor Danny Glover took the stage to introduce John. John started his remarks by establishing to whom the magnificent building belonged: "How do *you* like your new Peter Kiewit Concert Hall and the Holland Performing Arts Center?" he asked the audience. He paid tribute to the brick and mortar geniuses that put the Holland on the national entertainment venue map: "Omaha's own HDR formed a pre-eminent design team, including, Polshek Partnership Architects, Kierkegaard Associates (acousticians), Fischer Dachs Associates (lighting and staging). The design was brought to life by the craftsmanship of Kiewit construction and its subcontractors."

After a series of thank-yous to the project leaders and those who made opening night a true benchmark in Omaha city history, he turned his thoughts to community. "The Holland has something for everyone. As I reach the end of my journey through this phase of this grand project, I thank many friends and supporters who cheered us along as each hurdle was conquered, who applauded our daily victories, and whose constructive interest helped make this project a grand success. Thanks also for all of you who have been so generous in your praise of this wonderful result. I applaud you!"

∼

The Freedom Center

The *Omaha World-Herald* on Friday, August 31, 2001, featured a banner across the top of the front page which read, "Final Goss Press Run."

Few readers understood the significance of the headline or the occasion. But for John Gottschalk and the employees of the newspaper—past and present—August 31, 2001, and September 1, 2001, were transformational moments in the history of the *Omaha World-Herald*.

The newspaper was retiring its three, hulking letterpress Goss presses, fifty-three years old and well past their prime. For several decades they had been kept running with spare parts and, when the supply of those ran dry, by the wisdom and ingenuity of *World-Herald* machinists and pressmen.

Letterpress was literally the printing method for the ages, five hundred years old. It employed raised inked letters pressing against a surface to produce a reversed image. While metal type was most often associated with letterpress, printers had also used wood or stone blocks. The industrial development of massive rotary presses fueled the progress in newspaper production. The Goss presses at the *World-Herald* had printed more than four billion newspapers. But the sheer antiquity of the presses had made them increasingly impractical as the mainstay of the *World-Herald*'s seven daily editions. The potential for a catastrophic failure was not far from John's consciousness beginning with his very first days at the *World-Herald*. The presses were surviving day-to-day, part-to-part. The *World-Herald* had become the largest market for Goss parts in the country. "Our basement was littered with parts as our machinists kept those babies running. It was an amazing feat. Those presses went out in 2001, but they should have been out of there by at least 1970," he said. The Goss presses, which never missed one day of duty, were eventually sold for scrap.

John's sense of history and legacy was on full display the weekend the *World-Herald* shut down the old presses and fired up the new ones. He invited all former pressmen—some spanning a couple of generations—to be part of the final press run. It was a retirement party of sorts for the Goss presses. Many took him up on the offer. He told them as they gathered in the press room, "As much as we're looking forward to turning on the new presses, when you silence a press—when you darken it forever—it's almost a spiritual moment. As important as the machines were, they were nothing without their skilled operators. We cannot honor these machines without honoring those men who tamed them, repaired them, made them sing, and, on occasion, cursed them. I say, well done."

Russ Lambert, who spent nearly fifty years as a pressman and to whom John gave the honor of shutting down the Goss presses for the last time, told an industry trade journal that the change was necessary. "Running a press isn't about printing a product. It's about the teamwork and the other people on the press. It's what you go through every day to get the paper out." Of the *World-Herald*'s presses, he said, "We used wood shims to keep them in registration. Those old machines have done their duty. It's time for them to go to sleep."

On September 1, 2001, a new era began. Housed in the *World-Herald*'s state-of-the-art Freedom Center were three MAN Roland Geoman offset presses made in Germany and able to print seventy-five thousand newspapers an hour. Checking in at 1,661 tons and five stories high, the web offset presses, the gold standard in newspapers, were nonetheless sleek and stylish compared to the 300-ton Goss behemoths.

Offset, also called offset lithography, produced higher quality and more consistent images than letterpress. Its process transferred (offsets) images from metal plates onto rubber "blankets" on rollers and then, in the *World-Herald*'s case, onto newsprint. Because the newsprint did not touch the metal plates, the life of the plates was extended.

The Freedom Center's spectacular new technology replaced the old Goss presses, which printed millions of pages of newspapers.

In "web" offset printing, found at metropolitan newspapers and other high-volume printing operations, larger, higher-speed machines were used. These were fed with large rolls of paper, creating a web that ends at a folder where the pages were separated and trimmed. Web offset was efficient and cost effective for newspapers, whose content changed with each printing and requires high volume outputs.

The Freedom Center presses came with stunning technological capabilities, spurred by six thousand synchronized motors controlled by six computer consoles. They were frequently in motion, printing, in addition to the *World-Herald*, two daily newspapers and five weekly newspapers.

Perhaps even more impressive was the system of handling material built into the Freedom Center's operation. The material handling center was built to house three thousand rolls of newsprint, each roll ten miles long. Railroad cars delivered newsprint inside the material handling center.

The MAN Roland III double-wide press at the John Gottschalk Freedom Center is five stories tall and can print seventy-five thousand newspapers in an hour. When it opened in 2001, the Freedom Center was at the national forefront in newspaper production and printing.

The center was connected to the printing plant via a tunnel running under downtown Omaha's 13th Street. A robotic shuttle system retrieved paper rolls and inserts as needed. Human hands did not touch the newsprint until, in the form of individual newspapers, it was handled by five thousand carriers throughout the city and far beyond.

John's description of the process revealed a leading-edge technology. Machines not only did the heavy lifting, but also handled the accounting for every column inch of newsprint once it was delivered to the material handling center. "The roll of newsprint comes into the storage area, and the outside label on the cardboard wrapper is scanned so we know the weight of the thing, the number of the roll, and so on. Nobody has touched it. Nobody is writing on it. It's scanned, a sticker is made and slapped on."

That information on the sticker took its rightful place in the computer system's memory. A large crane then picked up the roll and moved it to the storage racks among dozens of other rolls, all safely and accurately catalogued in the system according to weight and quality. As each day's production was mapped out, the computers calculated the particular edition's needs: X amount of standard rolls, perhaps Y amount of short rolls, perhaps Z amount of particularly high-quality newsprint for section fronts and high-color pages.

The crane went to the storage center, read the bar codes and brought down the specific roll that was needed for production, placed it on a trolley that ran underneath 13th Street to the press room on 14th Street. John never tired of describing the process. "The trolley stopped. There's a machine that removed the wrapping. The roll of newsprint was still not touched. A robot arrived and picked it up, took it over to the press and slid it on, threading it into the web. Still not touched. It printed the paper, which then went through a series of elevator conveyors to get the printed papers up to the top. The papers then went through bundling and tying, down the spiral, into the bundled paper rack, which has wheels. The trucks are all lined up at the deck. The racks are pushed into the waiting trucks, so the paper gets touched by the guy who takes the bundle and that's it."

Anticipation of the Freedom Center's coming online was palpable at World-Herald Square for many weeks. John planned its opening celebration, attended by two thousand people. Former Secretary of State James Baker was the keynote speaker. John's five-year-old grandson, Austin, threw the switch to start the presses. The newspapers, which ran on September 1, 2001, carried with them the first redesign of the *World-Herald* in eleven years, including more color to show off the musculature and finesse of the new presses.

John had put together a team who collaborated on the Freedom Center, the new presses, and the transition into reality on September 1. Those closest to the front lines were John's eventual successor, Vice-President Terry Kroeger, the project manager; Production Manager Kristy Gerry was in charge of the massive number of integrations necessary to pull off the transition; Managing Editor Deanna Sands led the redesign project; and of course Donna Grimm, John's long-time and meticulous assistant, aided by Joel Long, the paper's community relations guru, on point when it came time to put together a celebration worthy of the moment in *World-Herald* history.

Baker's speech was particularly moving, perhaps even more so when weighed against the events of September 11, 2001, just a few days after the dedication. For John, the former secretary of state touched a nerve sometimes forgotten not only by readers of newspapers but also by those who produce them. "(The speech) was a discussion about freedom. It still rings in my ears. Never let someone convince you to trade security for freedom. Yet, just a few days later on 9/11, we were going through metal scanners and doing all kinds of things."

The dedication of the Freedom Center was completed five months later with a cornerstone-laying ceremony including the installation of a time capsule to be opened in twenty years. The capsule contained essays by judges, lawyers, and journalists underscoring the ideas and values associated with freedom; a flag of the *USS Nebraska*; the results of an essay contest for schoolchildren; memorabilia from Omaha's Henry Doorly Zoo; and a letter from John to his grandson, a "message for the future."

John had invited *World-Herald* readers to submit items to be placed in the time capsule. One of the most valued donations came from Jim Slater of Omaha. It was a union pin Slater had inherited from his grandfather, William J. Scott. As the story came down to Slater, his grandfather was the pressman for the old *Omaha Herald*. One day in 1889, Scott was told that the *Herald* had been sold to a competitor, the *Omaha World*. Thus, the task fell upon him to operate the press for the first edition of the new *Omaha World-Herald*. There could hardly have been an item in the capsule more symbolic of the *World-Herald*'s continuity from the nineteenth century to the twenty-first.

James Baker was the keynote speaker at the opening of the Freedom Center, the *Omaha World-Herald*'s state-of-the-art production plant. The plant was later named the John Gottschalk Freedom Center.

While the Freedom Center's technology and state-of-the-art systems were the envy of newspapers across the country, its inception was long overdue, John realized. With presses decades past their prime and reproduction getting "muddier" every year, he saw early on that replacing the presses would be critical to the *World-Herald*'s future. John said that although advertisers were not leaving, the general marketing movement was towards more powerful messaging, using color and reproduction unavailable in the old Goss system.

Weighing against that ever-increasing demand for action was employee ownership. "The fact is that we were going to invest millions of dollars in presses, but this wasn't somebody else's money. This wasn't an amorphous corporation. In an employee-owned company, this was you and me. And, if we're going to incur that demand on our profitability and, ergo, our stock growth, it would have quite a substantial effect," he said. The effect would be felt greatest among those with the most stock, many of whom—including John—had moved higher up in the company to places where major decisions were made.

Nevertheless, the decision to sink $125 million into the Freedom Center was John's, "The only place it was made," as he put it. He faced mandatory retirement in seven years, which would have been fine if they could pay off the presses over twenty or thirty years, but no deal like that was in the offing. His assets, too, were in play.

"The need to improve our product and our processes just lingered and lingered," John said. "And it was not going to solve itself. So, you've got to make a decision. I had the choice to kick the can down the road to another generation—or take the bull by the horns."

There was no serious pushback even though many of the primary stockholders were executives with whom he worked every day. "Everybody knew the jig was up. The idea of better reproduction, better speed, better deadlines, were all plusses. This was all opportunity."

The Freedom Center was on the drawing board for five years. It was partly a creature of the *World-Herald*'s need to move its technology into the twenty-first century and partly for the advancement of a vision that would move downtown Omaha forward. The *World-Herald*, with the First National Bank of Omaha and Union Pacific, anchored a twenty-eight-square block swath that was ripe for redevelopment in downtown Omaha. Their commitment to the core city was preserved in brick and mortar.

In 2008, working in a benign conspiracy and cone of silence, a group of *World-Herald* employees and friends outside the newspaper surprised John with a retirement "parade" party at the Embassy Suites in suburban LaVista. Lured to the hotel on the premise of dinner with friends, John soon found himself watching as a cavalcade of well-wishers representing every facet of his life as a consummate newspaperman, captain of business, philanthropist, and leader on national and local nonprofit boards.

Omaha World-Herald building (in the foreground), Union Pacific Headquarters in the center, and First National Bank Tower to the left.

Part of the Gottschalk family enjoying the
"parade" at John's retirement party.

Terry Kroeger, by then John's successor, was the parade's
"grand marshal" and host. Toward the end of the festivities
Kroeger announced that the newspaper had thought long
and hard about a gift to honor John. "We really scratched
our heads and struggled with what to do. Finally we came up
with an elegantly simple solution. From now on that building
(he was pointing to a photo of the Freedom Center), will be
known as the John Gottschalk Freedom Center."

John later admitted that putting his name on a building
was "not his style," conceding that some people see him more
as a "community guy or a publisher than just a raw newspaper
man. And I think my journalism, true journalism, as well
as business credentials, are just fine. I think I've always felt
comfortable I provided the right leadership. I think people
who worked at the *World-Herald* with me and for me respected
me and my ability to bring consensus to keep moving forward
instead of stopping and yammering. I made a lot of decisions
without going down to the last nut. With the Freedom Center
I could see the problem just as big as right smack in front of
you. So we built a new facility."

That facility was eventually called the John Gottschalk Freedom Center, even if its namesake—who appreciated the sentiment—would have never made that choice.

∾

Baxter Arena

Two days into John's temporary gig as interim president and CEO of the University of Nebraska Foundation he discovered a "contract" involving developers related to a parcel of Foundation-owned land near UNO, the University of Nebraska at Omaha. John's predecessor at the Foundation had agreed to a deal whereby the developers could buy the parcel from the Foundation and build a big box store—or anything else, apparently—if the university hadn't built on the land within two years. That deadline was drawing near. The developers had notified the Foundation that the new CEO needed to sign the document "right away."

John had no idea what any of this meant. Still, although it was only his second day at the Foundation, it was not his first rodeo. His instincts—honed from years on boards and as CEO of a major corporation—broke out the red flags. He knew a couple of things right away: He was not about to sign something blindly, and he was none too taken with the developers' concept. He knew Omaha. He knew the land in question, which was adjacent to the teeming new developments at Ak-Sar-Ben Village, should not be relinquished without serious study.

"I get to looking at this, and I'm thinking I'm here as a fiduciary, among other things, of the University of Nebraska's property," he said. "This was a document, a contractual document. It said if we don't build something there, the land use would ultimately default to this commercial development."

John had heard rumblings about the site in question. The ice hockey landscape in Omaha was changing. Mayor Jim Suttle had announced that the aging Omaha Civic Auditorium, with its insatiable appetite for maintenance costs, would close in 2014, two short years away. The popular UNO hockey team played most of its games at the sixteen-thousand-seat CenturyLink but practiced at the Civic. It was a tenuous arrangement. Given cost and availability, CenturyLink was not suitable for the team to use for practice and, realistically, was simply too large a venue for home games. Without a dedicated place to practice and unable to fill CenturyLink, UNO was looking for a single solution to a pair of problems. It was interested in putting a new ice arena near the campus and near Ak-Sar-Ben Village, which was already intertwined with the university because of geography.

John knew a big box store would not be a good fit given the direction the neighborhood was moving. Instead of signing the contract, he called one of the principals and said, "I've got this piece of paper down here that apparently needs to be signed today. I'm not so sure I ought to be signing it because I don't know enough about it. At a minimum, I don't know how or why you all negotiated this thing into a two-year standstill. I don't feel at all comfortable about that."

Then he called the chairman of the Foundation board. The chairman was unaware of the arrangement, which did not surprise John. Together, they decided to sign the document but only after extending by one year the deadline for action. John was grateful for the time and for the chance to end any exclusive relationship, real or implied. "I told the developers that the land would not automatically default to them. All it meant was that if we didn't build, we would create an opening where if they wanted to make an offer, they could. I said that's the best I could do for them."

The site was eventually to have a building, but it was, as John described it, "a difficult birth."

A few weeks later, John was asked to attend a Foundation staff meeting in Lincoln about a new ice arena. As it turned out, to John's bemusement, the staff artist had called the meeting to show off a rough version of a marketing piece for a hockey arena. John soon learned that few details had been decided.

He said, "I was looking at this rough brochure and there was no copy or anything. I said I understand that this is a new thing, but how many seats is this arena going to have? And somebody said five thousand. Then somebody else said it was going to have four thousand. Then another person said between two thousand and twenty-five hundred."

Wondering if this was simply another "vast project springing from a half-vast idea." John had other questions, not the least of which was: What was going on? How could you have a brochure on a new arena with indeterminate capacity? He asked the dozen staffers at the meeting where the arena was going to be built. He asked if they had a site picked out. The answer was no. Nor could they answer with much specificity how much an arena would cost. After they fumbled from $84 million to $100 million to $60 million, they admitted they really didn't have any costs pinned down.

John summed up what he had heard: "Okay, let me see what this meeting's about. We're going to prepare a sales brochure about why somebody ought to donate money to build some kind of ice facility the size, place, use, and cost of which is totally unknown. Why are we having this meeting?"

The group could not argue with his assessment. Or as John liked to tell it, "You'll keep running red lights until somebody steps in front of you."

John left the meeting still in the dark and didn't hear about the ice arena for nearly a year. Then he was asked to become involved, along with the UNO chancellor, the NU president and the Ak-Sar-Ben Trust board, an eventuality that precipitated a battle between two passionate forces.

At the behest of "outsiders" such as John and university president J.B. Milliken, the "insiders"—developers—held a meeting and invited others interested in the project. The hosts proceeded to offer up a PowerPoint presentation showing a crude layout of buildings on university property—not a square foot of which they owned. Once again John asked questions, which were once again answered without specifics as to what the rectangular shapes on the screen represented. The gist? "Well, we'll get it worked out."

John's earlier skepticism was proving prophetic.

About that time, the lid came off. University of Nebraska Regent Howard Hawks, who had not been at the meeting, was none too pleased when he heard the developers' particulars. The result was an impasse between the university and the Ak-Sar-Ben Trust. Neither could agree on a way forward for the land in question. It was prime real estate for a university structure, but also either an asset for a growing Ak-Sar-Ben Village—or a headache, depending on traffic, access, and aesthetics.

In 2013, a new entity, the UNO Arena Development Corporation, was formed to reconcile the competing interests, chaired by Regent Hawks and including John, Ken Stinson from the board of the Ak-Sar-Ben Trust, and UNO Chancellor John Christensen. UNO Athletic Director Trev Alberts and Heritage Services CEO Sue Morris worked closely with the group. Heritage Services saw an ice arena with a public access component as worthy of its time and money. Jean Stothert, who was elected mayor the same year the UNO Arena Development Corporation came into being, pledged $1 million out of the same fund former mayor Hal Daub had used to help seed the Orpheum Theater renovation and the Holland Performing Arts Center building.

Eventually, the university and the Ak-Sar-Ben Trust came to an understanding as to who would get what and for what. The university bonded its end of the costs. Heritage Services raised $40 million of the $90 million project.

What eventually became Baxter Arena, naming rights to which were sold to a group of Omaha area auto dealerships for $4 million, opened October 23, 2015. The arena had two sheets of ice: one for UNO hockey games—quite popular in Omaha—and a second for a UNO practice facility, which doubled as a public skating venue. While Baxter Arena was also home to UNO men's and women's basketball teams, its volleyball team, concerts, and a number of area high school graduations, its community ice sheet won a devoted following in Omaha.

The Baxter Arena saga was a near-accidental board membership for John, whose simple but frank questions helped to steer the arena into the right context and eventually into responsible hands in order to be conceived, designed, built, and, most important, enjoyed by the public.

Still, the project opened John's eyes, indicating to him that the undertaking of community development was changing in Omaha: the players, the process, the point. Not that Omaha stopped growing and progressing, but John sensed a difference from past projects.

"For me, Baxter Arena was a turning point," he said.

THIRTEEN

A Learned Compassion

John has touched a lot of people. We have better community leaders because of him. He and Carmen both have been role models. Take a look at what he's done in the community. And when I'm talking about community, I'm talking about Omaha and the state. First, his leadership at the *World-Herald* was the type of leadership that brings everybody together. He kept the whole state tied together because of his great concern for the entire state of Nebraska.

–MIKE YANNEY

When seventeen-year-old Anne Sluti was violently abducted from the Hilltop Mall parking lot in Kearney, Nebraska, on the evening of April 6, 2001, Nebraskans prayed for even a glimmer of hope. Like most of those keeping watch, John Gottschalk did not know the Sluti family. He knew only that he hoped for Anne's safe return.

Law enforcement officers tracked Anne and her kidnapper into the Rocky Mountains near Yellowstone. On April 12, they surrounded a cabin on Flathead Lake, Montana, and waited out the kidnapper in a ten-hour standoff. Anne emerged from her captivity; her terrible ordeal ended. She flew home the next day on a private jet, the same plane that had brought her parents, Don and Elaine Sluti, from Kearney in the hope of finding their daughter alive. The Slutis arrived to a cheering crowd of friends and well-wishers at the Kearney airport.

Few knew that the plane that whisked her parents to Montana and brought the three of them home to Kearney was John Gottschalk's.

Anne Sluti's story was emblematic of John's sense of compassion and responsibility, his desire to make situations better, to improve what was wanting, to right what was wrong, to help where help was needed. And to make sure his part in leaving a place better than he found it never became the story. No news outlets carried the story that he freely offered his plane to the Slutis. But Bill Kernen remembered and told the story years later.

His unsolicited assistance was quintessential John Gottschalk. It stemmed from a sense of compassion acquired in the Sandhills from two previous generations.

The following year, *Omaha World-Herald* columnist Mike Kelly got a phone call in the newsroom with word that his daughter Bridget had been sexually assaulted and left for dead in a Texas field. Within minutes and without prompting, John arranged for his jet to fly Kelly to his daughter's hospital room.

Such kindness and immediacy were a refined version of the example set by his grandfather, Bill Barnes. The three Gottschalk siblings learned the lesson early on from their parents, grandparents, and neighbors in Rushville: Helping hands build great communities; generosity keeps them strong.

While leadership, tinged with compassion and an acute sense of duty, steadied John's oars even in treacherous currents, his relationships inside and outside the *Omaha World-Herald* revealed a way to work—and a way to live.

High on his list of goals when he became CEO and publisher of the *World-Herald* was changing the culture at the company. His campaign to alter what he saw as a "top-down" managerial structure was moved along by his essays in the paper's internal newsletter, *Square Talk*. He used Tuesday executive meetings to tout the efficacy of managers making more decisions and providing more leadership. (He believed that finding the right person for the right job at the right time had a demonstrably positive effect on this aspect of culture change.) Finally, he knew people grew when they expected and received a healthy balance of reasoned criticism and sincere praise. Even though he clearly was the boss, he developed a reputation for eliciting what others on his team were thinking and being respectful of their ideas. Ann Burdette, his longtime assistant at the *World-Herald* and member of the board of directors of the Carmen and John Gottschalk Foundation after retirement, said, "John was a good listener. Too often CEOs talk more than they listen."

Those markers and more reveal that John's leadership style was displayed best in his relationships with people, inside and outside the paper.

Even to an outsider, Rushville's lessons of commitment and compassion went deep. Bob Kerrey spoke fondly of the three months he spent with the Gottschalks in Rushville. "John and I were very, very close friends," he said. "If you'd asked me at the time who was my best friend, he would have been high on the list. I learned about the culture of ranching and the culture of rural small towns. It was my first introduction to Native American culture, particularly the Lakota. I read Mari

Sandoz in particular. She had grown up not far from there. I read *Old Jules*. I would say it was much more an introduction to the culture than it was to politics."

Still, politics were never far from the lively evenings with the Gottschalks, discussing the world of the early 1960s. "His father, Phil, was one of a kind," Kerrey said. "Oh my gosh, yes. He'd come home—well, they printed with ink—he'd come home a mess. But it had to be the first time I'd ever engaged in political debates, well, political conversations, you couldn't really call it debate. This was before the Kennedy assassination. John's father was a Republican. He was not terribly fond of the Kennedy administration.

"I was not a Democrat. For my first vote, I registered as a Republican—maybe because of Phil."

Kerrey voted for Barry Goldwater in 1964. His early political views were constructed in the Sandhills. "The summer of 1963 was a formative summer for me," he said. "That's when I began developing my own political ideology about the role of government in our lives. John and his dad and brother Mike, they had a big impact on my ideology.... The summer of 1963, I heard an articulated political philosophy, which included Mari Sandoz's attitude toward our treatment of the Lakota. I think John has had an important impact on my political philosophy."

As the good friends moved their lives in different directions, they remained close. Kerrey finished his degree at Morningside College in Sioux City, Iowa. Despite his asthma, he passed a military physical and enlisted in the Navy. "I took the physical right after the first freeze and I had no asthma symptoms. So I ended up going into the service. I was in the military by fall of 1966. I was notified that I had passed my physical examination and that signaled I was about to be drafted. I had read Herman Wouk's *The Caine Mutiny*. That caused me to volunteer for the Navy."

Home on leave and about to be deployed to Vietnam, Kerrey stopped to see John and Carmen in Sidney, where John had become the newspaper's owner. He said what was true then was always true about them. "There's something about John and Carmen I just like. I could talk to them in ways I couldn't talk to other people. I don't know what it is about John, but I trust him completely."

Kerrey became a Navy Seal and helped lead a nighttime raid on a Viet Cong compound on Hon Tre Island near Nha Trang Bay on March 14, 1969. While losing blood from severe shrapnel wounds, Kerrey put together a successful counterattack. He lost his right leg below his knee as a result of his injuries. He was awarded the Congressional Medal of Honor by President Richard Nixon in 1970. After months in a VA hospital, Kerrey returned to Nebraska and eventually found his way into politics. The fact that he did so as a Democrat made no difference in his friendship with John.

"Maintaining a friendship might have been a little more difficult for John," Kerrey said. "I moved to the Democratic Party and John didn't, so we had some political differences compared to the good ol' days. But we were just good friends. It didn't matter. If John had moved hard right and I'd moved hard left, it would not have had an impact on our friendship. If we had a passionate disagreement on every issue of the day, our friendship would have survived. But we have both moved in a direction where it's hard for us to claim either party today. He would say he's not so much a Republican as a frustrated American. There's a lot to trust in somebody who's lived the life John's lived, to have to leave college to run the family business. I was quite impressed with his success at Sidney and at the *Omaha World-Herald*. And with the generosity he's shown. John's a real builder of communities. Some people are and some people aren't. He is. I've learned a lot from people who were builders."

The friends continued to discuss the topics of the day when they could, too. When Kerrey told John he was going to be a Democratic candidate for governor and asked his buddy if he had any thoughts, John said, "Yes. Change parties." But Kerrey won as a Democrat and then went on to serve twelve years in the United States Senate.

Neither Kerrey nor John was looking for anything beyond friendship. Kerrey was clear on what constituted the limits of their friendship. "I didn't require people to support me in politics to be my friend—I married a woman who didn't support me in politics. In my relationship with John, we expect each other to do one thing: To tell the truth and never trade on our friendship. I'd never trade on friendship with anybody. The older I get the more important they are. I don't recall, during the entire time I was governor and senator, that John Gottschalk ever asked me for anything."

Kerrey said many conversations with John in the 1990s centered on education. John was concerned about young people, about their willingness to work hard, the kind of parenting they were getting, and what could be done by leaders such as politicians and newspaper publishers to improve the quality of leadership coming from a new generation of professionals.

In the end, Kerrey, the Democrat, said party affiliation was no barrier to his deep, committed friendship with John, who remained a Republican. Nor would it have changed John—or Kerrey's view of him.

As a friend for nearly sixty years, Kerrey held no illusion that his take on John Gottschalk was singular. "I'd be surprised if (my experience with John) is unique," he said. "John is really reliable. If John tells you he's going to do something, he does it. That's how he treats all of his friends."

Politics be damned, too, because for Bob Kerrey, governor and U.S. senator, John's sweet spot had to do with building and bettering his community and his world, not endless political debates.

"This word 'builder' is an important one," Kerrey said. "John was a builder and a completely unselfish person on one level. On the level where it matters: When you stripped away all the things. He liked getting things done. You could count on him. He cared deeply about every community in which he was involved—the check for the baseball diamond in Rushville. My guess is he's still doing things in Sidney. He's done a lot of things in Omaha. He was a reliable community builder."

Bob Kerrey and Mike McCarthy were among John's closest friends.

John's service to his community, his state, and his nation was clearly defined: His work on national boards changed the landscape of the National Benevolent Association; energized the administration of the Boy Scouts; enhanced the commitment to excellence of his fraternity, Phi Gamma Delta; and improved the structure and scope of the USO. Closer to home, he was one of several driving forces that changed the Omaha skyline and refocused the direction of its downtown. His energy and vision for the arts community in Omaha became exemplified in the beauty and acoustic integrity of the Holland Performing Arts Center and the renewed and restored grandeur of the Orpheum Theater. As a volunteer, he spent eight months retooling the culture and securing the future of the University of Nebraska Foundation. His leadership with Omaha 2000 had a beneficial impact on K-12 public education in Omaha and Nebraska. His tireless work helped revitalize the city of Sidney and, by extension, the Nebraska Panhandle. For ten years his deft mastery of the River City Roundup's reins established Omaha's paean to a "Midwestern heritage" and helped make it a considerable success. John was also part of many other local ventures that relied on volunteers, private contributions, and, what he seemed to enjoy most, plenty of elbow grease.

As extensive as his résumé was as a national figure, John was clearly and mostly a Nebraskan. His close friend for many years and with whom John did plenty of business, Mike McCarthy, called John a "citizen of the state." Whether it was his time, his ingenuity, his checkbook, or his experience, John's relentless giving—and its clear attachment to his DNA—had an impact on McCarthy, too.

"I had never met anybody who was so committed to his community," he said. "I always thought, and probably still do, that he was overly generous. He gave time, money, attention, that's just the way it was, this was a part of life, you've got to do this. I've never met anybody like him. He has heavily influenced me. I'd say I don't think you can create a generosity of spirit; either it exists or it doesn't. But you can sure as hell nurture it, and I'm sure he did that for me."

∾

Mike Kelly was a fixture at the *Omaha World-Herald* for nearly five decades. His career in the newsroom, which began in 1970, encompassed covering cops, courts, and city hall. In 1981, he became sports editor, and a sports columnist. Ten years later he left sports and became the newspaper's featured columnist. Mike Kelly became synonymous with the *World-Herald* and remained so until he retired in 2018.

He did not have close daily contact with John, but they connected occasionally, chatting in the hallways or during John's visits to the newsroom. Sometimes he received a congratulatory note about his work, or would write John a note of thanks for a pay increase or stock opportunity.

What started on the morning of June 21, 2002, changed Kelly's life and how he came to know the kind of person John Gottschalk was.

"Around 10:30, I was joshing with somebody in the newsroom like you do, getting ready to write my weekend stuff. I get this call from a Detective Sharon Brank. She was from the Killeen (Texas) Police Department," he said. Kelly's daughter, Bridget, was a first-grade teacher in Killeen.

"She asked if I was the father of Bridget Kelly. I expected I was going to hear she had been killed by a drunk driver, that was the image that came. Then she told me that Bridget was involved in a crime." In the moment he was trying to process "involved in a crime," Brank told him Bridget had been raped and shot three times and was in the Army hospital.

"I asked if she was alive."

She gave Kelly the name of the nurse, a lieutenant at the hospital.

"So, I called and started jotting down everything. After I got off the phone, I turned to Anne Henderson, my editor, who was talking with some people, like you normally wouldn't interrupt, and I said, 'Anne.' She looked at me funny like 'can't you see I'm talking to people?' I told her what happened, and I had to go. Larry King (the newspaper's executive editor) came out, and I went into his office and called my wife, Barbara, who was in Cincinnati watching my elderly mother and starting to bake cookies."

In the whirlwind that was the next few moments, Kelly knew he needed to get to Texas in a hurry. An office assistant frantically called the airlines, but it was going to take all day to get a flight. Meanwhile, King had headed straight for John's office.

"King came out of John's office and said, 'Go home and get your stuff and get out to the airport on the private side. There's going to be a plane for you.' I said, 'What?' He said, 'John's calling for his plane.' I lived downtown, so I walked five blocks to my apartment. A couple of people were with me, I was just grabbing things. I called Barb again. Steve Jordon, a long-time friend and colleague, said, 'Do you want me to go with you?'"

Although Jordon asked three times, Kelly assured him he would be all right. He called his wife again in Cincinnati. He told her he was about to leave for Texas and that a private plane was ready for him. He said he'd call her when he arrived. "And I said, oh, by the way, Steve offered to go with me. 'Take him!' she said. She didn't trust me by myself."

By mid-afternoon, Kelly and Jordon, who took only the clothes on his back, arrived in Killeen on John's private jet. After renting a car they made it to the post hospital. "Who knows how long it would have taken me to get there. So, to get there fast was really, really great," he said.

Bridget was recovering from six hours of surgery, but Kelly was able to see her and talk with her that day, a day that had started like any other Friday in the newsroom of the *Omaha World-Herald*.

Kelly—who was unaware that he flew on John's private plane, only that John had arranged to get him there, nonetheless—wanted to call John and thank him and update him on Bridget's condition.

"Donna Grimm answered and said, 'Well, he's in the board meeting.' I said, 'Oh, I'm sorry, I didn't know there was a board meeting. I'll call back.' And she said, 'No, hold on, he'll take the call.' Which, I thought, oh, my gosh, that's kind of a shock. But, in retrospect, I would have taken the call if I were he. I don't know if he took it in the meeting or if he went to another room. I also don't remember clearly what we talked about, but I was thanking him effusively for getting me down there and he said, 'You would have done the same thing if you were in my position.' Which I thought was very nice to say, that he thought that was something he should do. He asked how she was doing and all of this and then, the other thing I remember him saying, that I appreciated was, 'Take care of your family. We'll see you when we see you.' I distinctly remember that as a direct quote. He wasn't trying to be quoted at the time, but I mean, I remember that's what he said. And I thought, you know, that's the kind of company and leader you want to work for."

Mike Kelly knew John Gottschalk as the publisher in the corner office, as the leader of the newspaper, and as the executive to be thanked when the employees' stock continued to grow in value. Still, through no fault of their own, bosses and employees often remain at arms-length given the structures and processes in any newspaper. When faced with a horrible, personal trial, Mike saw John for who he really was, and the kind of culture he, as leader, insisted on having at the *World-Herald*.

He said one of his favorite stories about John, one he wrote in detail in one of his columns, came about when an explosion downtown cut power on a Saturday night as the *World-Herald* was trying to put out its huge Sunday edition. It was all hands on deck in the pressroom getting machines to run and papers out the door in the middle of the night. David Kotok, longtime reporter who later rose to managing editor at the *World-Herald*, told Kelly that when he saw John next to him pitching in, he told him it was "great to see the general in the trenches next to the privates getting his hands dirty."

John said, "Yeah, the dirtier they get, the better I like it."

∾

Darius Morris was a custodian at the *World-Herald* for many years. "He was a go-getter, an African-American guy, and he loved sports. He was always going on about the Cardinals or the Dodgers or the Huskers, whatever it was. He loved them. He was a great guy," John said.

One day Darius was in John's office on a ladder changing a light bulb when the phone rang. John was at his desk. Shortly afterward Donna Grimm, who had taken the call, stepped in. Donna usually announced a call in person only if it was of some special urgency. This day it was the White House calling. "It was during the Clinton administration," John recalled. "Darius was still up on the ladder. Donna said, 'John, the office of the president wants to talk to you about coming in to meet with him about an education thing.' I wasn't too keen on Clinton anyway. I figured I didn't need that goat-rope, so I said, 'Well, tell him I'm not going to be able to make it.' Donna left, and I went back to working. Two nanoseconds later, Darius came down off the ladder, and asked, 'Was that THE president? And you told him no?'"

John nodded.

"Man," said Darius. "You got the juice."

∾

When Ann Burdette applied to the *Omaha World-Herald* in 1984, she had grown weary of the stresses and vagaries of selling real estate. She said that during her job interview at the *World-Herald* she was given questions in math, not her strong suit. "But the thing that worried me the most was my typing speed because I had not worked for anybody in an office in many years. I managed to get it to fifty-five words a minute, the minimum required."

John Gottschalk hired her. It didn't take long for her to get a read on her new boss. "My first impression of him was that this was a very intelligent man who had an idea of what he wanted and how to do it. And it seemed to me he had a lot of integrity. He was somebody I could be very proud to work for."

Her days were structured around the tasks at hand, which he spelled out each day with a specific plan. "Oh, yes. He had things he wanted to accomplish. He was great in reorganizing an organization or a company. He was really good at that. People would call on him to talk about that, and he would take a lot of time with these people. Sometimes, I would think, 'Why are you taking all of this time?' But, for some, like Child Saving Institute, and the National Benevolent Association, he made an enormous difference."

The year after Ann Burdette arrived, John became president of the company. For Burdette, the transition was exhilarating and a little scary. "I thought to myself, 'What am I doing working for the president of a big company?'" But, she said, "John was so kind to me. I know he was worried that I felt confined in the office all day. He suggested that maybe I'd like to take my lunch to the park and stay a little longer. He was really nice about all that. And, very, very understanding about things. And very patient with me. He would give me assignments to help me learn about the newspaper. He would send me off to do something, let's say, with the production department, that I really didn't need to know. But he knew, and I knew, that… it would be helpful if I just learned something more about how a newspaper is put together.

"Every year, employees came in to buy stock and, consequently, I got to meet a lot of people that way, people I never would have worked with," she said. "Particularly people in the newsroom because at that point John had very little to do with the newsroom. Even when Andy retired and John took over everything, Woody was still there as editor and there were very few in the way of newsroom personnel who came in to see John other than, you know, the managing editor and maybe a few other people. But the stock program helped me get to know all these people."

As the gatekeeper—a role that one might believe took on added significance when he became publisher in 1989—Burdette used common sense because John had no rules regarding who saw him or connected with him on the telephone. If it wasn't exactly an open-door policy, it was the next best thing. Burdette said she simply assessed how busy he was, where he was, and moved ahead, often walking into his office when it was a call from a local friend or somebody from Rushville. As he typically did, he trusted his co-worker, someone he had hired and trained. "He never gave me any guidelines," she recalled.

Burdette took to John's management style of accessibility. *World-Herald* employees from every department were welcome and encouraged to take their concerns and questions to the publisher. Also, John's office was often a stop on visiting executives' itineraries, for an Omahan looking for guidance, or by advocates of a civic project seeking financial help. "You could meet someone important, on a national basis, who was coming through town and needed to talk to the publisher of the *World-Herald*," Burdette said. "Or you could meet local people who were involved in wanting money from the World-Herald Foundation. I loved doing all that."

Burdette considered herself a city girl, having lived in Dallas, New York City suburbs, St. Louis, San Francisco, and

Honolulu. John thought an education in the ways of rural Nebraska was in order, so he got Burdette involved in 4-H. "I remember it had to do with young women who were being honored for their work in agriculture. At first I thought, oh, my goodness."

She came to love it as she began to know young people who had grown up on a ranch or a farm. Even though her first connection to rural Nebraska was as the result of a huge livestock show in Omaha, her eyes had been opened. "I got to know a lot of these people," she said. "It was never that I felt snobbish about it. I just didn't know what that life was like. That was my problem and he helped me get out of it. And it's made a big difference in my life. I understand the rest of the state far better than I would have otherwise. I did get outstate a little bit when he became involved with the New Seeds for Nebraska program, which had to do with discerning what Nebraskans wanted for an economic future."

As his assistant, Burdette saw John during successes and also when life in the publisher's chair was difficult, from the Franklin fiasco to the failed attempt to buy Stauffer. "John handled stress really well," she said. "But, it was there. They would be doing due diligence to acquire some company, you know, and there was a lot of hustle-bustle. Stauffer was really good planning. It set the tone for other projects. During Franklin, John worked hard behind the scenes because he was very concerned about the reputation of the paper."

Burdette retired in 1997 after nearly fourteen years as John's assistant. She was sixty-five and ready to slow down from the pace of working for John, a pace she once told him he needed to adjust for his own good. "One time I went in and I said to him, and he tolerated it, 'You wear five hats. You're the publisher of the *World-Herald*' and I rattled off the others and said, 'That's too many for any one person.' And he didn't get mad at me, he just kind of laughed. I knew it wasn't going to change him, but I felt like somebody ought to tell this man, 'You don't have to do everything yourself, you know.'"

Her benign scolding notwithstanding, Burdette said John always treated her well, and his guidance in her participation in the employee stock program left her with a comfortable retirement. "He was just kind about everything. But you know, he had certain things he thought you should be doing, and I always felt if people didn't get along with John, it was because they weren't doing those things that he was expecting of you. And, it wasn't that he was expecting way more than you could give, but he had high expectations for people and one of them was that they did their job."

Burdette said, too, that John was unique among corporate executives of his time when it came to women in the workplace. "He was really good working with women in a day when that wasn't always the case. It wasn't always the case by the people who worked at the *World-Herald*. But he understood that women had capabilities, and he let them go with it. As he got to know you and rely on you, he really relied on you to do what you were supposed to do. And so, of course, you didn't want to let him down. I'm not talking just about me, I'm talking about Connie Spellman and all kinds of other people."

Her observations were shared by others including members of John's management team Bill Donaldson said that John not only recognized the value of women working at the *World-Herald*, but also "made more room in the company for accomplished women." Bill Kernen said John was very appreciative of the role of women in the workplace.

Sue Morris, the Executive Director at Heritage Services, expressed similar views. "John empowered women. I'm not sure he knew he was doing it. He did more to advance women at the *Omaha World-Herald* than anyone before."

~

Sue Morris and Joan Squires with John at his retirement "parade" and party.

In the whirlwind that was John Gottschalk's schedule in 1995, he found time to drive completely out of his lane for one evening. That spring A.R. Gurney's touching play, *Love Letters*, graced the stage at the Omaha Community Playhouse for twenty-three performances.

There, twenty-three different couples—including a number of prominent Omahans, mostly non-actors—played the parts of Andrew and Melissa, friends from second grade, who live apart in boarding schools, marry others, and never quite make the romantic connection. The plot moves forward in a series of letters exchanged between the pair over many years. The action consists of the characters reading their letters aloud, back and forth.

On April 15, John played the role of Andrew with Omahan Dorene Butler taking the part of Melissa. For John, acting— even for a single night—was one more way to give back to the community and support the arts. He was also a member of the Omaha Community Playhouse Foundation board and its chairman from 1996 to 1998.

"Artistically," said Playhouse Artistic Director Charles Jones in a *World-Herald* interview, "having all these people binds the community to the arts here because each of them has a circle of friends to touch and influence. It's a community celebration."

∼

Donna Grimm had a certain grace—both in the sense that those who knew and worked with her were sure of her grace, and, perhaps more important, that it was unquestioned and indisputable.

She was John's assistant at the *Omaha World-Herald*, and, after his retirement, at the office where he carried on his civic and philanthropic activities. Hers was the first inviting voice and cheerful smile that greeted you when you reached the offices of the Carmen and John Gottschalk Foundation. She was as warm and genial with the FedEx man as she was with U.S. senators and captains of industry. Like her boss, she had an eye for detail and for the big picture as well, all with a genuine kindness, rarer and rarer in a coarser and coarser world.

In planning for his retirement in 2007, John bought an old mansion on North 86th Street near Cass Street. It had been home to an advertising agency, but John turned it into offices, landscaped the grounds, and christened it Three Cedars in homage to the towering conifers on the grounds. His first tenant was Bill Kernen, also retired, in 2006.

"I like to be busy. I like my work," Grimm said. "I've always enjoyed the job and the variety. Working for John, every day can be different. I've never dreaded waking up on Monday morning, or thinking Sunday night, 'Oh, my gosh, it's another Monday.' I have never, never, ever felt that."

Grimm grew up in Manning, Iowa, about one hundred miles across the river from Omaha. She moved to Omaha to attend business college and started her career at one, and then another, small insurance company. She learned about "teamwork, about sharpening my secretarial skills and understanding responsibility. You needed to show up every day on time and put in your 200 percent. All my bosses were wonderful people, so it was great training."

She moved on to Peter Kiewit Sons' in 1969 and stayed there for seventeen years, working primarily on the executive floor where she learned first-hand the rigors and responsibilities that come into play when serious decisions needed to be made. Those were the days of electric typewriters, shorthand, and manual accounting, when assistants taped together typed sheets of paper for tax returns.

In 1986, about the time her boss, the general counsel for Kiewit, was leaving, a friend who had earlier moved over to the *World-Herald* called and told her the newspaper was looking for a secretary in the executive offices. Grimm applied and accepted an offer. She worked for Woody Howe, the paper's editor, for twelve years before becoming John's assistant at the beginning of 1998, following Ann Burdette's retirement. She remained in that role through his retirement and the process of succession and the building and opening of the John Gottschalk Freedom Center.

Then it was on to Three Cedars.

Like many others, Grimm recognized John's focus on the future and the workload it took to keep his aim steady. As his assistant, this would become part of her focus, too. "When I started working for him, his vision was not one year or eighteen months," she said. "It was generational. He put together a strong team to grow people and put them in the right places around the U.S. to run all these companies. He had a huge job, a huge job. And every year, that became greater and greater. That alone would be enough for any CEO to be overwhelmed, but then he had all the community things, too."

Early on, working for John, Grimm realized that he "was a totally different personality and different person than Woody." While she was doing the best she could to keep up, the sledding was tough, especially trying to discern what "was needed of me so I could have it be right and to try to save John time and to be helpful." John gave Grimm direction and was helpful at every turn, but she had nagging doubts. Several months into her new job, John wrote her a memo.

"He said, 'I hope this will be helpful to you and for the both of us going forward.' He wrote about his role as a CEO and what he saw as his job, what was needed from him every day to run a company and how that might impact me. It was back and front, six pages long. He could have just said, 'This isn't quite working out for us. Maybe we should find a different spot for you.' But he wrote the memo. That was huge for him to do that, to give me that chance. He was actually trying to help me enormously. He didn't have to do that. Why would you do that for a secretary?"

Grimm still had the memo twenty years later.

Her mettle working for John was tested right out of the gate.

"My first week working for John directly, I got a call from Sen. Chuck Hagel's office. They were secretly going to nominate John for some honor. They had to supply some information to a committee to get John's name in front of them. So they asked me to pull together all this information on John. It was my second day on the job.

"They were on a deadline. They needed it in two days. It was all to be top secret. Every time John walked by my desk, which was a lot, because every time he went in and out of his office I'd be right in front of him, I'd have to watch out of the corner of my eye. He'd kind of casually look across my desk to see what I was working on. Well, he didn't see much going on because I had it all in secret, stuffed away. I remember that it was terrible for me, just terrible. I thought, 'Oh, I'm going to get fired for this, and I'm trying to do something for John.'"

Donna Grimm and Ann Burdette, long time assistants to John.

Grimm never told John the story, which was probably for the best. Whatever honor Hagel nominated him for, he never received.

After a while Grimm also became tuned into John's decision-making, which others outside their working circle might have seen as too quick or even rash. After years of experience with the process, Grimm saw it working in a variety of positive ways.

"Almost instantaneously, he gets the picture, completely. And he can know instantly what changes need to be implemented or what advice needs to be given. I think it's because the same concepts in life apply to a lot of things and those concepts immediately come to him, and he has a plan and a vision, and it fits. It didn't matter how large or small, it just seemed to fit."

Grimm, after two decades as John's assistant, reflected on advice he had given. She said it was always informal, a natural outgrowth of their relationship and perhaps more to the point, a product of John's personality. "As you are going about day-by-day and you're talking about things, sometimes you end up asking for advice and you don't even know you did," she said. "Just because John is who he is, I think people don't even realize that he's mentoring them and giving them advice when they happen to just be having a communication because he doesn't waste anything. If you listen carefully to his stories, there's always a lesson of some kind."

His standards were high, according to Grimm. "He expected a lot from people and there's nothing wrong with that. He expected people to keep moving and do a good job and there was a lot of work to be done. Do it well and be proud of what you're doing and get help when you need it."

As the gatekeeper for the CEO and publisher, Grimm became a student of human behavior, often encountering those who otherwise would have never ventured beyond their own department at the newspaper and surely never ended up in the CEO's office. They were often anxious about being there. A lot of them would start off by saying, 'Oh, Mr. Gottschalk. What an honor it is.' And he'd say, 'Call me John. Let's get that clear from the beginning here. I'm John.' And he would warmly shake their hand or give them a tap on the shoulder or something and then he'd say, 'Okay, now we're going to start over. I'm John.' So, he'd get them to chuckle a little bit."

Grimm saw him the same way outside the cocoon of the executive suite. "He wanted people to see him, whether it would be in the lunchroom or at the coffee machine or hallway. He wanted people to understand he knew who they were, what they did, and that he appreciated it. He was very visible."

She said John would "make the rounds" at the newspaper numerous times when he left his office. Sometimes the rounds began early. "Someone came to me and said, 'Guess who I ran into this morning at 5 o'clock and he greeted me? It was Mr. Gottschalk.' I realized that John was parking at the Freedom Center. We had three lots that he could have parked in, but that one was at the new Freedom Center. He knew a shift started at 5 a.m., and he wanted to walk in and greet those people at ten 'til five and say, 'thank you for what you're doing.' And, he would do that and at the end of the day, too, whomever he ran into on his way in or out. He wanted to know people. And, he wanted people to understand 'I know who you are.'"

Donna Grimm, who said the privilege was hers professionally and personally to work with John Gottschalk, learned, too, that he was not simply a product of his environment. He embodied it.

"John's grandfather sounds like the person John learned a lot from as far as being quiet, behind the scenes, and just helping. A lot of people leave their hometowns, but John took the best of both worlds there, and used that to be respectful of people and to be honorable. You find that stuff in Rushville, Nebraska. He was such a piece of the fabric of that place."

In the early spring of 2006, John was at the coffee machine, getting one of his twenty cups a day, when a co-worker said, "John, are you okay?" He went back to his desk and was noticeably dizzy. He realized that something was wrong. A trip to his physician, Dr. Joel Bessmer, revealed that he was diabetic. But Bessmer had more disturbing news. He had diagnosed John with chronic lymphocytic leukemia (CLL), a cancer of the blood and bone marrow. Dr. Jim Armitage was called in to deal with that discovery. Armitage told John the disease could go one of three ways.

"It could flare up immediately," John said. "Or you could be walking down the street ten years later and it could fire up. Or you could die of something else." For John, option three rang the truest. Still the diagnosis and aftermath got his attention, "stopped him in his tracks," so that in his personal diary he wondered if "spring would come again."

CLL forced him to make lifestyle changes as did the diabetes diagnosis. The coffee had to go. The disease brought him up close to his own mortality, to consider the end. As an especially private person, John shared his CLL diagnosis with only a few people. Mike McCarthy was one of them.

"He told me about it when we were at the *World-Herald* in his office," McCarthy said. "So you revert to your comfort zone, right? John and I used numbers. You've got an 80 percent chance of making it for ten years, to seventy-three, and a 20 percent chance of making it twenty years. So it's not like this is terminal, right? And your (tests suggest that) you've got a lot of running room here. On the other hand, we had that philosophical discussion, saying mortality was a fact so better make sure you're going to get done what you want to get done. John was very much about having a plan and maybe for the first time in his life, it was 'Okay, I really have to have an end game.' And then he immediately went into planning mode. He said, 'Okay, I'm going to have one, you know, and not be in denial.' I'd say he was certainly shaken by the diagnosis, but not despairing in any way."

McCarthy also speculated that John's reticence to be more forthcoming about his CLL was simply part of his nature, honed from a seat in the leader's chair and the soul of a problem solver. "John was conscious of not burdening other people with his problems because he was the receptacle, especially when he was the publisher and as a philanthropist, of people coming to him and saying, 'Here's my problem.' He gravitates towards solving those problems kind of instinctively, rather than pushing back and saying, 'Yeah, it is your problem.'"

John began regular blood tests, more frequently in the beginning because as a chronic disease, CLL had no cure.

The tests eventually became yearly events. Regarding his diabetes, he embarked on a lifelong plan to keep all his "numbers" in a healthy range.

~

Mike McCarthy called John Gottschalk a citizen of the state. Mike Yanney had the proof.

"John has touched a lot of people. We have better community leaders because of him. He and Carmen both have been role models. Take a look at what he's done in the community. And when I'm talking about community, I'm talking about Omaha and the state. First, his leadership at the *World-Herald* was the type of leadership that brings everybody together. He kept the whole state tied together because of his great concern for the entire state of Nebraska," Yanney said.

Yanney understood that this leadership was more than just a statewide circulation. Serving communities large and small throughout the state with a single unifying presence— the *Omaha World-Herald*—required foresight, vision, and a committed and keen understanding of its readers. He saw that in his friend John Gottschalk.

"Second, he took on projects that really made a difference," Yanney said. "Today, for example, we're recruiting people from all over the world for the Nebraska Medical Center. The Holland Performing Arts Center and the Orpheum Theater are huge assets for us when we're recruiting. And then if you look at education, he had Omaha 2000 way before people were focusing on K-12. It really helped Omaha get out in front of the game," he said.

Yanney owned and managed commercial banks, did extensive work for the East West Institute in bettering relations with Russia. He established America First Companies in Omaha in 1984, changing the name to Burlington Capital in 2006 when he became chairman emeritus. He was born in Kearney during the Depression, the youngest of nine children. Yanney was only eleven when his father died, but he learned from his mother the value of service to and compassion for others. When he was honored by Ak-Sar-Ben in 2015, he said, "Being a giver was right on the top of her list. She always used to say to me, you're not going to have a problem making money. I want you to focus on what you're going to do to make a difference."

So Yanney's fondness for philanthropy aligned with that of his friend John, whom he met shortly after John moved to Omaha. Soon they were working together on riverfront development projects. They also shared a love of hunting and fishing and spent time at each other's "retreats" in the Rockies.

When Yanney and his family wanted to build a park in Kearney to honor their parents, John was part of the team. "John was helpful in a number of ways," Yanney said. "When we first started we bought eighty acres. I think the *Kearney Hub*, which I still read all the time, had some questions whether this thing would get done. So they called John and asked him about it. He said, 'Get out of the way, it's going to get done.' That made a big difference. It was a monumental step in making that park happen."

Part of that difference was the John and Carmen Gottschalk Observation Tower, built by the Gottschalks as a gift to the Yanneys and the city of Kearney. The tower, which rose eighty feet into the clear Nebraska air, quickly became a favorite spot for marriage proposals and photo shoots, both personal and professional. Its panoramic views extended in all four directions until the horizon was gently swallowed by the sky, leaving one to imagine the rest of Nebraska stretching far and wide, a state loved—and understood—by two citizens: Mike Yanney and John Gottschalk.

~

As it was with many small towns in Nebraska, high-school football was part of the DNA in Rushville. The games captured the town's undivided attention on Friday nights in the fall. The Longhorns were a powerhouse during John's playing days, a force built and maintained by legendary coach Bill Stephenson. Stephenson began his coaching career at Cambridge, Nebraska, where he led an undefeated squad in 1951 and had his teams in 1952 and 1953 ranked in the top ten Class C rankings.

His 1959 Rushville team—John started at quarterback and linebacker—went undefeated. In 1960, John's senior year, the Longhorns were once again a top ten team. Stephenson went on to Lincoln Southeast High School where he coached for seven more years. He was the head coach for the North team in the 1961 Shrine Bowl and had a career record of 117-37.

John revered Stephenson, calling him a "giant" in a eulogy at his funeral in Lincoln in 2002. He spoke with a combination of reverence, humor, and gratitude in his remarks, which he headed, "The measure of a man is not what he takes, but rather what he gives; not what he has, but what he leaves." Some of his words follow here:

> I consider it an honor to have been asked to speak briefly about Bill Stephenson—a man who touched all in this room. To some here today he was a longtime friend. To some a neighbor. To others a teacher, a father, a grandfather. I knew him first as a young coach who came to Rushville from five successful years at Cambridge, where he launched his coaching and teaching career. He was a young father, a World War II vet, and a great athlete.
>
> My late father, a devoted football fan and editor of the Rushville newspaper, met him the first day he came to town. Having two sons who would soon be playing for Bill, he was vitally interested in the new coach. I remember him telling me after that first meeting with Bill. "John, you better be prepared to work. This guy

knows the game. He will have high expectations of you. He comes here to mold young men like you, and he will teach you to win in all you do."

No truer words could have been spoken. I played for Bill four of his five years in Rushville. He molded us into a team. He taught us to work—and work together. He demanded we think. He demanded we play hard and clean. He modeled all the characteristics we learned to mimic... how to be a winner at school and at home. We had guys who came to town from surrounding ranches who didn't know a thing about football—a couple didn't even know how to put on a supporter. No matter to Bill. He was a teacher and he could teach them more than football.

He set high standards for all he did. If enjoying his favorite pastime of hunting, he expected every shot to count. If joking and kidding with friends, he was prepared to take as much as he gave. When it came to raising his family, he set the rules clearly: work hard in school; respect your parents and elders; know and love your nation; do whatever you choose, but do it with all your heart. Celebrate victory; learn from defeat. Team. Persist.

There is not a one among us this morning who will not always remember his humor. He'd say something seemingly outrageous. If you learned to not respond immediately, and just looked in his eyes, pretty soon you'd see a twinkle and that memorable subtle smile. He occasionally had a little fun in the classroom, too.

I recall a time in his Government class a couple of us were not paying attention. Well, actually, we were goofing off. He stopped his lecture, walked to the board and drew two circles about five inches in diameter, three feet apart. He then invited us to step forward. Noting we seemed to have trouble focusing on what was going on in class,

Bill told us to put our noses in the circles. We felt stupid standing with our backsides to our friends, but we didn't have any trouble concentrating on what he was saying the remaining few minutes of the class.

We had a kid who grew up on a ranch and had never even seen a football game. No TV in those days down on the ranch. The first game of his freshman year was played on a dirt field that'd been used only a week before for an annual rodeo. The fella's name was Butch. When our team arrived at the neighboring town, we walked across the loose dirt, turned up by the hooves of horses and cattle. Butch ran over to Coach and remarked what a fine "arena" it was, noting that the loose dirt would be a lot easier on him when tackling. He asked Bill if all football fields were like this one. Bill, holding back a laugh with all his might replied: "Well, Butch, I asked them to remove the grass just so you would feel comfortable for your very first game." Butch walked away beaming. What a coach he thought, to do something special for him like that. By the way, that was my first start for a Bill Stephenson team. We won that opener and the next twenty-some games.

Each of you has a funny story about Bill. They will fill our conversations for our remaining years. He left us a rich treasure of fond memories. Before the day is out, we'll be laughing and sharing many of them with each other. Bill would cherish that.

By my measure he was a giant. Each of us can point to a gift we received from him. To his five sons and their families, thank you for sharing him with us.

The measure of this man is not what he took, but what he gave; not what he had, but what he left—to each of us.

∾

John's first real job outside the *Sheridan County Star* was as a scatter raker at the Forney Ranch, where he learned labor relations the hard way from Don Forney and a wondrous combination of grace, enthusiasm, and hospitality from Olive Forney. Fifty-four years later, when Olive died in April of 2002, Don asked John to speak at her service, where he remembered her as a treasure tucked away in the beauty of the Sandhills:

She left us with a clear understanding of what it was to have a zest for life... There is a special peace surrounding this small parcel of land today. Outside it is spring, Olive's favorite time—a time for gardening, branding, greening pastures, renewal, and fresh air. She loved these Sandhills, as do we all. She spent her entire adult life here devoted to her family, always ready to lend a hand to friends and neighbors.

Those of us who cannot be in this most special place all the time always looked forward to our visits to the ranch— as much because of Olive's consummate hospitality as for the comradeship we enjoyed as her guests. She sparkled whenever a neighbor or guest arrived at her door. There was nothing she wouldn't do to make you comfortable and welcome. It is rare that one is blessed with the presence of a woman so completely devoted to others.

Above all else, Olive Forney was genuine. She made no pretenses. If she didn't know something, she'd say so and learn what she needed. If she thought you had fallen short of expectations, she would tell you—not so much in a lecture, but in a positive lesson, encouraging you always to do better. If she found something pleasing, she would tell you about her enthusiasm for it. She was as honest and open as these great rolling hills.

I do not share the pastoral skills of Rev. Tom Dykes, but I know there was a special spiritual quality about

Olive. She just made you feel good about who you were, where you were, and the blessings you enjoyed. God surely put her among us to lift our spirits—and she fulfilled that mission in spades.

~

Jackson Hole, Wyoming, was John's long-time getaway from the rigors of newspapering and, in retirement, his home for a good portion of the year. Among its characters was "Teton Jack,"—Jack Langan—whom John came to know at the Silver Dollar Bar inside the historic Wort Hotel. The Wort's lobby, appointed in rich wood with western touches, looked like a place to encounter European royalty, a Hollywood starlet, or a dusty mountain man just down from the Tetons. The grand staircase dominated the entryway, plush, polished, and welcoming. Through the lobby and down a paneled hallway sat the Silver Dollar Bar, awaiting the thirsty and the curious, its countertop displaying 1,234 silver dollars embedded just below the lacquered surface. It was here, at the very western end of the bar, that John first met Teton Jack Langan.

Whenever John stopped in the Silver Dollar for a late dinner or nightcap, he found Teton Jack on the same barstool, dressed in fringed buckskin, a beer with tomato juice close at hand. With his white beard, flowing hair, and the occasional donning of a coonskin hat, Teton Jack would have made central casting proud. He wasn't simply a skilled outdoorsman and guide who more than looked the part; his was a full and fascinating life.

Jack Langan was born in 1921 in Chicago. After his father died, he left the Windy City at age six to live with his mother on the Pine Ridge Reservation, a day's ride on horseback from Rushville and bisected by the 100th meridian. According to Andrea Page in her book, *Sioux Code Talkers of World War II*, Jack was "half white, half Lakota… and learned the Lakota ways of life and how to speak the Lakota language." She met him in Jackson Hole while researching the code talkers. He encouraged her to write the book, which chronicles the heroism and contributions of Native Americans in World War II. Jack even had a Lakota name, Pahizi Wawoyaka, which translates to "yellow-haired storyteller."

Like John, Jack first visited the Tetons as a youngster. He wound up working for the National Park Service in Yellowstone before hitchhiking to Fort Bliss, Texas, in 1941, where he enlisted in the Army. His unit was the Seventh Cavalry—a throwback to the Old West in that they still used horses. After fighting in World War II, Jack returned to the Midwest, graduating from the University of Illinois, where he captained the cheerleading team. He worked in Chicago as a cub reporter, a journalistic connection John sensed during their conversations about newspapers. Jack also had stints as an advertising copywriter in Chicago and a magazine editor in San Francisco before returning to his beloved Wyoming as a radio broadcaster. In 1963 he co-wrote an article for the *Casper Tribune* about President Kennedy's visit to Jackson Hole, calling it the first by a president since Chester A. Arthur in the 1880s.

Teton Jack dabbled in politics and the counterculture, too, palling around with Wobblies and beatniks in San Francisco in the 1950s. He told Franklin Rosemont, author of *Joe Hill: The IWW & the Making of a Revolutionary Working Class Counterculture*, that he had been a "hobo, mountain man, wilderness guide, photographer, folk singer, poet, writer, and songwriter."

Jack's formative years on the reservation had a profound impact on his life. He was not only a noted speaker on Native American history and culture but also established the Sacred Pipe Indian Mission Foundation in Wyoming to foster support and understanding of Native American religion, traditions, and customs. He formed the Wind River Mountain Men, a group he led as they rode in President Lyndon Johnson's inaugural parade. He was listed in the 1972 *Who's Who in the West*. He spent better than two decades living in the Tetons as a guide. And, of course, he spent many nights at the Wort Hotel, holding court in his customary, somewhat cranky, but informed way.

John Gottschalk knew little of this remarkable history. But Teton Jack was simply too much of a character for a curious journalist like John to pass up. One evening, John decided to park himself near enough to the end of the bar so he could learn more.

That was the beginning of their acquaintance. Teton Jack proved to be often reticent and occasionally irascible, but a gifted raconteur nonetheless, spinning yarns of exotic travel, life in the mountains, and extraordinary stopping off places on his journey. Out of curiosity, John, after a few evenings near the end of the bar, asked Teton Jack why he always sat in the same seat. The man in buckskin replied he considered that particular seat to be his property.

Not everyone was taken with Teton Jack. He grew to have a notoriously hostile relationship with one of the bartenders at the Silver Dollar Bar, a woman who, as John described it, poured Teton Jack's drinks with a certain amount of disdain. One night, John and Mike McCarthy stopped into the Silver Dollar. Mike was in Jackson for one of his many fishing adventures with John. He, too, knew of the legend and had previously talked to the character known as Teton Jack. Both were surprised on this night, however.

The universe had shifted, ever so slightly. Teton Jack was not in his usual spot.

Instead, John and Mike found him on the opposite end of the bar, perched in his precarious way on the last stool on the bar's eastern terminus, a beer and tomato juice in front of him as usual. John broached the subject.

"Jack, why are you sitting here?"

"She hates me, so I moved."

While the logic made sense, the calculus did not add up. The same scowling bartender served the same scowling mountain man the same drink—whichever end of the bar he chose.

Jack Langan died in 2002 before he had chance to read Page's book on the code talkers that he had inspired. But the stories of Teton Jack Langan lived on in the culture and officially, too. The Jackson Hole Historical Society and Museum had a small collection of newspaper articles, photos, personal letters, diaries, and artifacts devoted to Teton Jack Langan. To John, he was an irrepressible element in the enduring appeal of the Tetons.

The Tetons have provided a lifelong scenic backdrop to John's life and needed sustenance for his love of fly fishing.

When John's daughter, Jodi Taylor, returned from California, she brought her two-year-old son Austin with her to Omaha. Taylor had been through a considerable rough patch and was now going through a divorce. She said she arrived home overwhelmed and "kind of broken." She said her parents "doted on Austin, but they also helped me mend. And that was important."

Taylor had been working in radio, writing content in California. She continued to do so as she and Austin set about putting down roots where she once had them. For Austin, childhood was filled with lots of time with John and Carmen, especially Friday night dinners with grandpa, which the two started when Austin was ten.

"I remember him working a lot," Austin said. "But never in the way that he did not have time for me. I often played with my Hot Wheels cars in his office, and it never disturbed him. Then we started every Friday having dinner at a Chinese place. I was always comfortable with him and he was always very open with me."

Austin, who graduated from Columbia College in Chicago and worked in film there, started after college as a gimbal operator. A gimbal permitted an object—in Austin's line of work, a camera—to pivot on a single axis and tilt in any direction all the while keeping the camera steady even when it was moving. Using gimbals in film eliminates blur when the camera, the object it was filming, or both move because the frame remained stable throughout the shot.

Austin displayed deftness behind the camera. Film was his art, and he was an exceptionally well-spoken young man. While language might be a gift of nature, considering his mother made a living writing radio copy, had her own blog for several years, and became a crackerjack teacher in middle school, nurture obviously was at work. Jodi Taylor suggested that other circumstances played a role, too, in Austin being poised and articulate from a young age. "I think growing up as the only grandchild, for a time, and the only child with me, he was thrust into a very adult world all the time," she said. "I took him everywhere. He had his first little baby tuxedo going to Dad's Ak-Sar-Ben thing (recognition as a mythical 'king' in the group's salute to exceptional community leadership), so he was used to being around people who converse. I talked to him like he was thirty, even when he didn't know how to talk."

John's grandson, Austin, pushes the button to start
the new presses at the Freedom Center.

John chose Austin to push the button that started the new
presses for the very first time at what was later to be named the
John Gottschalk Freedom Center. Austin was just five. Their
relationship continued to be strong even when Austin was
away at school and Friday dinners turned into phone calls. "We
still had lots of good conversations," Austin said.

Austin said those talks, and the aggregate of all those Friday
night dinners, and time together gave him many things. "I have
a good relationship with my father who is in California, but
(John) was the prominent male in my life. He taught me to
drive, shoot a gun, and shave," Austin said.

Austin said that his grandfather passed along more meaningful things, too. "Self-determination and self-motivation. He
taught me not to be scared of ambition. He taught me insight
and how to be aware. I admire the man so much. He taught me
a lot of things indirectly, too."

Whenever Austin Taylor returned to Omaha to see his
mother, he made sure dinner with his grandfather—Friday or
any night—was on the agenda.

FOURTEEN

Reality, Reflection, and the Future

He made a point of being around and wandering through the newsroom... shooting the breeze with people. At World-Herald Square everything was on two floors, and so nobody was very far away from anybody. Everybody used the same lunchroom and so you might run into John there, or he'd be in the newsroom. He wasn't hesitant about bringing an idea to (editors), but then he'd stop to say "hi" to somebody. He didn't malinger, he didn't hang around a long time, but he was friendly in that way, and seemed approachable that way.

–MIKE REILLY

The Inland Press Association gathered for its annual meeting at the Renaissance Hotel in Chicago in late October 2007. Inland had about one thousand dailies and weeklies on its membership rolls. The 122nd version of its yearly conference brimmed with an array of speakers and subjects: examining insights and observations on new media; gaining

Wall Street's view of the value of newspapers; tapping the Hispanic market; using vertical markets in online classifieds; exploring new revenue strategies; hearing a single-copy sales success story from Waco, Texas; and delving into how to find, lure, and keep the best and the brightest in the newsroom. National leaders from massive metros and productive community papers spoke. They included *Chicago Tribune* owner Sam Zell; Paul Ginocchio, director, Deutsche Bank Securities Inc. in New York; and the author and host of *A Prairie Home Companion*, Garrison Keillor. The presentations covered newspaper publishing from content to audience to finance to the internet to sales.

Every year, Inland honored a publisher who "brings about positive change while exemplifying the finest in journalism and community service." The honoree received the Ralph E. Casey Award, Inland's highest honor.

John Gottschalk, a year from retirement, was Inland's 2007 recipient. As such, he was asked to offer remarks at a luncheon in his honor. John delivered a fairly short and to the point speech, but surely long enough to give those in the room keen insight into the mind and experiences of a journalist and publisher about to close a career, which traced back more than five decades to the *Sheridan County Star*. His fellow publishers soon found that he was unsparing in his message to them.

He would later call his remarks his "eulogy to real newspapering."

"I have spent my life rooted in the daily exercise of serving readers," he said. "Digging out, reporting, and delivering information vital to sustain a self-governing people—telling stories well that lift the spirit, not just the barking dog, burning building, bleeding victim, or whistle blower 'news' so common in too many newspapers and in nearly the entire content of local TV news shows."

He quoted *Omaha World-Herald* founder Gilbert Hitchcock, telling the audience that he always tried to publish the "people's paper," a nod to the First Amendment and the unfettered flow of information to citizens. He then gave the publishers ten ideas to "ponder" as they "try to bring understanding and meaning to the increasing velocity of life." He dared them to be better.

John started by daring them to be credible (credibility being their "most precious asset"), to "give readers thoughtful and meaningful stories and worry less about entertaining them." He dared them to find more commonalities and fewer differences among readers, to reassess the value of their information to readers, and "to stop standing by while AP gives your valuable exclusive content away to the likes of Google." He implored them to edit ferociously while demanding that the basics of good reporting be the focus. He said that franchise and perpetuity should be their mission. "Newspapers aren't properties. They are perceived as people," a reference to the reality that too many newspaper owners no longer saw the responsibilities inherent in journalism but rather only the math of the bottom line. He urged them to be fully rooted in the community, to think not about next year but about the next generation of readers. "Play long," he implored.

Sales managers must be bold and forceful and insist on the same from their staffs. "If not, call in the ad director and light a fire under his fanny—or get a new one who knows more about selling than taking orders."

He dared them to shut down their mechanical switchboards, to employ a real human being as the newspaper's gatekeeper. "Give your switchboard operator a hug every day. She is the front door to the place people turn for help." All staff in every department, too, should understand that people want to talk to humans, not machines. Nor should the publisher ever become isolated from his or her employees, even in large metro papers, he told them. "Dare to get close to your employees." He told them Yogi Berra had it right: "You can observe a lot by just watching."

Having prepared for a thoughtful succession at the *World-Herald*, John urged publishers to do the same, accepting that the future of their newspapers and their legacies depended on it. "Look at yourself in the mirror and realize that the second you leave your present job, the value of your years of work will be established by your successor, not you," he said. "If you have done it well, your work will be reaffirmed and sustained by that successor. If you have one ounce of passion about our business, don't leave in a way that will relegate history to judge your stewardship as a failure because the business collapsed after you left. Either you left a weak business or you failed to prepare a worthy successor."

He closed by encouraging them to see that the time for reflection and self-appraisal was now. "Don't wait until your career is nearly over before you take some time to reflect upon what you would say if you were asked to make a speech to a highly engaged, capable, and knowledgeable group of publishers on short notice." He told them to do what he had done for nearly twenty years: Take two or three days each year to reflect on what was important and if a course correction was necessary, do it. "Don't let the drift I sense in much of our industry rob you of the satisfaction you deserve from holding one of the most honorable, demanding, and rewarding jobs in our nation."

John's news values and principles were not matters that evolved over time, arriving as a crystalized philosophy just in time for him to pass them along to national publishers as he approached his final year as publisher. In a memo to news executives at the *World-Herald* in 1990, less than a year into his tenure as publisher and CEO, he had delivered a similar message, telling them that their newspaper should be "truthful, accurate, fair, balanced, and necessary." In other words, a critical cog in the daily life of a community. He eschewed "herd journalism," practiced by lesser outlets aiming for "conflict journalism" rather than telling stories that impact readers.

He told them the *World-Herald* needed assignment editors who "knew something about real life outside the newsroom," who were "in touch with average people" who largely constituted their readership. He said news management must insist copy editors be teachers, reporters write with clarity and precision, and senior editors ensure the newspaper presented to readers each day was "useful, relevant, and complete."

He made it clear, too, that not only would personnel selection be key, so too would the development of all staff. "Good people must be given a chance to grow. Poor performers must be culled."

Even then, just steps into his nearly two-decade journey as publisher, John told his team that he would make himself available to be part of the decisions and work necessary to strengthen these core values and principles.

Twenty-eight years after he wrote the memo—with social media entrenched in society and inextricably entwined with journalism, with newspapers increasingly being referred to as "properties" and rated on their profit potential rather than on principles embodied in the First Amendment, or their integrity, or their journalistic effectiveness—John sang the same tune, still warning against the atrophy of news gathering and reporting, yet touting the gifts of freedom of the press.

The occasion was his induction into the Nebraska Journalism Hall of Fame in October 2018. Nearly four hundred people crammed into a ballroom at the Cornhusker Marriott Hotel in downtown Lincoln to celebrate the First Amendment, newspapers, and community journalism. John was part of an induction class of three and spoke second on the evening's program.

Among the honorees was Allen Beermann. Although not a journalist, Beermann was the popular and long-serving executive director of the Nebraska Press Association. Many of Beermann's friends sang his praises that night, from the emcee to the evening's entertainment to the keynote speaker. While the adulation for Beermann was genuine, a couple of times it teetered precariously close to being over the top.

As was his custom, John started making notes for his remarks during dinner before the inductions. He filled the side of a manila file folder with thoughts and musings. When his name was called, however, he ambled forward to the podium leaving his "speech" lying on the table next to a basket of rolls.

"What a wonderful night," he began, pausing briefly—"*if* you're Allen Beermann." The quip brought down the house, defusing whatever awkwardness might have been building in the ballroom and giving his friend Beermann a good laugh.

He then turned to more serious matters, praising the continued strength of community newspapers and paying homage to his friend, mentor, and long-ago colleague at the *Sidney Telegraph*, Jack Lowe. Lowe and John were co-owners of the *Telegraph* for four years before Lowe retired and sold his interest to John. In a wonderful twist of fate, John had established the Jack Lowe Community Journalism Fund at the University of Nebraska in 1974. It was the genesis for the Nebraska Journalism Hall of Fame, which, forty-four years later, would be honoring John Gottschalk.

When Lowe died in 1999, John's public statement revealed a deep, personal loss and previewed observations to which he would return that night at the Cornhusker Hotel:

> *My heart is heavy. I feel a deep sense of loss today.*
> *How blessed I was to have him as a friend and a mentor.*
> *People across Nebraska knew Jack Lowe as "Mr. Sidney,"*
> *as a gentle man and servant of his neighbors.*

His writing alone would have endeared him to us all, but he gave us so much more. He gave us, by example, a deep respect for duty and service to our community … and civility to one another. He made us laugh, he inspired us to undertake and accomplish things we never thought we could.

Across the lips of all who knew him, today passes a common expression: Thank you Lord for sending this special man to us. He left so much good, we will be carried by his deeds and kindness for years after this passing....

John also briefly cautioned the audience at the Hall of Fame Awards that in many ways the big newspapers seem to have lost their way, but community journalism was thriving because it emulated editors such as Jack Lowe. Surely not everyone there shared his assessment of the nation's metros in general or the *Omaha World-Herald* specifically, but clearly one could draw a straight line from what was on John Gottschalk's mind then to his remarks to the publishers at the Inland conference in 2007.

∼

John carried the admonition to owners, publishers, and newspaper executives in boardrooms as well. "If you have done it well, your work will be reaffirmed and sustained by that successor." A smart plan of succession, he believed, was the footing on which any organization could move toward the future while bringing with it the best of the past.

John moved effortlessly in both the corporate boardroom and the world of nonprofit agencies, often downplaying his leadership role, pointing out that great teams achieve great success. Having the skill set and temperament to move back and forth between business and civic leadership was not unusual, but doing it at the level and with the success as John did was exemplary, though not unique in John's circle. He served on a number of boards with local civic and business leaders who had similar skills and attitudes. Indeed, Heritage Services was a meeting of like minds with a common purpose, a civic passion to better a community, state, and nation, and a notable track record in the corporate boardroom.

Chief among John's principles—and he had years of experience practicing it—was the strength and efficacy of choosing the right person for the right job at the right time, whether that be a company's leadership team, an executive director of a nonprofit, or a local fishing guide.

Such a philosophy required John to spend considerable time from 2002 to 2007 grooming and teaching and preparing Terry Kroeger to succeed him as CEO at the Omaha World-Herald Co. and publisher of the *Omaha World-Herald* newspaper. As 2007 began, he told his executive staff that his primary focus for the next twelve months would be preparation for the transition when his retirement arrived in 2008. Consequently, it was with great disappointment to John ten years later when part of a management change included the departure of Kroeger. John believed strongly that the brightest line of his legacy was tied directly to the triumph or failure of his successor. Berkshire Hathaway, which bought the *World-Herald* from its employees in 2011, went on to hire Lee Publications, a competitor, to manage the company, leading to Kroeger's departure.

While John had questioned the changing nature of journalism in general and the grounding of the *World-Herald* in particular, he, like many others, was caught off guard when the paper's top management responsibility was "leased" to another company.

Clearly, he knew change was inevitable and often preferable to a status quo based on narrow justification, "That's how we've always done it." One of his primary goals was to change what he called the "culture" at the *World-Herald*. To do that meant far more than several company-wide emails or a series of come-to-Jesus department meetings. For John, culture change and culture maintenance constituted a planned, ongoing exercise designed to help staff work efficiently, effectively, and ethically, tapping into the best of each worker. He believed leaders set the tone—whether the subject was effort, intellect, efficiency, problem-solving, relationships, vision, or doing the right thing at the right time for the right reason.

Nowhere was that more apparent than in John's practice of assembling the *OWH* executives once a year in Tucson to review the past, consider the current state of the company, and plan for the next decade, or even the next generation of newspapers and the men and women who would run them.

Bill Kernen, former *OWH* senior vice president and board member, remembered John's skill for seeing the future. Kernen and senior vice president Bill Donaldson were the "Dollar Bills," John's closest confidantes at the *World-Herald*, part of the inner circle that expanded the company dramatically under John's leadership.

"He had the ability to look over the hill to know where he thought the company needed to go," Kernen said. "Early on, after he was promoted to CEO, each year he would get away for a week annually. He would hole up someplace and just spend a week bringing people in and talking to them about the industry and other things. And I remember he'd bring back a thick stack of papers from his gathering of information and, out of that, set the agenda for many strategic planning sessions the executives and John held annually in Tucson."

They used page summaries of his detailed notes, not simply as an agenda for the Tucson meetings, but also as a roadmap for the company's future.

Donaldson said John's forward-looking approach was evident early on, with his leadership on the newspaper's printing and computer changes. "His future-oriented approach took him to have an early interest in technology," Donaldson said. "We did some things early on trying to anticipate how they would affect us. We knew we had to do something or technology would kill us. He had a goal of growing the company. He had looked at other organizations, using the computer to evaluate acquisitions. He was on a long-term mission, not just a year or five years."

Retired *World-Herald* editor Woody Howe (left) with the
Dollar Bills—Bill Kernen (center) and Bill Donaldson—
during the "parade" at John's retirement party.

Kernen said John's approach also included being open to the ideas of others when gathering information, even though it was clear who the boss was. "You always knew that John was in charge, I mean, there was no question about that. He was very confident, he was intelligent, he was a great speaker, great writer. I don't know if he ever spoke from a draft. It was a testament to his trying to get closure on where he thought the company should be going. He was definitely a good listener. He saw a need to move responsibility after he became CEO and, as I perceived it, probably expanded on that need in two or three ways. Number one, he saw a need that we, as an executive group, needed to go away for some period of time in the fall, or in the winter, after our annual meeting with the stockholders and hold our annual strategic meeting." High on the agenda, Kernen said, was the question, "Who are going to be the next folks in line?"

These yearly books comprised a number of sections. The book prepared for 1994's Tucson meeting had sections on news, miscellaneous concerns, image, reorganization (as needed), people, confidential topics, and cultural change. A couple of pages at the beginning were devoted to the previous year's "history," but the books were forward-thinking documents, designed to assure a successful future for the newspaper and its employee owners.

To that end, John was especially keen on company executives knowing that a significant responsibility of their roles as company leaders was to assure smooth and efficient transitions when they left. That required choosing the right successor. And while "fit" was a product of skill, smarts, and character, any heir apparent for a leadership position in the company needed not simply to understand "culture" was a critical component to the company's financial success; they also needed to have demonstrated the will and wisdom to maintain it.

Consequently, under John's leadership, company executives made succession a priority. Most of the heavy lifting fell to John and the Dollar Bills to make choices. Even then, John had the final say, none of which was news to any *World-Herald* executive during John's tenure as CEO. As Kernen said, everyone knew John was the leader, the man in charge. Still, the process of and focus on efficient and effective succession meant most promotions were not only smooth, but also rather unremarkable.

"The Dollar Bills and I would go down a day early, and we initiated the tracking and the whole approach to transition. It was really an issue of age. Kernen and Donaldson and I weren't that far apart. They were a few years ahead of me. So, we were all going to retire at roughly the same time. And, so we had three jobs to fill that were important jobs, really important jobs."

Donaldson was the first to retire. He did many things and did them well. "Donaldson was a great all-around player. I mean, he led the ad division, he handled circulation, he did labor relations. When I got to the *World-Herald* in 1975, we were in the middle of the typographer's strike and Bill was managing that issue."

The process was open-ended in the sense that John and his team realized that not everyone wanted to be a vice president or even the CEO. He, Kernen, and Donaldson maintained a list of young prospects in the company, detailing their obvious strengths, such as finance or sales. Some they threw into the "all-arounder" pile. It was necessary to remain realistic about changing circumstances in the lives of the up-and-comers they were evaluating. "Maybe over the course of ten years, everything changed," John said. "So, we had to test these guys and gals."

They were up-front with the potential executives. "We told them we were beginning to think about transition. It may have seemed like a long way away, but the time would come quicker than they thought. We said we wanted to develop a program with some of our best people, to move them around in different assignments within the company and the paper. We told them we wanted to see what they excelled at and get an idea of what the future might hold for them. But, I told them up front, they had a choice. They could get in the game or not. Well, everybody wanted in the game. Over the course of time, we'd move them around. We spent ten years going over these people all the time, moving them around and getting them a variety of exposure." John's successor, Terry Kroeger, was a case in point, starting fresh out of college as an assistant purchasing agent, moving to a variety of management positions within the company at newspapers including Columbus, Kearney, and Stockton, California, where he was publisher. He returned to Omaha to become John's deputy in charge of building the printing plant before becoming publisher and CEO when John retired in 2008. He was head of the BH Media Group in 2018, but left the company after Berkshire Hathaway turned over management of the Omaha World-Herald Co. and its newspapers to Lee Enterprises.

Because transition was a numbers game, if someone wanted to retire early, John wanted to know, making no judgment one way or the other. "Don't be bashful, we told them. If you want to retire early, tell me that. If you want to retire late, tell me that. We had to stay current where succession was concerned."

While succession strategy considered the past but happened in the present, its focus, where it demonstrates its success, was in the future. John's own ascent to the corner office came in stages, illustrating the importance of having a critical strategy for succession. By 1985, he held the title of executive vice president, and the board of directors was about to meet. "Harold Andersen called me into his office and said, 'The board's going to elect you as chief operating officer of the company.' The first thing I said to Andy was, 'Well, I'm very pleased about that. It comes as a surprise to me at this stage.'" The promotion positioned John at the head of the line to become Andersen's successor four years later when Andersen reached the company's mandatory retirement age for its CEO of sixty-six. At one point during those four years, discussing John's eventual succession, Andersen said, "You know, John, the first thing you got to do is find a John Gottschalk." John responded immediately. "I said, 'Andy, if I stay in this job as long as you've stayed in this job, my successor is in the seventh grade. I cannot see him yet.'"

The succession strategy was rooted in mathematics, which John loved. "Generally, you retire at age sixty-three or sixty-four or sixty-five," he said. "You've got some good young people and you've got to get them seasoned and ready. We need a little time to move them around, look at them, really check them out. We'd like to have them ready to move up between ages forty and fifty, leaving fifteen years to retirement. And, so, you take that fifteen years we want them to work after we select them, plus the ten years of preparation, that's twenty-five years. If they're going to retire at sixty-five after fifteen years on the job and ten years of preparation, we have to have them spotted by the time they're forty."

Not all successions and transitions went smoothly. At a meeting of managers and executives at Tucson just before his retirement, John, after serious consideration, told one of the group that the position to which he hoped to be promoted was not going to be filled. The individual took the news poorly. "I guess his reaction was really not surprising, because his hopes and expectations were high," John said. "But we never indicated to anybody that they were in. You weren't in until you were in." Later, following a dinner attended by participants in the meeting, the group headed for the parking lot. The disappointed manager, his wife at his side, approached John. "He said to me, 'John, you're wrong. I'm going to prove you wrong.' I said, 'Perfect. That's what I want you to do. Because if you're going to prove me wrong, you've got to do it right. So, have at it.' But I retired without filling the spot because I didn't think he was the right guy."

The man stayed with the *World-Herald* for many years afterward, advancing after John retired to what he thought was his rightful place. John said it was nothing personal, but his view of succession was that it underpinned the organization's success, so decisions he made, he made for the company.

Former Executive Editor Mike Reilly remembered a time when John turned him down for a promotion, but this time the landing was soft.

A native of St. Louis, Reilly was waiting for an offer from the *Post-Dispatch* after a stint with the Columbia, Missouri, *Daily Tribune*, where one of his colleagues was John's father, Phil Gottschalk. He met John at Phil's retirement party in 1987. Reilly stayed at the *Daily Tribune* until 1989 when he left for another St. Louis paper that went under a year later. That gave him plenty of time to drive the editors at the *Post-Dispatch* to distraction.

"I wasn't getting anywhere bugging the editors there," Reilly said. "One of them there knew the managing editor at the *World-Herald*, Bob Pearman. He called Pearman and said, 'Have you got anything for this guy? He's really driving me crazy.'" The *World-Herald* offered Reilly a job. "But, I didn't know anything about Omaha. I was on the fence about it. John's dad called me and said, 'Why are you holding out to work for a paper that pretends to cover the state when you can go work for a paper that really covers the state?' He kind of nudged me, and I took the job in Omaha. So, I was probably more than the random reporter hire."

While John didn't interview Reilly, he did make a point to see him when he came for the interview, a touch that impressed the young St. Louisan. "I thought John was very nice. He just came out and met me. He knew I was there. He wasn't interviewing me, but he was very gracious to me for my whole career while he was publisher."

He also found the publisher to be available, formally if necessary, and clearly as someone who was an obvious and visible part of the ongoing work at World-Herald Square. "I thought he wanted to be accessible," Reilly said. "He made a point of being around and wandering through the newsroom and, you know, shooting the breeze with people. At World-Herald Square everything was on two floors and so nobody was very far away from anybody. Everybody used the same lunchroom and so, you know, you might run into John there, or he'd be in the newsroom. He wasn't hesitant about bringing an idea to Mike Finney or Larry King (*OWH* editors), but then he'd stop to say 'hi' to somebody. He didn't malinger, he didn't hang around a long time, but he was friendly in that way, and seemed approachable that way."

So it was odd that Reilly found a degree of trepidation about John among a number of his co-workers. He chalked it up to history. "John was a strong figure in the community and in the company. I don't think I feared him, but I was amazed when I arrived at how much fear there was of John and Woody both. And I didn't fear Woody, either. I found John approachable and easy to talk to. But it was a culture there that maybe predated either of them."

Reilly put his reading of John's non-threatening manner to the test. "Once, in the newsroom, I had to say something to him. I knew before I said it that it wasn't exactly what he was going to want to hear. I don't remember how I said it, but it was with a little bit of care. He looked at me and said, 'Well, that was elegantly put.'"

Reilly worked his way through the newsroom and found himself as an assistant managing editor late in John's tenure as publisher. That's when he decided that being Editorial Page Editor was the next logical step for him, so he spent four months reading and researching in anticipation of applying for the vacancy, which John would fill after Frank Partsch retired. He threw his hat in the ring. John chose Geitner Simmons, who had been an editorial writer under Partsch.

Reilly's disappointment was palpable, but John made sure he knew why he wasn't chosen and how the decision fit into a larger plan for the newspaper—and for Mike Reilly.

"John turned me down. It was between Geitner and me. Geitner was picked. But, it was John's decision and I think, even then, he had his eye on me to be the managing editor and the executive editor. But, I didn't see that. I wasn't as confident in myself, maybe, as he was confident in me. I don't remember exactly what he said, but I remember how good I felt after he turned me down. He came into my office. The gist of what he said to me was that this wasn't the job for me. 'I'm going to disappoint you about this today,' he said, 'but you have a bright future here. Your field of play is very broad. Don't lose heart over this.' The way he handled that was a lesson to me as a manager and a leader about how important those kinds of moments can be. When you have to disappoint somebody, how being caring and careful about it can pay off dividends."

The next day Reilly sent John an email, following up on their conversation. It read in part:

One of the less appreciated traits of good leaders is the ability to disappoint people well. You've disappointed me about possible promotions three times now.

Each time, you did it well.

Each time, my let-down was tempered by your kind words about my contributions and by your willingness to share what has always sounded like clear thinking behind your decision.

I thank you for both.

I feel a need to tell you, though, that this latest disappointment came as a shock.

I've spent the last four months fully expecting to become your next editorial page editor. I had the passion for it. I would have done a great job.

But I acknowledge you have the better vantage point to see the whole picture, including Geitner's strengths and how my talents can be used better in the newsroom.

I trust your judgment and your sincerity about my future prospects here.

John followed up with his own email, which said, in part: "Your intensity about this vocation, and this newspaper particularly, is a characteristic few hold, and thus, it further sharpens why I told you we need you here, fully engaged. I know you were disappointed....

"I know you have high standards, Mike, and I admire you so much for that. I have come to know you as one who moves forward in most any circumstance, and I know you will continue to do well in your present assignment. Nonetheless, I too feel the need to stretch Mike Reilly—and I am comfortable that he has much left to give this newspaper. You want that and so do I."

∽

In December 1997, the *Omaha World-Herald* printed a five-day series called "Farm to Fork." It began with an ominous observation, tinged with reality.

> *An invisible villain lurks on the pastoral horizon of the Great Plains. It breeds in the bellies of cattle, and it likes to attack children.*
>
> *It is Escherichia coli O157:H7 (E. coli), a genetically mutated, microscopic bacteria that worms its way into the food we eat, especially ground beef. Every year in the United States it causes an estimated ten thousand to twenty thousand illnesses and one hundred to two hundred deaths.*
>
> *It starts and spreads on the farm. But policymakers in government and the beef industry have done almost nothing to try to stop it there.*
>
> *That is just one of the problems the* World-Herald *discovered in a three-month investigation of the nation's methods for keeping beef safe.*

Mike Reilly was the lead editor on the series, which included bylines from *World-Herald* staff writers David Hendee, Henry Cordes, Paul Hammel, and Jake Thompson. Jeff Beierman and Jeff Carney were the photographers.

Impetus for the series came from the closing of a Hudson Foods meat processing plant in Columbus, Nebraska. The Arkansas-based company had recalled 25 million pounds of beef in August 1997 after inspectors suspected the meat could be contaminated with E. coli. Tests on 1.2 million pounds of Hudson beef revealed the presence of the deadly bacteria.

The recall of beef in such dramatic quantities had a chilling ripple effect across Nebraska, from pastures and pens in ranch country to the meat counter in grocery stores to dining room tables everywhere. Reilly's team of reporters set out to determine the extent of the problem, the depth of its consequences, and how it would affect not simply ag producers but also consumers' decisions at the market.

The award-winning series set off a chain of events, during which Reilly came to know John Gottschalk as more than just an executive in a big office. Those events began with widespread unhappiness among livestock producers. While not taking direct aim at the reporting, representatives of the industry asked to meet with John. Reilly said they wanted to dictate what should come next. "They were asking for some friendly follow-up stories that kind of indirectly apologized for how harsh these stories were. You know, to set the record straight as they perceived it on what a great industry this was."

Kathy Pilling, who was the farm advertising rep for the *World-Herald's* classified ad division, said beef producers told her they had no quibble with the accuracy of the content, but they believed the newspaper unnecessarily "sensationalized" headlines and graphics. "They felt the series portrayed a negative picture of the beef industry."

The livestock producers in effect demanded to dictate story assignments, and they did so under cover of a very real threat: Either write follow-up stories to make the industry look better than they believed "Farm to Fork" had, or they would pull their considerable advertising dollars.

Surely few if any livestock producers in the late 1990s had much knowledge of the "milk wars" in and around Sheridan County almost forty years earlier. That's when a sixteen-year-old John Gottschalk stared down an angry group of dairy farmers at the counter of the *Sheridan County Star* on a Saturday morning in Rushville. The farmers were demanding the retraction of a story that had run in the *Star* that week. John gave them the same answer then that he would give the livestock producers who complained to the *World-Herald*.

No. No new set of stories would be written to undo or condition what had been reported in "Farm to Fork."

John remembered the livestock producers wanting more than a massaging of their industry's image.

"They wanted a retraction. Yet they could not offer one single error of fact in the stories. They were just of the opinion that it made them look bad. This story came on the heels of several E. coli outbreaks. People knew little of what it was or how it got into the food chain. The livestock guys then said they would pressure all livestock sale barns across the state to withdraw their advertising from the *Omaha World-Herald*, presumably to force us to stop the series. I told them we truthfully printed the facts as to how E. coli migrated from farm to fork. The stories did not make any accusations. I don't recall the exact amount of business lost, but it was well over $1 million a year—forever. I understood that would happen at the outset and was willing to forgo that revenue forever before I would bow to threats being the arbiter of the paper's credibility. Our pen, and the truth, was never for sale."

The fallout was swift. True to their word, the beef industry boycotted the *World-Herald*, pulling all its advertising. For Pilling, the boycott meant the loss of her job as her accounts dried up. She resigned three months later. In her resignation letter to Classified Advertising Manager Dale Harris and copied to John, Pilling said, "It doesn't really matter at this point whether (the beef industry) overreacted or acted upon legitimate concerns, they felt they needed to pull their advertising—and they did. In the last two months, I've lost my position and the trust of livestock advertisers I've worked with for the last ten years. Credibility takes a long time to restore and I can't afford to wait any longer. It seems incredible to me that the number one industry in the state of Nebraska is of so little concern to the largest newspaper in the state. More important than the loss of revenue is the loss of trust of the industry. It is not in the best interest of the newspaper to disregard this fact."

Pilling went on, however, to thank John for helping her earlier and for "being accessible, understanding, and fair."

John said her predicament obviously had become clear to her early on as the series ran. "I imagine she was quite uncomfortable to be under attack by a bunch of hotheads. She certainly had no responsibilities or experience with policy or unpleasantries. Even before (her letter) reached me, I imagine she had connected the dots between their threats and her job being at stake."

The Nebraska beef producers' reaction to the series revealed not only the pressure a large advertiser can put on a newspaper but also—as John explained—the push-pull between advertising and news. "I have never known a newspaper in which there was not constant tension between the ad department wanting to love their customers, and the newsroom wanting to love their readers. Neither knows much about the other's responsibilities. The ad department says, 'Why won't they write positive pieces about my grocery account?' The news room says, 'Why is the ad department always bellyaching about ad placement?'"

For Reilly, John's reaction to "Farm to Fork" and the ensuing nastiness brought on by the state's beef industry underscored both the accuracy of the reporting and the importance of journalism. "It was very gratifying," Reilly said. "But I don't know that I honestly was surprised. As a reporter, you're constantly questioning your own judgment, your own accuracy, your own fairness. So there's always an insecurity that's associated the night before you publish a big story, or in the aftermath when people start complaining about it. There's always some thought if you did everything right. Could I have done more? You know, if you're a conscientious journalist, you're going through that all the time." For Reilly, it was "a very affirming, gratifying moment" when John told the beef producers there would be no retraction.

He said that it was only later that he learned how much money was at stake, with word spreading quickly throughout the newsroom regarding what had transpired between the publisher and the big advertisers.

∼

Standing just inside the door to the *Omaha World-Herald*'s fifteenth floor executive offices was *Good News*, a thirteen-hundred-pound bronze sculpture of a paper carrier, a satchel of newspapers slung over his shoulder, his faithful dog at his side, and his right arm extended, newspaper in hand.

George Lundeen was the sculptor, the same artist who created *Outta Here*, the spectacular bronze statue outside Modisett Park baseball field in John Gottschalk's hometown of Rushville, Nebraska. John was the driving force and primary financier behind Rushville's push to rebuild the venerable baseball park. Lundeen's bronze of a baseball player swinging for the fences captured not only the drama and beauty of the sport but also the effort by the town of Rushville to raise the money to build an outstanding sports venue.

Good News greeted everyone who had business on the fifteenth floor. But John, who commissioned Lundeen to create the sculpture, said the image of the young boy was also a reminder that the multi-billion-dollar industry that was America's newspapers was then totally dependent on children—subteens in many instances—to distribute its product. While newspapers logged and analyzed circulation in numbers and formulas that may have been over the head of an eleven-year-old carrier, youngsters were nonetheless a critical cog in the process of getting newspapers to readers in Omaha, across Nebraska, and beyond.

For the *Omaha World-Herald*, that process reached a stunning milestone in late 1986 when the newspaper's November 9th Sunday edition went over the three hundred thousand circulation mark. In honor of the occasion, John sent champagne to Bill Donaldson, then in charge of circulation. In a handwritten response to John, Donaldson said, "Your gift of champagne is very much appreciated. It has been distributed among those in circulation most responsible for the record sale. We popped a cork Friday night. That's good stuff."

Obviously, none of the bubbly was shared with the hundreds of carriers who braved a morning temperature of twenty-five degrees on November 9 to get the *World-Herald* into the hands of the readers, more that day than had ever been in the paper's circulation.

Those were heady days for the newspaper industry and for carriers. According to the Pew Research Center, weekday circulation in American newspapers peaked in 1984 at nearly 64.5 million. Sunday circulation peaked in 1993 at 62.6 million. Circulation, for a variety of reasons, slid steadily thereafter. Since those salad days in the 1980s, the *World-Herald*'s circulation had fallen to just under 98,000 daily and about 113,000 Sunday by September 2018.

John Gottschalk and Bill Donaldson experienced a painful, tragic low when circulation was running high—the loss of a carrier.

Danny Joe Eberle, a thirteen-year-old from Bellevue, an Omaha suburb, was delivering his Sunday morning route, September 18, 1983, when serial killer John Joubert kidnapped and brutally murdered him. Danny Joe had made it to only three of the seventy houses on the route. His body was found on September 21 along a gravel road four miles from his paper route. He had been stabbed nine times. Joubert was a radar technician stationed at Offutt Air Force Base in Bellevue.

"(Danny Joe's death) really impacted all of us," John said. "Bill (Donaldson) was so good working with the family afterward, but it was a terrible time."

Nearly three months later a twelve-year-old boy from suburban Papillion, Christopher Walden, went missing just a few miles from where police found Danny Joe's body. Joubert had killed Christopher and hid his body even further out of town. Authorities found Christopher after two days.

Joubert, who had earlier murdered an eleven-year-old boy in Maine, was arrested a month later after police responded to a report of a suspicious person near a Bellevue preschool. He confessed to the two Nebraska murders and, after numerous delays and appeals, was put to death in Nebraska's electric chair on July 17, 1996.

Danny Joe's murder was among a dozen abductions, sexual assaults, and deaths among young newspaper carriers nationwide between 1970 and 1993. Since 1992, forty-five carriers of all ages were killed doing their job. Of that, twenty-three were "murdered or killed violently." Circulation decline played a significant role in fewer numbers of carriers, too. The fact remains that the idealized image of a newspaper carrier— the same one George Lundeen captured in *Good News*—was truly a portrayal of the past. Most newspapers now were delivered by adults or contract carriers in vehicles, as a result of the swing from afternoon to morning publications interfering with school schedules. Child carriers had become a rarity.

When John retired from the *World-Herald*, he left the sculpture, thinking its message still should be preserved. True, the demographics of news carriers had changed. But there was more. Ten years after his retirement, Berkshire Hathaway, the owner of the *Omaha World-Herald*, entered into a management agreement with Lee Enterprises of Davenport, Iowa, to run the *World-Herald*. John decided that the time and values depicted in *Good News* were no longer a true reflection of reality. He had the statue moved to his home.

When John read about Tatyana Goryachova, the idea of a free press went beyond a democratic principle: it was life or death.

Goryachova was editor-in-chief at the *Berdyansk Delovoy*, the only independent newspaper in Berdyansk, the Ukrainian port city of 133,000 on the northern coast of the Sea of Azov. The *Delovoy*, by reporting on corruption and ineptitude in local government, earned the enmity of officials and five competing newspapers, which were owned by political parties or government entities. The editor's specific sin was giving equal coverage to challengers in local elections, thereby infuriating incumbents. Goryachova and her family were targeted by death threats. The paper's publisher was injured in an automobile accident caused by someone tampering with the steering.

One night early in 2002, while Editor Goryachova was walking home from work, she happened upon another pedestrian on the darkened sidewalk. The stranger threw a jar of hydrochloric acid over his shoulder and into Goryachova's face, blinding her for two months. She would need two surgeries, one about eight months later and one again in 2017. Acid attacks had become a staple to settle political scores in Russia and other parts of Europe.

Undaunted, Goryachova continued to lead the *Delovoy*, but she had no press and was required to use government printers. She struggled to meet the considerable challenge of corruption in government. Elections to foster democracy were imminent. John Gottschalk was in touch with Hal Foster, who worked in the *World-Herald* newsroom years earlier. Foster knew Goryachova from a journalism seminar in Kiev. John put together a team of executives at the *World-Herald* led by Doug Hiemstra, who made it possible for a restored offset press from the *Papillion Times* to be sent to Berdyansk. Over the course of about a year getting the press there and up and running, the *World-Herald* also sent press technician Tracy Levstik to the Ukraine for three weeks. Another press mechanic, John Dean, also spent time in Ukraine setting up the press. John wrote to Goryachova in early 2005:

> *Tatyana: I have followed your country's struggles closely and I applaud your continuing courage to seek what is right for the Ukraine... and congratulate you and your countrymen on the tedious but important recent election victory. Many friends in Omaha are pulling for your fragile democracy.*

She replied:

> *Thank you (Doug) and Mr. John Gottschalk for the nice words. It was very difficult victory for our country and for all honest journalists of our country. We are really proud of our new democracy and our new president Victor Yushchenko. We were at the Maidan (Independence Square) in Kiev. We wrote about all the events regarding dirty struggle of Victor Yanucovich in our newspaper. A bank account of our newspaper was (frozen)... But we are winners. We are very happy and independent now.*

Yushchenko survived an assassination attempt and led Ukraine until 2010 when Yanucovich was elected.

For her determination Tatyana Goryachova won the Courage in Journalism Award from the International Women's Media Foundation and a similar award from Human Rights Watch.

The *Berdyansk Delovoy* continued to publish every week.

~

The tools of democracy at the *Sheridan County Star* in the 1950s.

To the astonishment of many in Sheridan County, in 1940, Mayre Modisett, known before then for his devotion to parsimony, footed the $10,000 bill for a new baseball park in Rushville. Modisett and his brother Albert had made a fortune in the Sandhills, Mayre in banking and Albert in ranching. Albert, a close friend of author Mari Sandoz, was killed in an automobile accident in 1935 traveling to the Modisetts' native West Virginia.

The new field, Modisett Park, elevated Rushville's baseball fever by several degrees and burnished the town's reputation. It brought in teams from around the state as word spread that the new field was the best in Nebraska outside Omaha. Baseball flourished in Rushville in the 1940s and into the 1950s. Modisett Park was a driving force in its popularity. In 1953 local businessman, Gene Leahy, who had played for years for the Rushville town team, met a scout for the Milwaukee Braves through his brother, Notre Dame football coach Frank Leahy. The chance meeting led the Braves to open a professional baseball school in Rushville. It brought talented young players from all over the United States, Canada, and Latin America to Rushville. Such schools were a vehicle of hope for aspiring baseball stars. Rushville rolled out the red carpet to make the players' experience memorable.

Over the decade of the Rushville Baseball Schools, the Los Angeles Dodgers and the New York Yankees added their names as hosts. The era ended after 1965, leaving Modisett Park to host American Legion games and an occasional pickup game on a warm summer morning. Age and upkeep were factors in the health of any ball field. Modisett was no exception. In 2013, Mayor Chris Heiser called John and asked if the Carmen and John Gottschalk Foundation would help save the historic structure, badly in need of repair and updating.

Jeff Barnes, in his 2014 book, *Extra Innings: The Story of Modisett Ball Park*, chronicled John's headfirst slide into building the structure anew, exactly as the original. The Gottschalk Foundation made an initial $350,000 donation (ultimately to grow to nearly $2 million). Another $126,000 was raised in Rushville, and $100,000 was sent to the Foundation by donors in Omaha and across the state and country. Modisett's future looked bright. John enlisted the help of his friends at the HDR architecture and engineering firm in Omaha to make his vision—drawn on the back of a napkin in 2013—come alive in his hometown. Rushville did its part, too, raising more than enough to ensure the rebirth of one of its most important landmarks.

On August 31, 2014, hundreds showed up to witness the dedication of the new Modisett Park and to watch some baseball—a game between PONY Leaguers from Chadron and Rushville. Once again, a fine "field of dreams" graced the western edge of the town and baseball reclaimed its rightful place in Rushville history.

~

Ak-Sar-Ben Village was a thriving area with outdoor concerts, a farmers market, and enough retail traffic to make it a hot destination in Omaha. Baxter Arena was nearby as was the headquarters of HDR, as well as a variety of shops, eateries, and a movie complex. Just a few years earlier, the neighborhood was a destination of a different sort. Until the late 1990s, it was the site of the Ak-Sar-Ben Coliseum and Racetrack, one of the country's top ten venues for Thoroughbred horse racing and a major local mecca for stage shows, ice-skating events, and an annual stock show and rodeo.

The racetrack had its record attendance in 1985. But by the 1990s, with racing fans increasingly forsaking the ponies and crossing the Missouri River to bet on the greyhounds in Council Bluffs, Iowa, the owners of the racetrack decided it was time to get out of the horse racing business. The owners were the Knights of Ak-Sar-Ben, a philanthropic organization with a long history of generating money and exerting community leadership. Their decision to give up on Thoroughbred racing was to have dramatic effects.

For one thing, not everybody thought a horse track was a loser. Douglas County commissioners coveted the racetrack and its park-like, central-Omaha campus. They saw the site as a potential recreational asset for the county and a moneymaker that, they were sure, could pay for itself, and more, through its racetrack revenues. To raise money for the purchase, the commissioners issued revenue bonds. The Knights were a willing seller of the park and racetrack; Douglas County took possession in 1992, continuing the racetrack operations. But the effort was short-lived. Casino gambling took root in Council Bluffs, enticing more gamblers to Iowa in search of the faster action of the slot machines and gaming tables. In 1995, Douglas County admitted that the racetrack was failing financially and had to be shut down.

This meant an end to the revenue stream that the commissioners had counted on to pay for park development and, more important, to service the bonds with which they had bought the property in the first place. The county's financial situation was precarious. Rumors spread that the county might default on the bonds. Other rumors suggested that the county might be tempted to unload the property to unscrupulous developers who might exploit it without appreciating its potential value as a public amenity.

Still another scenario—and this was more than rumor—had it that Nebraska horse racing interests were cementing an alliance with the casino industry to push for legalization of casino gambling in Nebraska. These groups envisioned a refurbished racetrack surrounded by banks of slot machines whose profits would subsidize the racetrack purses, thereby attracting higher-quality horses and, in turn, restore track attendance to that of the glory days of the 1980s.

Samson finally stirred. Samson was a mythical figure in the Knights of Ak-Sar-Ben. His purpose was to advance civic and community causes in the name of the Knights—and not to receive any personal credit for these accomplishments. John had been an Ak-Sar-Ben councilor from 1987 to 1989. He also had been honored as the organization's "king of the mythical kingdom of Quivira," in the early 1990s. By 1995, some people, including John, thought the organization had an additional opportunity for service.

So Samson, in the person of John Gottschalk, put together "Samson's Centennial Vision," a roadmap to solve the growing Ak-Sar-Ben problem and stifle the bid to bring casino gambling to Nebraska. John had long been an opponent of expanded gambling and his editorial positions at the *World-Herald* were consistent to that end.

Samson's vision was clear and concise, almost matter of fact, beginning with a five-part hypothesis that clarified the players and the problem:

1. The fear of Douglas County defaulting on bonds was being used by politicians to escalate gambling in Omaha.

2. The current fervent argument that further gambling was needed to "make racing a success" could not be sustained by logic or morality.

3. The notion that county ownership of Ak-Sar-Ben needed to generate revenue dissuades the community from developing a truly functional new convention center.

4. The belief that Omaha would be best served by reducing rather than increasing gambling.

5. The promise for the public good to come from the Ak-Sar-Ben site, when it was sold to Douglas County, had not been kept and it needed to be.

Samson had defined the problem. Then he went about detailing the solutions, which included heading off gambling interests seen as "fulcrums for leveraging more gambling." He argued that restoring ownership of Ak-Sar-Ben to non-government entities would best serve the interests of the community and give the Knights of Ak-Sar-Ben, who could parlay that into development, a chance to reinvigorate their historic commitment to community leadership. Such a plan would lessen the rancor caused by the sale of the property to the county. It also would "resolve the uncertainties of bond holders," some of which were nonprofit institutions to which bonds had been donated by the original purchasers. Finally, Samson declared that this plan was "the right thing to do for Omaha."

He laid out a plan to tackle the problem and described what success looked like for the county, the city, the Knights, and the people of Omaha. Then Samson slipped his vision into the right hands, giving hope and a plan to those searching for an answer—and surely causing heartburn to those hoping to plant casino gambling smack dab in the middle of Omaha.

As King of Ak-Sar-Ben's annual fall gala in 1994, John had a team of escorts
in the mythical "kingdom of Quivira." The event raised scholarship money
for the Knights of Ak-Sar-Ben, a long-time philanthropic group in Omaha.

Thirteen years after "Samson's Vision" made the rounds to a select few, John sent an email to Mike McCarthy, who had become instrumental in Ak-Sar-Ben's rebirth and redevelopment—but had never seen the original "vision." John had retired from the *Omaha World-Herald* several weeks earlier but remained as chairman of the board. He came across

"Samson's Vision" in his files. The email to his close friend was both praiseworthy and reflective.

>*Mike:*
>
>*I'm in the periodic stages of reordering my life and affairs including some file cleaning and general "dunging out." (Isn't that old Midwestern term just perfect?)*
>
>*I came across the attached (Samson's Vision), written by a lone ranger at the time everyone was fully resigned to the County Commissioners' thirst for revenue via gambling—feeling nothing could be done with Ak-Sar-Ben but to turn it into a casino. It was a foregone conclusion. It was depressing.*
>
>*The document is footnoted "Samson's Vision." Samson was a mythological figure omnipresent in the early days of Ak-Sar-Ben. Good things would happen for Omaha and attribution was usually given to "Samson." I believe it was a way of giving credit to the "brand" rather than any individual. Samson did a lot of really good things including dumping the toll bridge that was detrimental to cross-river marketing development for Omaha.*
>
>*Anyhow, Samson carried this document to only about a half dozen people at the height of the "railroading." One was John Nelson, to whom he inquired about Paul Bryant perhaps having interest in acquiring bonds for defeasance. The second was a meeting with Bryant (who by the way said he would be helpful because it was the right thing to do for Omaha). Next it was a Sunday visit with Bob Daugherty, seeking money for acquiring the bonds. He said he'd help. And finally with the bulk of the money needed, a discussion with Walter (Scott), who appropriately took an interest and committed the remainder of the money needed and talked with Ken (Stinson), then the most influential governor.*

This morning I drove by the busy (Ak-Sar-Ben) site. It prompted me to write you with gratitude. I send it to you to tell you how proud I am of the extraordinary work you have done to shepherd the harvesting of a dream in bringing Ak-Sar-Ben Village into reality. Your unheralded efforts should be very satisfying to you. But, I want you to know that your "Samson-esque" contributions to our city do not go unnoticed. I am one who understands real results are a more meaningful measure of civic contribution than the mere applause given to those who seek vain recognition.

Gratefully, John G.

⁓

Phil Gottschalk, John's father, died Saturday evening, February 12, 2000, in Columbia, Missouri, at the Lenoir Home. He was seventy-nine. He had fought cancer for three years, buoyed by those who loved him, a considerable group drawn from friends and family. Phil was both hero and mentor to John, a guiding light both as a journalist and a father. John wrote Phil's obituary, which appeared first in the *Columbia Daily Tribune*, Phil's last stop on his journey, a life trek John described as living in "twenty-year increments." Phil grew up in Missouri and attended the University of Missouri before heading off to the U.S. Army in 1942.

The second score of life found him, with his wife Mary Jane, raising a family in Rushville, Nebraska, where they owned and published the *Sheridan County Star*. He returned to Columbia in 1966 following his divorce from Mary Jane. There he became a father and grandfather to a second family and worked mostly as the wire editor at the *Columbia Tribune*, writing his popular seasonal column on MU football called "Fan in the Stands." (In Rushville he had written a column called "Pigskin Roundup.") John and Phil reunited every year for Nebraska's football game against Phil's beloved Missouri Tigers. Phil retired in 1985, but remained active during the final stage of his life, devoting much of his time to *In Deadly Earnest*, his award-winning history book of Gen. Francis Cockrell's Missouri Brigade in the Civil War.

Aside from Phil's lengthy obituary, John would also detail the magnified moments of February 5, 2000, which he spent with Phil.

Phil Gottschalk, at age 62.

Today I said goodbye to my father. I entered his room at Lenoir about 1 p.m. and found him in bed, eyes half open, staring at the ceiling. His mouth was half open, each exhale was accompanied by a moan. I didn't know, as his lips moved, whether the moan was an attempt to talk to me or just a noise accompanied by the exit of air.

I stood over him and announced myself, 'Dad it's me. John.' After a couple of times, he noticed. I asked if he was in pain, if he was uncomfortable. Only moans came out. I was worried he would not speak, but he managed to let me know he was not in pain and not uncomfortable.

John told Phil that he'd heard the day before had been rough. He had spoken with the new hospice nurse by telephone. She said Phil had been talking better in the morning.

John reassured his father that he would be there for him and asked if he needed anything, a request answered with only a mumble. Moving closer, John heard Phil tell him he needed nothing.

"I wanted to give him permission to die, if he needed it and if he was 'ready.' He didn't answer.

"I told him he had played a great game against an unrelenting opponent. It was the fourth quarter and his opponent would soon score a victory. I said it was impossible to prevent that victory. I told him his defense had been on the field too long, now that opponent could no longer be held at bay. I said it was no sin to lose this game as long as he had given his all and lost honorably. I told him he would have that distinction. He understood what I said."

John described a steady stream of visitors that day who came to see Phil, some resigned to reality, a few still holding out hope, but all saddened and heartsick that the robust, gruff, cigar-chomping, 280-pound journalist, historian, and unyielding friend now lay quietly in a nursing home bed, shrunk to 117 pounds. After leaving to finish some paperwork at Parker Funeral Home, John returned to Lenoir where he found Roseann Echternacht, the daughter-in-law of Phil's wife, Patty, distraught at Phil's bedside. In the ensuing conversation, John assured her that Phil indeed "knew Jesus intimately." At 6 p.m., John asked Roseann if she could give him a few minutes alone with his father before he had to head back to Omaha.

"I bent over the frail skeleton of a man who was always a giant to me. The sun had set, and only the hospital bed light lit the room. I took his hand, bent over, and got his attention. His eyes were wide open. He saw and heard me clearly.

"'Dad, you gave me life and you gave me a family. You brought me on a long journey from Dayton to Rushville. I will always love you for that. I told you long ago that I would 'walk this last path at your side.' The moaning stopped. The open mouth closed. His eyes closed, and he gave me that memorable warm smile.

"I tightened the grip on his hand. His grip was remarkably firm on mine. I continued, 'Although I must stop walking now, I will still be with you. And you will always be in my heart.' Another smile but no words.

"Silence fell over both of us for a few seconds. I began to notice my gentle attempt to pull my hand away was met with some resistance. 'I have traveled with you as far as I can now. The rest of the journey you must make by yourself. Are you ready for that?' Again a smile as I reached to gently pry his grip from mine. I crossed his hands and placed both of mine over his.

"'I'll see you again Friday, Dad.'"

John did see his father again. With Lynn and Jodi, he was with Phil Gottschalk when he passed away the following Saturday.

≈

While the salute and parade at the Embassy Suites was a spectacular sendoff for John, his last meeting with shareholders as chairman was on January 25, 2008. Gathered that day were shareholder employees, whose toil, ingenuity, and pluck were the backbone of the company's stunning growth. Some in the audience that day would leave the *World-Herald* as millionaires, as a number of their colleagues had already done. John spoke to those co-workers and friends:

> *Well, the hour comes.*
>
> *You cannot know how deeply I respect the owners of this company. Both time and talent fail me to adequately tell you all that is in my heart today.*
>
> *I have lived a dream… doing something I looked forward to every morning… running the "people's paper." Never have I felt a moment of drudgery. Seeing you, the great bearers of our daily efforts, brought joy to me. I had fun, and I laughed one thousand times more than I wept.*
>
> *To be able to come to this highly respected newspaper— to be able to sustain the respect and significantly grow the enterprise—I could never have envisioned all that we have accomplished in these thirty-two years.*
>
> *Growing up in a small-town newspaper family, I learned early about self-reliance, initiative, hard work, and persistence. I learned, too, that deeds speak much louder than words, and that humility was the supreme trait of the successful leaders I admired most.*
>
> *You have given me the privilege to lead the establishment and first generation of an employee-ownership culture for this great newspaper.*
>
> *Years from now, your efforts will be looked upon as the earliest and most successful pioneering in the art of both winning and operating a substantial enterprise. Scholars will study how we did it… and I believe admire*

the unselfish commitment you made to this institution… well above and beyond self-interest.

The example of our infrastructure renewal comes quickly to mind. It is a gift to the next two generations. You had the respect for this great institution—and the courage—to invest in building something for the future instead of just selfishly stuffing it all in your pockets and turning your head to sustaining the enterprise.

You must always be proud of that.

My most fervent hope is that the passion for our mission of public service will remain with this company forever—looking forward—honoring the past but not living in it.

The Omaha World-Herald *is so much bigger than me—and you. It is over a century of public service to this state's good people. It is the most trusted beacon of truth. It has earned and held the trust and respect for the common man and the aristocrat—for its honesty, its integrity, and its credibility. These precious jewels are our most important treasure. They must never be bargained away or their luster allowed to dull.*

I cannot bring my day-to-day active career to completion without telling you how much you mean to me.

You are my sun and my rain… the nourishment of all ideas and vision that made real the many victories we have shared.

You have allowed my life to have great meaning by engaging in something enduring and worthwhile.

Nothing can come close to the power for good a great newspaper commands. Careful exercise of that great power will remain the primary difference between continuing to distinguish ourselves from all the other media or sinking into a useless, missionless, inconsequential rag.

I owe much to Ann Burdette and particularly Donna Grimm, both of whom worked tirelessly to manage me. Both of whom represented me and the company with the highest standards of discretion and integrity. Thank you, Ann and Donna.

Collectively our new leadership team gives me great pride—because of their character and values. You will never be ashamed of these leaders, and they will live every day knowing your future as well as this great newspaper's reputation are a very special and demanding stewardship.

Just as the four generations of my four predecessors carried the reputation of this newspaper to greater heights—so too will you and Terry. You—and Terry— are ready.

I know not how many days are left to me—but they all will be warmed by my memories and my faith and belief that you will raise this great enterprise to new heights.

So now—I retreat to spend those remaining days with my high-school sweetheart—to whom I owe the attention too often diverted over these thirty-two years. Thank you for waiting, Carmen.

And, instead of the usual phone call after so many long days at the office, I'll tell you personally this time: "I'll be home soon."

God bless you all.

FIFTEEN

The Confluence

Gottschalk, literally "Servant of God"
in Old German.

Among the treasures found in Omaha's Joslyn Art Museum was a nearly seven-foot bronze cast of Auguste Rodin's *Andrieu d'Andres*, a gift from John and Carmen Gottschalk and Woody and Anda Howe.

The statue was part of Rodin's most famous sculpture, *The Burghers of Calais*, which depicts six prominent residents of Calais on the way to their death during the Hundred Years' War. Rodin typically set apart components of his larger groupings and turned them into individual and magnificent works of art. So, it was with *Andrieu d'Andres*. Rodin instructed that his works be cast no more than twelve times. Each was considered an original. Joslyn's *Andrieu d'Andres* was numbered "6/8," meaning it was sixth of a group of eight.

While the statue was a stunning piece of art and rare indeed, the narrative behind its inception was what drew the Gottschalks and the Howes to *Andrieu d'Andres*.

An eleven-month siege of the city of Calais, just across the English Channel from Dover, brought the townspeople perilously close to starvation in early August 1347. England's King Edward III, who personally oversaw the siege, said he would end the horror if Calais sent six of its most prominent citizens to deliver the keys of the city to him and face certain death. The king insisted the men be barefoot with ropes around their necks. Six men, burghers—community leaders—volunteered. Among them was Andrieu d'Andres.

With a wailing citizenry watching from the gate behind them, the six burghers delivered the keys, essentially signing their death warrants. That was when Edward's wife, Queen Philippa de Hainault, pregnant and adamant about not bringing a child into the world under the stain of such violence, persuaded her husband to free the burghers, saving their lives.

While the story had a happy ending, Rodin captured the courage and anguish of the burghers as they made their way from their beloved Calais on a journey to save it.

Woody Howe wrote at the statue's dedication, "The lesson of the burghers has a special appeal to John and Carmen and to Anda and me. John and I are both newspapermen. In our careers, our basic goal has been the dissemination of news, information, and ideas that help people understand their world. In a sense we have been teachers. At the very least, we have been stewards of an institution with deep roots in the community. It seemed to us fitting that newspaper families donate this statue to Omaha and Nebraska and Iowa, communities we have tried to serve in our own way. We hope it will be a gift that will teach the value of patriotism, courage, and sacrifice."

Sue Morris, whose help in securing the statue included a trip with Woody Howe to New York to see the work of art at Christie's, said, "I have had many opportunities to share philanthropic gifts with donors. This was one of my favorites." Morris said she thought immediately of Woody and John when she heard the Rodin was going to be available.

Morris had worked often with John in public and philanthropic ventures. She said the gift was reflective of John's commitment to public service.

John, too, believed that Rodin's *Andrieu d'Andres* carried a message that would resonate many years into the future.

"Some may wonder, why this and why now?" he said. "The answer is found in this powerful piece and the story of how it came to be. The burghers of Calais volunteered to sacrifice their lives to save their community. It is our hope that generations will forever be inspired by associating this sculpture with selfless service to others. If so inspired, a lifetime of professional and personal actions will greatly advance civilization. The most profound principles are those one stands by when it is inconvenient. Service to others is such a profound principle."

When several streams finally merged, the confluence, the whole of the rushing river, looked as if it was one singular body of water. But back upstream, as the rivulets sought the low ground at the urging of gravity and nature, each carved its own niche into the mountainside. So it was with John Gottschalk's tributaries—compassion, service, duty, humility—as they formed a single, impressive life.

And while friends, colleagues, observers, even biographers, might have attempted to capture his days in a single phrase or concise sentence, the eventual river was too large and moved too fast to lend itself to a singular summation. Sue Morris's accurate observation that the Rodin gift encapsulated John's life of service provides a key to understanding the man and his life story. Service was a powerful force in John's makeup, influencing his accomplished career as a newspaperman; his impact as a captain of business; his embrace of his role of husband, father, and grandfather; and his insistence on life-long learning, ever curious about this thing called the human experience. Perhaps above all, his commitment to service was central to his natural affinity and skill as a leader.

John's remarkable journey from Dayton, Ohio, to the rolling hills of Sheridan County and the town of Rushville, Nebraska, was the stuff of legend, a drama filled with birth and rebirth. Then followed a glorious childhood spent along the 100th meridian in a place where neighbor was a verb, where triumphs and tragedies were shared experiences.

Phil and Mary Jane Gottschalk's kids, John, Mike, and Lynn, grew up smart and capable—leaders, professionals, difference makers—but never far from the streets, schools, and playing fields of Rushville. What some see as the suffocating closeness of small-town life, they experienced as a nurturing "village," raising its sons and daughters straight and strong and giving every opportunity to a child of Rushville to conquer Sheridan County—or the world.

John with Mike and Lynn, about 1950.

When John came to know the spectacular story of his own beginnings, he chose to move forward rather than get mired in the what-ifs and whys. While periodically curious, he never lingered over his days in Dayton or his temporary "adopted" status. Rushville was always home and family.

There, he learned the newspaper business from his grandfather, Bill Barnes, and his mother and father. He mastered the details of production and reporting. By sixteen he could hang a line of type and write a concise lead. He picked up and eventually perfected the art of balancing advertising and news, business and information, making money and minding the principle of the First Amendment. When the John Gottschalk Freedom Center was dedicated, John insisted that the celebration was, above all, a reminder that underneath all the state-of-the-art engineering and technology remained the tools of democracy.

John also learned from his grandfather and others in Rushville that giving and being of service was to be approached neither haphazardly nor by default, but rather carried out as a purposeful part of a full life. Through the Boys Scouts, he found ways to turn words such as honor and duty into skills. Long after he left Rushville, he was able, as the national leader of the Boy Scouts of America, to again practice its principles on a much larger stage, principles he had cherished throughout his life.

With his newspaper education in hand—at least the how and why of it—John began his own career when he left possibilities he and Carmen had in Lincoln to return to western Nebraska, taking the reins of the *Sidney Telegraph*. There, his mentor, Jack Lowe, taught him the importance of good community journalism.

Although John had witnessed civic engagement, civic duty, and civic pride in Rushville, Sidney was where he first put both oars in the water, propelling himself forward in running a successful newspaper and in providing public service to his community. Stints as a young newspaper owner/publisher while being a city councilman and mayor prepared him for a fully-engaged business and civic life when he left Sidney for Omaha in 1975. Perhaps even more important was John's ability to keep a professional perspective both as a local, elected leader and as a manager for those charged with reporting on local, elected leaders. Some would believe that the natural, adversarial relationship between government and journalism would, in Sidney, have stymied municipal progress, quality journalism, or both. John, however, was able to hit a sweet spot of sorts, leaving to *Telegraph* Editor Frank Partsch most of the newspaper's editorial positions and news decision-making as regarded the city council and mayor's office. The shorthand the pair developed during those years came in handy when they found themselves in a similar editorial dynamic some years later at the *Omaha World-Herald*.

John's one foray into traditional politics started and stopped with an unsuccessful bid for a seat on the University of Nebraska Board of Regents. Even though he finished among the also-rans, John's experience of campaigning across the vast district gave him keen insights into what Nebraskans valued. As publisher and CEO of the "state's newspaper," John put his regent's campaign experience to work, too. It proved invaluable because more than any entity in Nebraska, the *Omaha World-Herald* set the agenda for civic discourse in the state.

When John, Carmen, and daughters Jodi and Christina arrived in Omaha in 1975, the bend in the river was life-changing. Publisher Harold Andersen gave John a number of tasks, all of which John accomplished with the determination that he first found at the end of a broom and the encouragement of his father at the *Sheridan County Star*. John knew how to get things done. So just a few years after arriving at the *World-Herald*, he led a team in the installation of a new front-end system for the newspaper. His efforts earned him praise and a vice presidency, but perhaps most important was how John went about his business: motivated, decisive, fair, thorough, meticulous, and always open to the ideas of others he was leading or with whom he was a working peer. These habits came not simply to define John, but also to underpin hundreds of relationships at the newspaper, in Omaha civic engagements, and on national boards such as the National Benevolent Association and the USO.

For some the real test of leadership and character comes when the current turns white and life's eddies threaten to strand or sink projects or people. John never stayed too long recounting missteps nor wallowing in an excessive examination of failure. He moved ahead, the lesson of losses filed for the future, whether he led a team that lost a deal after considerable time and effort; said goodbye to a huge advertising account after standing his ethical ground; found himself hauled into court for no apparent good reason by those within the sphere of the *World-Herald* family; or was asked to take one for the team when it was time to make him whole with his stock buyback at retirement. While disappointed, even angry at times, he instead chose to drill down on the positive, often with a generous dose of John Gottschalk pragmatism.

One of his great joys as CEO and publisher of the *World-Herald* was to see employee owners at the *World-Herald* accumulate a nest egg through the employee-ownership program. More than a few retired as millionaires. While the sheer magnitude of the numbers was thrilling, John felt a kinship to each of them both as their leader, but more important, as their co-worker. These were people he knew from their efforts, but also from his insistence on being a visible, approachable leader. He was often out of his office, down with the production team talking machines and technology. Or he was in the newsroom, bending an editor's ear with a story idea or handing out attaboys and attagirls to reporters. He rarely overstayed his welcome, resuming his place in the background, where he was comfortable as a leader.

His files were filled with hundreds of thank-you notes and letters from employees who obviously liked their retirement resources, but who often spoke, too, about John's making them feel a part of something bigger than the job. Those employees were not simply grateful for their jobs; they were grateful for having a purpose at those jobs.

Still other notes thanked John for his time and his wisdom. A John Gottschalk calendar was a thing of beauty, crunched to the very minute, given his responsibilities at the newspaper, his duties to civic projects such as the Holland Performing Arts Center, his commitment to a number of national boards, even his temporary gig leading the University of Nebraska Foundation. But John made time for those who needed it, especially those starting out, finding their way. Sure, some wanted him to write a check, too, but many were just seeking John's input. So he made time, much as mentors had made time for him from his grandfather to Majorie Wasserberger to Jack Lowe to Harold Andersen.

Education was important in the home of Mary Jane and Phil Gottschalk. John carried that ideal with him into stints leading Omaha 2000 as a model for other cities and brokering a deal to keep Omaha's school district from a disastrous trisection. He started the *Omaha World-Herald*'s Academic All-State teams, which became the gold standard in Nebraska for honoring high-school scholars. He led reforms as a national board member for his college fraternity, Phi Gamma Delta.

Defining a life was an inexact science. Answering the questions of who someone was and what he did were often a matter of record: Résumés, personal vitae, trophies and news accounts reveal plenty about those whose lives were public and pronounced.

Measuring whether any of it made a difference, however, could be tricky. Plato said the real measure of a man was what he did with power. Some, using the typical metrics of status, wealth, and influence, would see John Gottschalk's life as one of power. Certainly, as the leader of the *Omaha World-Herald*, John had a professional footprint that was considerable in business, journalism, politics, and any number of issues important to Nebraskans.

But Rushville was never far from John's perspective—toning, conditioning, and clarifying life and its waterways, sometimes still and serene, sometimes foaming and fierce. John was skilled at reading whatever river on which he found himself, but his approach was always the same: put together a team, move forward, work hard, solve the problem, do what's right, understand the human side, and be honest about it all. For John, the problems were often complex; his solutions—his process—were detailed, meticulous, successful, and, to some, inexplicably simple.

Travelers heading north from Jackson Hole, Wyoming, would find that the highway bends left at Warm Springs Road. Suddenly filling the spectacular panorama was an unobstructed view of Grand Teton, rising 13,775 feet into the pristine mountain air. On clear mornings, when the clouds had moved off the peak and the sun streamed from behind the driver, Grand Teton took on a particularly clear and stunning patina. Grand is the highest peak in the Tetons, a subrange of the Rocky Mountains. To the west lies Idaho, to the north Yellowstone National Park, the nation's best-known natural wonder.

For newcomers to the area, Grand Teton's unfolding majesty could stir the soul. The mountain could move regulars, too, like John Gottschalk, who, after the late 1970s, spent every chance he could in Jackson. He was there primarily to fish but clearly also to recharge his batteries and renew his lifelong affection for the Tetons and natural beauty unfolding beneath them. In 1987, he and Carmen bought a house in the hills along the Snake River just below the Teton Pass. While at the *World-Herald*, John tried to get to Jackson at least one weekend every summer month. He reveled in hosting family, friends, and business associates, or simply spending a couple of days with his fishing guide and close friend Scott Hocking on one of the nearby rivers. After he retired, John spent the better part of four months—June through September—in Jackson Hole, fishing and welcoming guests from all over the world.

Scott Hocking

He had first arrived in northwest Wyoming as a Boy Scout, camping there and catching his first trout in Jenny Lake, a postcard-beautiful two square miles of water at the base of Grand Teton. Jenny Lake was at the north end of the valley or "hole," a nod to the argot of nineteenth century trappers who traipsed through the high flatlands below the Tetons, fifty miles from the town of Jackson to the southern entrance to Yellowstone National Park.

Nearly seven decades later, John's time on the rivers in and around Jackson numbered in the thousands of days, many with Hocking. John estimated his catch-and-release totals the tens of thousands, preferably cutties, but lake trout, brownies, and rainbows, too, and all on flies. John and Hocking's friendship grew from a love of fly fishing into one of mutual respect and shared wisdom. On the river, and later over drinks and dinner, they talked about everything from politics to history, philosophy to fishing. A frequent topic was the grandeur of Jackson Hole and the various pressures on its existence, from recreation to development to management of its treasures.

David Jackson gave the valley its name, when, as local legend had it, he spent the winter of 1829 at what was now Jackson Lake. Among his contemporaries were trappers Jim Bridger, Jedediah Smith, and William Sublette. They came to call the valley cut by the Snake River below Grand Teton, "Jackson's Hole." Sharing the valley with the trappers were Native American tribes—Shoshoni, Crow, and Blackfoot—who spent their summers hunting for their winter provisions. Nearly two hundred years later, Teton County was home to Yellowstone National Park in the north, Bridger-Teton National Forest on the east, Grand Teton National Park just above the town of Jackson, and Gros Ventre Wilderness to the southeast. The majesty of and recreational opportunities in Teton County—including a world class ski resort in Teton Village, west of Jackson—brought nearly four million visitors to the area each year, many of whom, when they reached Warm Springs Road going north, were awestruck by Grand Teton's magnificence.

John never tired of the views nor took for granted the valley and its environs. When he hosted visitors, his knowledge of the area was detailed and expansive, including how to experience the most dazzling scenic views at certain times of the day in certain places and at certain angles. A self-confessed impresario of sorts, he said sometimes, with the right music playing in his vehicle and the right panorama before him, he had been moved to tears. (He was partial to a recording of the Mormon Tabernacle Choir singing "Amazing Grace.")

Aside from being a consummate fly fisherman and promoter for the wonder of the Tetons, John was also a bit of a local historian, able to offer visitors insights on local legends, from cowboys to bikers to the wealthy transplants whose mansions blink on the mountainside as dusk swallows the Tetons and stills the night in the hole.

Rushville, two degrees west of the 100th or Dirt Meridian, was nearly equidistant between Jackson Hole and Omaha. The symmetry was more than lines on a map. It was a metaphorical balance for the journey downstream of John Gottschalk and his considerable life: as CEO and publisher of the nation's fifty-second largest newspaper, as chairman and change agent on national boards, as committed, dependable leader for Omaha's civic progress, and as the quintessential fly fisherman, home on the rivers below his beloved Tetons.

Sheridan County, Nebraska—right on the Dirt Meridian—was always present as he made his way, no matter the task at hand, the problem to solve, the joy to experience, the loss to accept, or the longitude at which he found himself. John Gottschalk traveled the world but truly was never far from home, from the values and experiences of Rushville, from a family steeped in publishing newspapers and developing character, from Wefso Drug or the Forney Ranch or the Quick Serv Drive-In. He carried, too, lessons from his playing fields and coaches, from an English teacher willing to prod him, from his fraternity where others looked to him for guidance, from his friends whose numbers were legion.

He saw the world through lenses provided by necessary leadership as a young publisher when most others were just starting out, by chance encounters and dumb luck—both of which he used to make his way, by seeing the hill from above and below before charging up its side, and by a grandfather who taught him that compassion need not be merely an act of selflessness, but rather a tenet by which a leader lived his life.

His details lived in harmony with his big picture, whether in a business meeting, acquiring a new newspaper, or in the middle of a mountain stream stalking cutthroats from a dory.

John Gottschalk's river sprang from Rushville in Nebraska's Sandhills, flowing south to Sidney, east to Omaha, and then west to Jackson Hole, Wyoming. It also moved with purpose and meaning to distant points around the country, picking up pace and volume as tributaries joined the gathering confluence.

INDEX